ROUTLEDGE LIBRARY EDITIONS: MODERN FICTION

Volume 8

BECOMING A WOMAN THROUGH ROMANCE

BECOMING A WOMAN THROUGH ROMANCE

LINDA K. CHRISTIAN-SMITH

LONDON AND NEW YORK

First published in 1990 by Routledge

This edition first published in 2020
by Routledge
2 Park Square, Milton Park, Abingdon, Oxon OX14 4RN

and by Routledge
52 Vanderbilt Avenue, New York, NY 10017

Routledge is an imprint of the Taylor & Francis Group, an informa business

© 1990 by Routledge, Chapman and Hall, Inc.

All rights reserved. No part of this book may be reprinted or reproduced or utilised in any form or by any electronic, mechanical, or other means, now known or hereafter invented, including photocopying and recording, or in any information storage or retrieval system, without permission in writing from the publishers.

Trademark notice: Product or corporate names may be trademarks or registered trademarks, and are used only for identification and explanation without intent to infringe.

British Library Cataloguing in Publication Data
A catalogue record for this book is available from the British Library

ISBN: 978-0-367-26004-0 (Set)
ISBN: 978-0-429-34150-2 (Set) (ebk)
ISBN: 978-0-367-33898-5 (Volume 8) (hbk)
ISBN: 978-0-367-33909-8 (Volume 8) (pbk)
ISBN: 978-0-429-32277-8 (Volume 8) (ebk)

Publisher's Note
The publisher has gone to great lengths to ensure the quality of this reprint but points out that some imperfections in the original copies may be apparent.

Disclaimer
The publisher has made every effort to trace copyright holders and would welcome correspondence from those they have been unable to trace.

BECOMING A WOMAN THROUGH *Romance*

LINDA K. CHRISTIAN-SMITH

ROUTLEDGE New York and London

Published in 1990 by

Routledge
An imprint of Routledge, Chapman and Hall, Inc.
29 West 35 Street
New York, NY 10001

Published in Great Britain by

Routledge
11 New Fetter Lane
London EC4P 4EE

Copyright © 1990 by Routledge, Chapman and Hall, Inc.

Printed in the United States of America

All rights reserved. No part of this book may be reprinted or reproduced or utilized in any form or by any electronic, mechanical or other means, now known or hereafter invented, including photocopying and recording, or in any information storage or retrieval system, without permission in writing from the publishers.

Library of Congress Cataloging in Publication Data

Christian-Smith, Linda K.
    Becoming a women through romance / Linda K. Christian-Smith.
      p. cm. — (Critical social thought)
    Includes bibliographical references.
    ISBN 0-415-90103-0—ISBN 0-415-90104-9 (pbk.) :
    1. Young women—Books and reading. 2. Love stores—History and criticism. 3. Young adult fiction—History and criticism.
4. Popular literature—History and criticism. 5. Young women—Education. I. Title. II. Series.
Z1039.W65C47   1990
028.5'35—dc20   90-8124
                                                                               CIP

British Library Cataloguing in Publication Data also available

To the young women readers of the romance

Contents

Series Editor's Introduction	ix
Acknowledgments	xv
1 Overview	1
2 Love Makes the World Go 'Round: The Code of Romance	16
3 Sealed with a Kiss: The Code of Sexuality	30
4 Mirror, Mirror on the Wall: The Code of Beautification	43
5 Keepers of Heart and Hearth: Gender, Class, and Race in Romance Fiction	56
6 Becoming a Woman: Narrative and Femininity	80
7 Romancing Girls: Romance Fiction and Its Readers	98
8 The World of Romance and Beyond	117
9 A Place in the World	130
Appendices	144
Notes	175
Bibliography	186
Index	199

Series Editor's Introduction

We are in the midst of a conservative restoration. In a number of countries, the New Right has gained a good deal of power in shifting debate over public policy and private life significantly in a rightist direction.[1] One of the major areas of contention has been that surrounding gender roles. "Real men" are "masters" and individuals who support "the free market, unregulated growth, and a militarized high-tech corporate economy." "Real women" are wives and mothers, unselfishly nurturing the traditional, heterosexual family. Gender differences, including the split between the male "public" world and the female "private" world, are natural and fundamental. To challenge them is to "break with God and nature; when liberals, feminists, and secular humanists prevent [women and men] from fulfilling these roles they undermine the divine and natural supports upon which society rests."[2]

Phyllis Schlafly pictures what the rightist vision of the danger looks like in graphic terms.

> Women's liberationists operate as Typhoid Marys carrying a germ called lost identity. They try to persuade wives that they have missed something in life because they are known by their husband's name and play second fiddle to his career. As a home-wrecker, women's liberation is far in the lead over "the other man," "the other woman," or "incompatibility."[3]

For Schlafly and other conservatives, feminism is anti-family, a symbol of the "me-decade," and negates the role of the woman as "homemaker." Total fulfillment can be found instead, however, in exactly this—in taking care of hearth, home, and husband.

How do women learn that such is the "real" path to fulfillment? *Becoming a Woman Through Romance* provides a detailed and nuanced look at how significant elements of popular culture construct an image of femininity that provides important support for such conservative ideologies.

Walk into a bookstore in any of the multitude of malls that stand as shrines to capitalism's consumer culture and stroll over to the section set aside for books for adolescents. You may not find large numbers of books many of you might consider classics, books that adolescents "should read." What you will decidedly find, however, especially in the increasingly dominant chain bookstores, is shelf after shelf of adolescent romance novels. Of course, romance novels in general are immensely popular and profitable. The audience for these kinds of books has expanded markedly among girls ages nine through fifteen, however. Teen romance novels now rank within the very top categories of books read and purchased by girls.[4]

The economics of publishing plays a major role here. Profitability and short term appeal increasingly structure the decisions of publishing houses. Short term profits, rapid turnover, and the minimization of risks rather than long term perspectives and a cultural vision serve to organize the life of many firms in the industry. In the words of a recent analysis of the publishing industry, financial capital is more important than symbolic capital. Intense competition has made it even more important that the former, not the latter, dominate.[5]

In this context, the popularity of romance novels can be gleaned from a few simple statistics. Sales of adult romances account for more than two hundred million dollars annually. Over twenty million people read them in over ninety countries. As Christian-Smith notes, this makes romance fiction "the most lucrative segment of paperback publishing today." Adolescent romances themselves now constitute the third most widely read books by teenagers and represent 35 percent of the total non-adult booksales at the major national bookstore chains. One series of books, Sweet Valley High, currently has over twenty-six million books in print.

How these novels are written is of considerable interest as well. Like the Harlequin and Silhouette romances that have become so popular with women readers, the novels for teenagers are designed, written, and produced in an almost factory-like fashion. Strict formulas exist for plots, topics, length, marketing, and so on. Like the assembly line art that is often produced by multiple painters—each one in charge of a specific part of a picture—these novels too are often produced by an entire stable of writers. The process gives the political idea of the "cultural worker" a whole new meaning as form and content are tightly controlled and the craft of writing is reduced to its atomistic components.[6]

Even with this process of writing, large numbers of adolescent romance novels are not only found in bookstores and libraries, but they also have taken a significant place in the school curriculum. Generally seen as what are called "H/Ls"—that is, high interest/low ability books—they are often used as reading material for those girls who are doing poorly in reading and who need to be "kept interested" in the reading process. Class and race issues surface here almost naturally, since it is often young women from working-class, poor, and "minority" homes who are labeled as poor readers. Yet the issues cut across the lives of all teenage girls as well.

As a number of feminists have argued, romance in general plays a particularly important role in teenage girls' lives. Investigating the place held by the meaning of romance, and how it is constructed, offers us an opportunity to understand more about the processes through which adolescent girls' gender identities are formed through their experiences with it.[7] In essence, Christian-Smith argues that the popular romance novels so eagerly consumed by these young women construct a particular definition of femininity. "Teen romances center their versions of femininity on devotion to home, heart and hearth." In them, "a woman is incomplete without a man, . . . motherhood is women's destiny, and women's rightful place is in the home."[8]

Becoming a Woman Through Romance provides an insightful textual analysis of the stabilities and changes in these books for half a century. It demonstrates how themes of gender, race, class, and sexuality are articulated and how these respond to alterations in society and women's struggles over time. In the process, the author clearly shows why we need to take adolescent romance novels *seriously*, both ideologically and economically.

Even if Christian-Smith had stopped there, with her provocative reading of the ways femininity is produced in these novels, *Becoming a Woman Through Romance* would have been a significant book. But she goes much further. She recognizes that texts have many possible meanings. They have "open horizons" and readers do not passively take in the ideological meanings that are supposedly there for all to see. Rather, readers help *construct* the text. At times, the meanings that are constructed may be surprising. Indeed, they may not totally mirror the problematic versions of femininity that organize these romance novels.

Series Editor's Introduction

Readers may construct alternative or oppositional meanings from the texts. This is exactly what Christian-Smith finds when she goes beyond the books and discusses how a group of adolescents actually reads them. These girls use the novels to partly contest unequal relations of power in their schools and daily lives.

This is one of the reasons why it is so important that we combine textual analysis with what people actually do with the cultural commodities made available to them. For we should not always assume that "the message sent is the message received." This is especially true when we are dealing with groups who have been subject to historical forms of oppression.[9]

For one thing, there is a politics of pleasure operating here. Many young women like these books and they use them in different ways, reconstructing the book's meanings as they go along. This is an important point. Readers of these and other kinds of romance novels are not unthinking dupes, people who are wholly taken in by the gender, race, and class ideologies "represented" in the texts. In fact, as some analysts have argued, one of the benefits of romance novels is that they enable women to control their own pleasure. In much the same ways as soap operas on television are geared to the temporal and emotional structure of household labor,[10] and thus are more contradictory than their critics allow for, so too do romance novels allow for a more complex set of meanings than we might imagine.

However, Christian-Smith asks us not to be too sanguine about these more liberatory possibilities. As she puts it, after spending a good deal of time with adolescent girls who read these books, these young women's "final acceptance of romantic love and its power structure, undercuts the political potential of these insights. Romance reading alters neither the girls' present nor future circumstances, but is deeply implicated in reconciling them to the social structure." Patriarchal relations may be contested and even partly reconstructed. But that does not mean that they will be defeated.

Where does this leave us? Young women *do* read these novels. The ideological effects are often contradictory, but the effects are real. They will not simply disappear. Given this, what are we to do? Should we banish adolescent romance novels from our schools and homes? Place them on special shelves in bookstores and libraries on which we attach a large sign that says "ideologically incorrect"? Linda Christian-Smith faces these questions head on. She suggests a number of strategies for engaging young women in critical readings of these books. Educators at all levels will find such critical pedagogical recommendations more than a little useful.

The act of reading and interpreting the language and meaning of a text is a form of cultural politics. Popular culture is not immune from such politics. The construction of femininity in ways that deny the long struggles against what Schlafly and others called "divine and natural" is part of this politics. In larger political terms, why then should we care about popular culture? Popular cultural forms matter because of what they themselves do and what people do with them.

> They are involved intimately in securing and producing the consent of women and men to particular hegemonic meanings for gender . . . and sexual difference. At stake in the struggles and contestations over these meanings are not only textual representations of femininity and gender relations in particular cultural commodities, but also their place and significance in the lives of the actual women and men who consume, use, and make sense of them in the contexts of their daily practices and social relations.[11]

The meanings that are produced in popular cultural forms, then, do make a difference in the daily lives of people. But the issue is even more important than that.

> The struggle for girls and women, then (whether they are feminist or not), over the gendered meanings, representations, and ideologies in popular cultural forms is nothing less than a struggle to understand and hopefully transform the historical contradictions of becoming feminine within the contexts of conflicting sets of power relations. The process of becoming feminine involves not only the unequal gendered power relations between men and women, but also those of class, race, age, and sexual orientation.[12]

Becoming a Woman Through Romance takes us a considerable distance toward understanding what is at stake in the lives of young women, and all of us, in an increasingly important area of popular culture, the political world of romance novels. This is a book that will be of great interest to readers in women's studies, cultural studies, education, and to all those who care about the question of whose perspectives are made available to our youth.

Michael W. Apple
The University of Wisconsin, Madison

Acknowledgments

I wish to take this occasion to express my appreciation to my colleagues and students who have offered support and encouragement during the writing of this book. The idea of studying teen romance fiction stemmed from the reading interests of my own middle-school students many years ago. Their initial insights made a strong impact on me then and now and I acknowledge their important influence. The teachers and students in the study of readers gave generously of their time and I wish to thank them. I particularly thank series editor Michael Apple for his insightful comments on the various drafts of this manuscript and his support through the years. I also thank Maureen MacGrogan and the editorial staff at Routledge, Chapman and Hall for their assistance. At Marian College of Fond du Lac Dr. Henry Lindborg and Sr. Deborah Golias were instrumental in providing a series of faculty development grants adjusting my teaching duties to include more time for writing. Colleagues Ann Egan, Nancy Riley, and Jan Ohlemacher provided much encouragement. I especially owe a debt to my spouse, Kenneth Smith for proofreading this book, and his patience, understanding, and assumption of many of the household tasks so that I could write. I would also like to thank my colleagues in the College of Education and Human Services at the University of Wisconsin Oshkosh for their interest and continuing support. These acknowledgments would not be complete without special recognition going to my faithful felines who kept me company during the writing of this book.

1
Overview

It's funny what a boy can do. One day you're nobody and the next day you're the girl some fellow goes with and the other fellows look at you harder and wonder what you've got and wish that they'd been the one to take you out first. And the girls say hello and want to walk down to the drugstore to have cokes with them because the boy who likes you might come along and he might have other boys with him. Going with a boy gives you a new identity—especially going with a fellow like Jack Duluth. (*Seventeenth Summer*, 1942, p. 60)

In a few years you'll love someone, Julia, and it will make a great difference in you. You'll see. A woman is never completely developed until she has loved a man; when that happens in the right way she is happy in other people's love as well as her own; she is more generous and understanding about the feelings of others. You might say that she knows completeness. (*Up a Road Slowly*, 1966, p. 103)

In one short day, I had turned pretty. . .Just the night before I'd been practicing my smile, and it had been just as rigid as it had always been. But Paul had said my smile was beautiful—sure enough, now it was. (*P.S. I Love You*, 1981, p. 60)

It's just when you're reading you're in some other world, well, not really, physically, I mean but you imagine you are. Sometimes I feel like I am the person going on dates, having loads of fun (Annie, a twelve-year-old romance reader).

We're selling jeans on the outside and happy family stories on the inside; but you have to sell the books the way the jeans are

Overview

sold (Ron Buehl, editor of "Sweet Dreams" teen romance series as quoted in Pollack, 1981, p. 28).

When young women read teen romance novels similar to these above, they enter the world of a half-billion-dollar-a-year industry (Market Facts, 1984) whose stock in trade is not only fantasies of love and specialness, but also politics. Teen romance fiction articulates the longstanding fears and resentments of segments of society regarding feminism and women's growing independence. The rapid rise to prominence of teen romance novels in only ten years parallels the shift in the political climate in the United States to the right-wing positions of Reaganism characterized by traditional perspectives on gender relations (Hunter, 1984). For woven throughout teen romance fiction's saga of hearts and flowers is an accompanying discourse that a woman is incomplete without a man, that motherhood is women's destiny, and that a woman's rightful place is at home. These themes are part and parcel of the New Right's political and cultural agenda regarding women, representing the conservative restoration of women to their "proper" place in society. Although I do not believe that there is an outright conspiracy between teen romance publishers and the New Right, one worked out over champagne and caviar, it is the case that more and more segments of the culture industry, particularly publishing, are owned by large corporations whose interests are politically conservative (Coser, Kadushin & Powell, 1982). These interests make their way into books like teen romances, which then become the site of ideological struggles for young women's hearts and minds.

In early 1980 the first new teen romance series "Wildfire," published by Scholastic Books, appeared in the bookstores. In the same year, Ronald Reagan was elected to the presidency of the United States during the worst economic crisis since the 1930s. Reagan entered office with an agenda supporting business and the restoration of traditional gender and family sentiments as a response to the economic crisis and pressure from conservative interest groups (Gordon & Hunter, 1977/78; Plotke, 1986). Reagan must be seen as one element in the New Right's longterm attempts to restructure the American economy and construct a conservative cultural accord (Hunter, 1985). According to Hall (1985), a key element in restructuring economic relations is winning the consent of the public by tapping into its fears, needs, and dreams, and then using them to shape a new consensus. Apple (1989) contends that the New Right has been very successful in both articulating the themes of loss of control that many groups feel regarding family, security, and authority, and in building coalitions based on these concerns.

Through New Right rhetoric, worries over family and authority have become translated into the defense of the family, promotion of traditional gender interactions and a general antifeminist stance. Concerned Women of America, Life Amendment PAC, Phyllis Schlafly's Eagle Forum, the Conservative Caucus, and Right to Life movement are among the prominent right-wing organizations that mobilize popular fears over the growing independence and political power of women. These fears are also seen in the "return to romance" themes in fashion, dating, and music (Schneider, 1983) as well as in popular slogans such as "A Homemaker and Damn Proud of It" and "ERA, NO." The burgeoning home-party system for selling Tupperware, lingerie, and cosmetics promote the modern-day version of "true womanhood" by idealizing women as wife/mother/sex object. The resurgence in importance of the home as women's privileged space is seen in the popularity of community college courses in creative child-rearing and interior decoration. "Cocooning" or spending time at home is touted as the new form of leisure. A home made comfortable and beautiful by a woman's hand is the unstated requirement here.

Yet there are tensions within this ideology of femininity ones that surface within popular romance fiction. For as Radway (1984) notes, the act of reading romance novels becomes a form of mild protest against patriarchy: in romance novels women triumph and their sense of competence is validated. Above and beyond this, the adult "erotic romance," as developed over the past ten years (Thurston, 1987) offers readers heroines who seek career satisfaction, economic independence, and more equitable relationships with men. Teen romance fiction reading involves the shaping of consciousness and provides the occasion for young women to reflect on their fears, hopes, and dreams.

While many films, soap operas, and popular songs explore the relationships between women and men, literature has a particularly long history of being concerned with the romantic and sexual aspects of these relationships (Robinson, 1978). The experiences of women in romance and marriage, and the power relations between the sexes, are abundantly described in the novels of Jane Austen, George Eliot, and the Brontës. This strong interest in romantic motifs has found expression in today's adult romance novels from Harlequin and Silhouette. Lately, teen romance novels in serial form have appeared in bookstores and school bookclubs. This fiction has astounded the publishing world by its popularity and actual sales. Although there have been several critical studies of adult romance novels and their readers,[1] it is only recently that teen romance novels been critically analyzed despite their popularity (Christian-Smith, 1986, 1987).

Becoming a Woman Through Romance is about femininity, about how thirty-four adolescent romance novels (see Appendix B) written in the United States from 1942 to 1982 define feminine identity for young women readers. I explore this topic through a close textual analysis of the fiction and by reference to a study of young women readers of the romance. Gender is only one aspect of women's identity. Social class membership, sexual orientation, and racial/ethnic background also contribute to one's social identity. I will explore how each of these shape the version of femininity in teen romance fiction.

When I analyzed each of the thirty-four novels, certain themes or codes recurred throughout all the novels: the codes of *romance, sexuality,* and *beautification.* Romance not only refers to the emotional and caring aspects of a special human relationship, but also involves patterns of power between women and men. Sexuality concerns various expressions of intimacy such as kissing, cuddling, and intercourse, expressions that like romance, include power relations between the sexes. On one level, beautification has to do with ways of getting and maintaining male attention. On another level, every stroke of the hairbrush and twist of the mascara-wand centers feminine consciousness in the body and converts women into consumers. There are two sets of oppositions, Good/Bad and Strong/Weak, that form the characters in the novels. Good/Bad and Strong/Weak have to do with the dominant characteristics of the heroine and her counterpart, the "other girl." The "good" heroine is dutiful, weak, shy, and naive about boys, whereas the other girl is assertive, self-confident, and very experienced with boys. Moreover, these codes represent how other people view female characters once they are no longer either totally good or bad. Together, these codes structure form and content, as well as the novels' version of femininity. These novels contained certain changes in the codes that fall into a chronological pattern. The novels can then be grouped into three periods: Period 1, 1942–59; Period 2, 1963–79; and Period 3, 1980–82. This periodization permits the detection of any changes that occur in the ways in which novels depict femininity over forty years.

Overview

Textual analysis alone cannot account for how individuals read romances or the range of responses to this fiction (Moi, 1985). I have therefore incorporated ethnographic data collected during the 1985–86 school year in three schools in Lakeview, a large midwestern city.[2] Through surveying, interviewing, and observing, I was able both to account for the complex meanings young women readers made during romance-fiction reading and to speculate on the implications of this reading for their developing social identities.

Themes and issues

Becoming a Woman Through Romance explores seven central questions that involve the representation of femininity in popular fiction: What views of femininity do the books present to readers? What patterns of power and control are implicit in textual definitions of femininity? What are the connections between gender identity and one's class and racial membership? How do adolescent girls interpret romance novels? What are the social, economic, and political implications of this fiction? How can teachers and parents help readers to read these books critically? How can a political practice be developed around popular culture? This book is divided into nine chapters that analyze the ways in which symbolic forms such as popular romance fiction both shape and regulate definitions of femininity, class, race, sexuality, and age.

This chapter introduces the theoretical framework from cultural studies and reviews the development of teen romance fiction in the context of massive changes in the publishing industry. Chapter 2 describes how the code of *romance* structures teen romance fiction and helps construct the version of femininity that the novels contain. This code gives to emotions and romance key roles in heroines' lives and has boys granting meaning to girls' lives. Although romance and the emotions give heroines a sense of belonging, they also contribute to their social subordination. In Chapter 3 I explore the code of *sexuality* and its role in rendering sexuality as synonymous with heterosexuality. I then connect sexuality to romance and power, describing how the code of *sexuality* defines pleasure and regulates sexual practices. The practices involved in becoming beautiful are analyzed in Chapter 4: I discuss how beautification centers feminine consciousness in the body and lays the groundwork for

Overview

heroines' sexual objectification. Beautification also makes heroines into consumers and establishes consumption as a distinctively feminine activity. On the surface, femininity seems to be of one piece in romance fiction. However, in Chapter 5 I demonstrate that social class and race contribute significantly to the heroine's gender identity. I argue that romance fiction's version of femininity is actually rooted in a particular class and race, although it masquerades as a universal identity. From this perspective, being a "proper" woman means putting home and family first and all other interests last.

Each of these chapters exemplifies a very consistent representation of femininity despite the fact that the novels span a forty-year period and contain two plot variations that have their heroines unsure of the virtues of romance. This consistency is due in part to the central qualities of the heroine and her counterpart, the "other girl" and to a central motif of "becoming a woman through romance." Chapter 6 explores the aspects of romance fiction that constitute its narrative form and analyzes the kind of feminine personality the novels extol. In Chapter 7, I move beyond the world of the romance text to twenty-nine actual teenage female readers of romances. I discuss school as a setting for this reading and the impact romance-reading has on how school officials view these girls. I then account for the reasons for romance-reading and the role of romance-reading in constructing these girls' femininity as well as their plans for the future. I argue that their romance-reading provides not only a way of fulfilling romantic fantasies, but also an occasion for self-examination. Chapter 8 places romance fiction within its historical context, focusing on the domestic, work-related, and political aspects of women's lives in the United States from 1942 to 1982. I draw parallels between key historical events and the content of romance fiction, arguing that the novels re-code larger social tensions, especially those represented by the New Right regarding women's place. I further argue that romance fiction is contradictory: it reconciles women to their social subordination while providing an escape from it. The final chapter places many of the issues from previous chapters in relation to one another, and considers the important practical concerns of teachers and parents. I argue here that in view of the pervasiveness of popular culture in the lives of young people and its importance in shaping modern consciousness, political struggles must be conducted around it. A methodological appendix contains pertinent theoretical and methodological background to both studies.

Cultural studies, femininism and popular fiction

The theories and methodologies of cultural studies yield much of use for the analysis of popular teen romance fiction and its readers.[3] Developed in the mid-1960s at the University of Birmingham, England, cultural studies provide an interdisciplinary approach, utilizing theory and interpretive methods from literary studies, anthropology, sociology, economics, psychology, philosophy, and feminist studies. The culturalist perspective drew heavily on the writings of Antonio Gramsci (1980), particularly those relating to hegemony and popular culture. Gramsci's theory of hegemony becomes the framework for analyzing the role of cultural processes in securing people's consent to existing social arrangements and as a source of opposition. For Gramsci, hegemony refers to the variety of ways in which dominant social groups (the ruling class) achieve and maintain power and control within a society. While maintaining power by force has always been historically important, for power to be truly consolidated the hearts and minds of people must be won. Gramsci singles out culture, especially the popular cultures of the working class, as a key element in this struggle for rule by consent. In Gramsci's view, these cultures are not only aspects of class-affirmation and "good sense," but also the site where the ruling class seeks to win favor. Cultural studies' research and its political agenda emanates from this problematic, as is evident in Johnson's important essay, "What is Cultural Studies Anyway?":

> The first [premise] is that cultural processes are intimately connected with social relations, especially with class relations and . . . formations, with sexual divisions, with the racial structuring of social relations and with age oppressions as a form of dependency. The second is that culture involves power and helps to produce asymmetries in the abilities of individuals and social groups to define and realise their needs. And the third, which follows the other two, is that culture is neither an autonomous nor an externally determined field, but a site of social differences and struggles (Johnson, 1983, p. 3).

> For me cultural studies is about the historical forms of consciousness or subjectivity, or the subjective forms we live by (Johnson, 1983, p. 11).

Overview

Studies by Hall and Jefferson (1976), Hebdige (1976), and Willis (1977) focus on the identity formation of youth through work and social class membership.[4] However, much of this research relegates questions of gender, race, age, sexual orientation, family, and personal life to secondary status. That cultural studies came to include these topics is largely due to the influence of feminist criticism and the reaction against racism.

The essays in *Women Take Issue* (Women's Studies Group, 1978) were among the first to examine how gender differentiation is linked to class, race, and age. Important for the analysis of romance fiction is McRobbie's study of girls at a Birmingham youth club (1978b), which situates them within a "culture of femininity" organized around domestic duties, consumption, personal life, and above all, romance. The girls' immersion in romance and beauty routines were responsible for the prominent positions these girls occupied within the home and family and their marginal status in the work-force. Although many of the girls questioned aspects of this mode of femininity, they ultimately endorsed a conventional femininity because they saw housework and children as "unavoidable, unalterable aspects of life" (McRobbie, 1978b, p. 98). The girls equally well recognized the mismatch between idealized versions of romance in the music and teen magazines they consumed and actual romantic relations. However, this insight did not prevent the girls from endorsing romance and marriage. They did so out of economic necessity and an understanding of the plight of single working-class women in a society largely structured by marriage and family networks. Although girls' lived experiences were vital in cementing their gender, class, and race identities, McRobbie's semiotic analysis (see Appendix A) of the popular British teen magazine *Jackie* (a magazine similar to the American *Seventeen* and *Co-ed*) (McRobbie, 1978a) pointed to the equal importance of written forms in reconciling girls to their futures.

Like teen romance fiction in the United States, *Jackie* is part of a publishing conglomerate composed of newspapers, comics, and other magazines. McRobbie argues that a distinct feminine culture is shaped throughout its pages. Using semiotic analysis,[5] she identifies four codes as forming the content of the magazine: those of fashion/beauty, romance, personal/domestic life, and pop music. McRobbie contends that the code of romance not only occupies a central position in the magazine's text, but also funnels sexuality toward a heterosexual model. *Jackie's* themes involves attracting boys and solving problems inherent in romantic relationships. In the short stories, romance is defined as "great moments," such as the first date and kiss, that serve as reference points in the lives of heroines. One of McRobbie's important insights has to do with the contradictory nature of romance for girls. On one level, romance softens the often sexist attitudes of boyfriends, allowing girls some measure of negotiation for power and control. However, romance always contains the possibility that a boy can experience the same emotions for other girls. This sets in motion a competition among girls for boys and generates a continual anxiety over loss of love and worry about the meaning of boys' actions.

Jackie also defines adolescent femininity in ways that are class- and gender-specific. In promoting the newest fashions, latest beauty trends, and current pop music as essential to a girl's romantic future, *Jackie* lays the groundwork for the consumerism and domestic labor required to maintain individual attractiveness. In reinforcing the domestic training girls receive at home, *Jackie* helps to solidify girls' future roles as housewives and mothers. This domestic identity becomes partially unglued through the consumerism the magazine promotes. Working-class girls' futures will require some paid work to make ends meet and to purchase little extras. Although the tone of *Jackie* is one of camraderie and girls sharing their "trade secrets," it actually addresses the individual girl, and how she can further her romantic prospects at other girls' expense.

Several studies have probed how popular culture constructs gender subjectivity, one's awareness of sexual differences. Subjectivity can also be thought of in the sense of being subject to someone's will or being controlled by another. Both notions of subjectivity appear in the research reported by Carter (1984), Kaplan (1985), Walkerdine (1984), and Winship (1987). These studies emphasize the importance of fantasy in mental life and how fantasy contributes to human social and emotional development. Popular fiction, a literary fantasy in which one can dream about an identity and pleasures often beyond what is socially possible or acceptable, especially facilitates this development. It also encourages reflection on problems from everyday life and on various alternatives in the imagination. This is especially true of romance novels, which encourage fantasies of love and sexuality. These qualities of popular fiction allow it to be an expression of resistance to patterns of domination. However, as McRobbie's analysis of *Jackie* shows, popular literature also reconciles individuals to prevailing social arrangements.[6]

Another theme in cultural studies concerns the connection between culture and economic and political forces. Forms of popular culture such as literature are commodity forms of capitalism, especially today when ownership is dominated by multinational corporations. Lovell (1987) argues that from the very beginning books were merchandise designed in part to make money. Only by analyzing the economic and social factors of publishing can one understand the connections between economic structure and the social relations expressed in and maintained by literature. The mercantile aspects of literature are especially apparent in the teen romance fiction industry where the bottom line has assumed new importance.

Publishing is big business

When one speaks of books, what is often conjured up are images of reams of paper bound between colorful or somber covers and the anticipation of a good read. As Coser, Kadushin, and Powell (1982) observe, publishing has always been both a cultural activity and a business. Schick (1958) notes that the availability of a wide range of books at increasingly inexpensive prices was made possible by technological developments producing sturdy but cheap bindings and by the increasing importance of the private bookseller. Although these paper editions allowed a greater number of entrepreneurs to become involved in book publishing, the fact is that the control of publishing has always been dominated by a small cultural elite (Lefevre & Martin, 1976). This pattern has intensified in the wake of trends toward increased consolidation of the ownership of book publishing through acquisition by multinational communications conglomerates (Apple, 1985). In this section I discuss the effects of mergers on patterns of power and control within publishing, especially in the romance fiction industry.

Who owns whom?

Anyone casually interested in the activity of the American corporate sector over the past eight years cannot fail to notice the phenomenal rate of corporate merging.[7] Almost every day we are greeted with yet another media message: Sears has acquired Dean-Whitter and Coca-Cola now owns Columbia Pictures, Gold Horizon Music, and Screen Gems. The list of corporations merging into megacorporate concerns seems to go on endlessly.[8] The publishing industry has not been exempt from this "merger mania."

Publishing has developed from small, independent, and often family-owned firms to megapublishing concerns that link numerous houses under the corporate banners of RCA, Gulf+Western, CBS and Xerox. The current ownership of houses publishing most of the books available to adults and children reads like the Fortune 500 list: CBS owns Holt, Popular Library, and Praeger. In addition to radio and TV stations and networks. Gulf+Western became the world's largest publisher of educational materials through its recent acquisition of Prentice-Hall and Simon and Schuster. This increased concentration of ownership of publishing in the hands of the few is characteristic of current events within the culture industry in general. The concentrated ownership of film, music, television, and book publishing has brought cultural production firmly within the dominant interests of the corporate sector—instant appeal and quick profits. It has also bound the fortunes of each sector to one another as is evident in Warner Books' recent purchase of the rights to the sequel to *Gone With the Wind* for a record 4.5 million dollars.

On the one hand, this megamerging may be regarded as an opportunity for infusion of substantial capital into publishing, which has always been an uneven industry as to profit-making. On the other hand, publishing observers such as Coser, Kadushin, and Powell (1982) have noted that as money is channeled into publishing houses, they are expected to turn large profits. The very ways that people speak about publishing today displays a distinct business mentality. Prime concerns are profit and loss sheets, five-year plans, advertising campaigns and readers who have become "the market." Editors in the old-fashioned sense—those who lovingly supervise a manuscript's journey in becoming a book—are now being replaced by specialists with business or legal backgrounds. The power of decision-making now rests with people who are at times unfamiliar with the specialness of books and with the time-honored practice of publishing initially unprofitable but important books. One outcome of this "bottom line" mentality is evident in what Whiteside (1981) terms the "blockbuster complex." Where houses once published bestsellers *and* modest sellers, the emphasis has turned to books with large immediate sale potential by popular authors such as Sidney Sheldon, Judith Krantz, Mario Puzo, and Stephen King. Nowhere is the

Overview

corporate "touch" more apparent than in the romance-fiction industry. Harlequin, Silhouette and the new adolescent romance series patterned after them are a response to these dominant publishing interests.

Adult romance fiction

With sales of more than two hundred million dollars annually and a readership of over twenty million in at least twenty countries, romance fiction represents the most lucrative segment of paperback publishing today.[9] Harlequin Enterprises, a subsidiary of the $550 million Canadian communications giant Torstar, is a cornerstone of the series romance industry, with its marketing expertise, profits, and the sheer magnitude of operation (Thurston, 1987, p. 192). Harlequin merits special attention here in light of its successful adoption of mass-production models to book publishing and it is an excellent example of the book as merchandise.

Harlequin Enterprises of Canada was established in 1949 as a reprinter and distributor of books; it became a romance publisher in 1971 when it acquired the inventory of an English firm specializing in romance fiction.[10] By 1966, Harlequin romances was selling fourteen thousand romance novels yearly. By 1979 the figure had risen to fifty million (Douglas, 1980, p. 26); in 1980 almost three million books were sold ("Harlequin," 1981, p. 94). Today Harlequin has a virtual worldwide monopoly of the series romance market, having recently absorbed its competitors Mills and Boon and Simon and Schuster's Silhouette Books.

The production of Harlequin romances occurs within a corporate model of maximum profit, low-cost labor, uniform production, and astute consumer marketing. Books are often written assembly-line style by a collective of writers who author under a single pseudonym. Advances and royalties range from $5,000 to $30,000 per book, which is an extremely modest figure in view of tremendous sales and the nearly 500,000-per-book press run. Bestselling authors such as Sidney Sheldon, Steven King and Judith Kranz receive one million dollars or more per book. The promotion and packaging of Harlequins follow a uniform format modeled on consumer products like toothpaste and soap. The strategic placement of the romances near checkout counters with other small items removes these books from the privileged position that books often occupy. Harlequin does not market particular books or authors, only its own name, which signifies a particular product to consumers.

Overview

Content is similarly standardized through the use of the formula approach, which locks all books into 190 pages and features the theme of romance in all its variations. The formula requires that the heroine be young, modest and inexperienced. The significant themes of the novels feature women's physical and emotional domination by men and men's cruel behavior towards women. The novels concern themselves with the heroine's loss of control through romance. A prevalent pattern in the novels has the heroine giving up a more independent lifestyle upon her marriage. The novels are also the site for the struggle between the sexes over control of the woman's sexuality. Marriage is the vehicle for making women men's sexual property and for confining her within the home. The kind of femininity featured in Harlequin novels is best summed up by Barbara Cartland, the "Queen of Romantic Fiction," in her comments on women's struggles for independence: "Women don't want that. . . .Women are happier when they're in the shadow of the throne and are pushing a man rather than pushing him out of the way" (O'Toole, 1979, p. 65).

Adolescent series romances

Market research conducted in the early 1980s revealed that teenagers were also reading Harlequin and Silhouette romances. Corporate business strategies have transformed juvenile divisions of publishing houses from barely profitable to highly lucrative; serial romances represent the third most widely read type of book by teens only superceded by mysteries and adventure books (Market Facts, 1984). Teen romance fiction also constitutes thirty-five percent of Dalton and Walden's non-adult book sales (Harvey, 1982). One series alone, Bantam's "Sweet Valley High," averages a first print-run of more than 350,000 books; it currently has printed over twenty-six million books since its inception in 1983 (Crossen, 1988).

Teen series romance fiction is the product of market research originally conducted by Scholastic Books' *TAB* teenage bookclub. Noticing that books with strong romantic motifs were the top-sellers, Scholastic developed "Wildfire," the first series romance for teens in 1980 (Lanes, 1981). Since then more than a dozen romance series have appeared—going by the names of "Sweet Dreams" (Bantam), "Young Love" (Dell), "First Love" (Simon & Schuster) and "Sweet Valley High" (Bantam). Teen romance fiction is actually nothing new. Books featuring girls' first love experiences date back to the 1940s and 1950s with the books of Maureen Daly, Betty Cavanna, Rosamond Du Jardin, and Anne Emery. What distinguishes these new romances is their production procedures which are similar to those for adult romance novels, and their large-budget marketing campaigns.

For the first time in publishing history, publishers are engaging in marketing acrobatics to harness the purchasing power of teenage girls. Teen romances are examples of "packaged" books, where each aspect of the books' development has been carefully supervised by a cadre of public-relations firms and marketing experts. The comments by Ron Buehl (editor of "Sweet Dreams") quoted in the epigraph to this chapter indicate that teen romance fiction has strong connections to other aspects of teenage popular culture. Indeed these novels read like a series of commercials for designer clothing and cosmetics, as flawless teenage girls smile happily from the covers. VCRs, motorcycles, CD players, and an array of other consumer products are indispensable aspects of the world of teen romance fiction. Because the financial stakes are too large to be left to chance, Simon & Schuster has channeled over one million dollars into its campaign to promote its "First Love" series and has made use of short tag-ons at the end of television commercials promoting its adult Silhouette romances. Publishers claim that book content reflects the results of their market research: girls ages nine to sixteen want to read about boys and clothes (Harvey, 1981).

The appearance of the romances has not been without controversy. Lanes (1981) notes that in her interviews with educators, parents, and librarians the general reactions ranged from annoyance to rage. These romance novels have been criticized for their "limited roles for females" and their depiction of "a narrow, little world" in which virtue is rewarded with the love of the right boy (Lanes, 1981, p. 7). The most vocal critics, the Council on Interracial Books for Children, claims that the books teach girls to put boys' interests above their own, encourage girls to compete against each other for boys, and depict only the life of suburban white middle-class nuclear families (Smith, W., 1981, p. 60). Others identify the new romances with the conservative political ideology represented by the New Right.[11] Still others have criticized the way in which the romances get into the hands of young readers—primarily through the school bookclubs.

The heavy promotion of the teen romance series in school book clubs like *TAB* and their inclusion within classroom libraries has caused concern.[12] Harty (1979) notes that the schools constitute a lucrative market for publishers. According to *Publishers Weekly*, in 1984 the schools spent 695.6 million dollars on books, making them the third largest account for the publishing industry surpassed only by general retailers and college book stores. Although textbooks comprise the bulk of these sales, the trade division is growing steadily as more schools use these general-interest books for instruction along with or in place of textbooks.[13] Acutely aware of sales trends, mass-market publishers have entered the school market via the popular teen romances, choose-your-own-adventure, and how-to-do-it books. Both traditional educational publishers, like Scholastic and Xerox, and the mass-market publishers have borne the brunt of critics' claims that the school is not the proper setting for these books (Lanes, 1981). The reputation of Scholastic and Xerox for supplying quality educational materials has been tarnished by the controversy over the romances and their editoral policies (Keresey, 1984).[14]

Despite these controversies and adults' misgivings, teen romance fiction remains a force to be reckoned with, given its immense popularity with readers and the kinds of gender messages it sends them. One message is that of the importance of romance in shaping femininity, and is the topic of the next chapter.

2
Love Makes the World Go 'Round: The Code of Romance

"Love makes the world go 'round," the old song goes. Although romance may not be the center of the universe for some, it is one of the "organizing principles" of the home and school lives of teenage girls.[1] It is also the dominant ideology of adolescent romance fiction. Except for a handful of studies,[2] much of the research on youth has not had much to say about this crucial aspect of teenage girls' lives, even though Gaskell (1983) and Millman (1985) emphasize that the decisions girls make about their futures often stem from their romantic expectations.

In this chapter I discuss how in selected teen romance novels adolescent femininity is constructed through the code of romance. The code of romance not only involves emotion and caring, it is also about the negotiation of patterns of power and control between young women and men. My analysis confirms several of McRobbie's claims about the relationship between personal life, romance and power. The personal and private realm have been implicated in the formation of femininity; this realm generates structures that control women (Griffin, 1985; McRobbie, 1978b). One important structure is romance which often operates in private life outside of public scrutiny, drawing its strength from feelings and emotions. This makes the power underlying private life invisible so that romance appears to be innocent and is not readily identified with the iron hand of control.

As previously indicated, I have grouped the forty-two novels into three periods according to the specific characteristics of the codes of *romance, sexuality,* and *beautification* in each period. I now provide a brief overview of the content of the codes in each period.

Period 1 (1942–59) fiction chronicles the introduction of the adolescent heroine into a world that she had only known as an onlooker. It is a world of proms, the malt shop, Saturday night dates, and above all, attaining the affection of the boy of her dreams. To this end she spends many hours before the mirror transforming herself into a vision of beauty. She and her boyfriend share a common perception regarding how each should act toward the other. He leads, she follows. She does not directly assert herself, but is rather heard through her informal influence. They share a love that is signified by an occasional chaste kiss, and through this love she changes from an uncertain girl into a poised young woman.

In period 2 (1963–79) novels, heroines continue to immerse themselves in romance. However, romance itself is now fraught with conflict and disappointment for them. Heroines and their boyfriends no longer share views as to how to relate to one another. Pressures towards genital sexuality cause intense struggles for power and control between the sexes. The experience of having to take a stand in these matters makes heroines more assertive than their counterparts in the previous period. However, this assertiveness is only apparent in matters of romance and rarely extends to other areas of heroines' lives. In the novels of this period, there is a noticeable decline in references to the processes through which heroines become beautiful. However, heroines continue to be pleased by compliments about their prettiness.

In period 3 romance (1980–82) continues to be the experience that forms femininity. Romance proceeds rather smoothly; the previous strenuous conflicts replaced with more harmony in romantic relationships. In order to influence the course of their romances, heroines have now returned to the use of informal influence (characteristic of period 1) that stops short of actual confrontation. In a manner reminiscent of period 1, the novels of period 3 contain extensive descriptions of the daily routines that make heroines beautiful. The chaste kiss and hug characterize sexuality in this period.

Several themes appear in the novels regarding romance. They structure the code of romance in the novels. These are:

1. Romance is a market relationship.
2. Romance is a heterosexual practice.
3. Romance manages sexuality while privileging nongenital forms of sexual expression.
4. Romance is a transforming experience giving meaning to heroines' lives and endowing heroines with prestige.
5. Romance is about the dominance of men and the subordination of women.

6. Romance is about learning to relate to men.
7. Romance is a personal, private experience.

In the following sections I discuss the meaning of the code of romance over this forty-year period, showing how it forms the one particular conception of femininity that these novels offer.

Romance is a market relationship

In each period, romance is organized as a market relationship in which the terms of a fair exchange are established. The interactions between girlfriends and boyfriends can be regarded as transactions that are coded as to the gender qualities each brings to romance. The feminine terms involve fidelity and devotion, which are exchanged for the support and prestige one has as the girlfriend of a popular boy. Getting a boyfriend confers status on heroines and gives them special privileges. This is graphically seen in several novels where boys are presented as the popular leaders of a mixed-sex crowd.

The exchange relationship is very apparent in novels like B. Cavanna's *Paintbox Summer* (1:1949)[3] and I. Hunt's *Up a Road Slowly* (2:1966), in which boys are the ticket into local society. In the first novel, Manuel Silva and Bill Edmond are very popular with friends and make heroines part of their friendship networks.[4] In M. Pollowitz's *Princess Amy* (3:1981) Guy Wetherington and Pete Demarest compete for the devotion of Amy Painter, a newcomer to the posh society of Mackinac Island's summer residents. Amy is introduced into this society through her aunt and uncle, who are among the wealthy residents. Amy is cast in the role of ingenue, bewildered by a life of maids and parties that is very remote from the pizza parlor that her own family runs. Guy wastes no time in establishing Amy as his girlfriend, dubbing her his "princess." Amy becomes popular through her association with Guy. However, this popularity comes with a price. Guy demands absolute loyalty and that she not so much as look at another boy.

In R. Du Jardin's *Wait for Marcy* (1:1950) Marcy Rhodes's romance with Steve Judson becomes strained when he fails to devote sufficient time and energy to maintaining the relationship. By arriving at the big school dance with another boy, Marcy signals the withdrawal of her loyalty to Steve. Marcy's actions are represented as legitimate because he has already violated the terms of their agreement. That boyfriends insist upon absolute fidelity is also evident in M. Daly's *Seventeenth Summer* (1:1942). Inexperienced heroine Angie Morrow is unaware of this requirement and dates another boy. Her actions cause boyfriend Jack Duluth to withdraw his support. That Angie's femininity is threatened is apparent from this powerful passage: "I didn't even feel like a girl anymore. And all my thoughts turned into little prayers which I meant so much that it made me ache all over" (1: 1942, p. 114). In similar fashion, when Donnie Mueller (J. Eyerly, *Drop-Out* 2:1963) becomes disillusioned with her boyfriend Mitch's inability to comfort her about familial problems, their romance falls apart. In each of these cases, the success or failure of romantic relationships hinges on the maintenance of a fair exchange, one that remains balanced as long as partners live up to its terms.

Although heroines understand the emotional exchange occurring in romance, they only dimly glimpse the fact that romance involves economic factors as well. The only novel where this insight surfaces is *Wait for Marcy*, where economic issues are conveyed through a character who is the adolescent version of a "vamp."[5] Unlike Marcy Rhodes, Devon Merriott is only too well aware of her attractiveness, and she collects strings of boys. Devon's various romances involve a strong economic component: she expects boys to spend lavishly for the privilege of her companionship. A telling episode involves her birthday—she had previously hinted at several gifts which she hopes to receive. That her expectations are realized is later seen from the room full of roses and expensive presents. It is clear that romance for Devon involves the exchange of a good time for her companionship. However, the text negates the importance of Devon's insight through her identity as a vamp whose actions and opinions are neither legitimate nor representative of "proper" adolescent femininity.

In a majority of the novels of period 1 the fair exchange involves fidelity and support. In most of the novels, heroines expect to be cherished and protected, and indeed they are. Much of this changes in period 2 novels, as pressures for intercourse within romance cause much conflict between heroines and boys. F. Pascal's *My First Love and Other Disasters* (2:1979) features Victoria Martin's plans to become popular by attracting the attention of Jim, the captain of the basketball team. Victoria's plan succeeds beyond her wildest hopes when Jim asks her for a date, but just when her romantic expectations are about to be realized, Victoria begins to discover some disturbing things about Jim. On their first date Jim tries to undress her. On subsequent dates, he makes it clear that he expects sex in exchange for his providing her with a good time. Victoria is caught between her fear of acquiring a "bad reputation" and her actual desire for Jim. Similar situations prevail in P. Zindel's *My Darling, My Hamburger* (2:1971) and N. F. Mazer's *Up in Seth's Room* (2:1979), where heroines Liz Carstensen and Finn Rousseau view intercourse as an unfair term of exchange in romance. Part of their actions stem from their perception of proper sexuality in romance as limited to hugging and kissing. They also fear pregnancy and parental reprisals. In the cases of Victoria and Liz, the strong desire to maintain the "good girl" reputation is bound up with being sexually inexperienced. Hence, the framework for the fair exchange involves some very traditional views of romantic and sexual relationships that I will pursue again at a later point.

Romance is a heterosexual practice

In all of the novels, especially those of period 1 (1942–59) and period 3 (1980–82), romance is solely a heterosexual relationship. In both of these periods, heterosexuality is legitimated through the absence of other sexual practices. That boys will be the exclusive objects of heroines' desires is taken for granted in the texts. This "naturalization" of heterosexuality is accomplished through specific statements that elevate heterosexuality, exclude other forms of sexual desire, and place limits on the relationships occurring between heroines. At this point, I will just sketch the contours of the romance-sexuality connection. I will elaborate on them in the next chapter.

The fiction of period 1 and 3 represents a virtually heterosexual universe. In *Wait for Marcy*, fifteen-year-old Marcy's initial lack of interest in boys and preference for female friends prompts concern on the part of her parents as to whether she is developing in the "normal direction" (p. 14). The parents breathe a sigh of relief once she begins dating Steve Judson. In S. Benson's *Junior Miss* (1:1942, 1969), Judy Graves stubbornly refuses her family's attempts to interest her in clothes and boys, preferring instead the company of her girlfriend Fluffy. Nothing that Judy accomplishes is as gratifying to her parents as when she departs for her first formal dance on the arm of Haskell Cummings. In B. Cleary's *Jean and Johnny* (1:1959), Jean's closest friend Elaine persuades Jean to pursue a romantic relationship with Johnny. Jean's misgivings about her readiness for romance give way to Elaine's pressures.

Although period 2 novels also endorse heterosexuality, its legitimation actually occurs through two novels that explicitly deal with heroines' struggles over sexual orientation. Both R. Guy's *Ruby* (2:1976) and D. Hautzig's *Hey, Dollface* (2:1978) contain the most direct statements made in the novels regarding heterosexual primacy by focusing on the relationships between two sets of black heroines: Ruby Cathy and Daphne Duprey in *Ruby* and Val Hoffman and Chloe Fox in *Hey, Dollface*. In *Ruby*, the relationship between Ruby and Daphne is formed against the backdrop of the racial struggles of the 1970s and Ruby's struggles against domination by her father, Calvin. Calvin has distrusted women and girls ever since he glimpsed Ruby and her former boyfriend Orlando kissing, and Ruby's movements are now strictly controlled. Ruby's friendship with Daphne evolves into a strong relationship marked by love and tenderness. Similarly, Val Hoffman's relationship with Chloe Fox evolves from friendship to love. Although both heroines derive much satisfaction from the relationship, it is also a source of confusion for them, especially regarding the strong sexual component of their feelings. Neither novel grants the "romances" of the heroines any legitimacy, and their relationships are vigorously censured by parents and teachers. In their eyes it is morally wrong that heroines have such feelings for one another, let alone act on them. Both novels express a virulent homophobia, but this is strongest in *Ruby*, in a scene where Ed Brooks, a schoolmate of Ruby and Daphne, discovers the nature of the heroines' relationship. He confronts Ruby with these words: "I knew something was wrong with you. Dykes is your thing. He put his hand to his forever swollen crotch. You want to feel the real thing? Here, I'll let you feel it" (2: 1976, p. 58).

Here the "real thing" symbolized by the penis becomes a larger symbol of legitimate sexual desire. The subsequent attempts of Daphne's mother to compel her "to go straight" establish the lesbian relationship as a stage to be outgrown. Ruby's father's lifting his ban on her dating boys is designed to steer Ruby toward "normal" sexuality.

Heterosexuality is established as the privileged form of pleasure and desire in the novels also through the character traits of heroines. By characterizing both pairs of heroines as alone, aloof, and unsettled, the novels are then able to present the heroines' lesbian tendencies as the symbol of their "strangeness" and confused thinking. This also allows the reader to perceive the heroines' relationship as a misguided extension of their search for answers. The practice of describing the heroines' sexual encounters, feelings, and interactions through heterosexual metaphors serve to prevent the uniqueness of relationships between women from attaining any voice in the texts. The patterns of domination and subordination in the interactions between the "strong and powerful" Daphne and the "weak and indecisive" Ruby simply reproduce the power dynamics characteristic of heterosexual romance in all the other romance novels.

Romance manages sexuality

Romance has a double-edged quality where sexuality is concerned. It controls the forms of and occasions for sexuality, and gives heroines some way of controlling boys' sexual demands. The novels' promotion of heterosexuality as the only legitimate form of sexual orientation is one aspect of the management of heroines' sexuality. By making romance synonymous with love between the sexes, the novels promote the idea that sexual orientation is naturally heterosexual. Such sexual meanings forestall any major questioning of heterosexuality or render such questioning deviant, the product of confused thinking, as in *Ruby* and *Hey, Dollface*.

In the novels of period 1 and period 3 heroines express tremendous consternation if boys attempt a kiss without prior professions of love and fidelity. For example, Jane Howard of B. Cavanna's *The Boy Next Door* (1:1956) demands that Ken Sanderson go through the rituals of romance before he kisses her. His spontaneous kiss embarrasses and angers Jane. In J. Quin-Harkin's *Princess Amy* (3:1981), Amy Painter's outrage at Guy Wetherington's kiss can only be understood within this larger context that links sexuality with romance. Amy will only permit a repeat performance after Guy has christened her "his girl." These novels clearly establish that sexuality without romance is taboo.

Sexuality is the implied central element in the market relationship of romance as well. The good-night kiss in period 1 and period 3 fiction becomes boys' demands for more than this in period 2 novels. Although heroines understand that sexual favors are a part of romance, they are by no means happy about this. Jean Burnaby of A. Emery's *Sorority Girl* (1:1952, p. 142) notes that one is expected to pay for an evening's entertainment with kisses. However, heroines have strong reservations about sexuality when it goes beyond chaste hugs and kisses, even when this is contextualized within romance. The storminess of the period 2 romances of Liz Carstensen and Sean Collins (*My Darling, My Hamburger*, 1969), Natalie Field and Owen Griffiths (*Very Far Away from Anywhere Else*, 1976), and Finn Rousseau and Seth Warnecke (*Up in Seth's Room*, 1979) are magnified by the conflicts heroines have over intercourse in romance. Heroine's struggles with the pressure boyfriends apply in the above novels and in *Up a Road Slowly* (2:1966) and A. Head's *Mr. & Mrs. Bo Jo Jones* (2:1967) provide additional evidence for how troublesome sexuality is in romance for heroines.

The emerging sexual discourse in period 2 novels throws into relief one of the purposes of romance, as revealed by Liz Carstensen's reflections:

> I want you, but I think we should be engaged first. I want to be your wife and have children and live with you the rest of my life. But I don't want to do everything now when we should wait. You wouldn't respect me if I did. (2:1969, pp. 44–45)

Romance is a way of circumscribing boys' sexual demands within traditional notions of permitted sexuality by compelling them to make emotional commitments to heroines. These emotional commitments, however, do not mean *carte blanche* when it comes to the form of sexual expression. Legitimate sexuality remains nongenital. Sexual struggles of heroines such as Liz Carstensen and Victoria Martin legitimate conventional sexuality by bringing divergent forms of teenage sexual expression (read: intercourse) in line with larger social views of appropriate sexual conduct. Conventional sexuality then provides a way for heroines to manage the sexual exploitation that hovers around the edges of romance.

Romance endows girls' lives with meaning and importance

Just as romance has these darker aspects, it also functions as a larger field in which heroines are singled out and given recognition by virtue of becoming a "girlfriend."[6] The very practical side of specialness is

Love makes the world go 'round

evident in Jean Burnaby's observation (*Sorority Girl*, 1:1952, p. 143) that boyfriend Tom Kitchell "had brought her to a pinnacle of repute; she had become known as one of the popular heroines who . . . was seen everywhere that mattered." This sentiment is echoed in *Seventeenth Summer*, where becoming popular with peers is but part of this "individual specialness" that girlfriends experience. That romance is clearly the turning point in heroines' lives is seen in the following passage, where Angie Morrow becomes Jack Duluth's girlfriend:

> It's funny what a boy can do. One day you're nobody and the next you're the girl some fellow goes with and the other fellows look at you harder and wonder what you've got. . . . And the girls say hello and want you to walk down to the drugstore to have cokes with them because the boy who likes you might come along and he might have other boys with him. Going with a boy gives you a new identity—especially going with a fellow like Jack Duluth.[7] (1:1942, p. 60)

Romantic recognition contains a certain magic occurring the moment the girl is assured of the boy's love. The magic of this moment is captured in *Seventeenth Summer* where Angie and Jack's romance is sealed with a kiss:

> I felt a new, breathless caution as if I were sitting in a bubble. . . . In the loveliness of the next moment I think I grew up. . . . Sitting on the cool grass in my new sprigged dimity with the little blue and white bachelor's buttons pinned in my hair. Jack kissed me and his lips were as smooth and babysoft as a new raspberry. (1: 1942, p. 59)

Romance has this power even in period 2 novels, where many heroines challenge several of the conventions of romance. Despite their actions, a dominant attitude towards romance prevails, as in *Up a Road Slowly*:

> Aunt Cordelia smiled. "In a few years you'll love someone, Julia, and it will make a great difference in you . . . . A woman is never completely developed until she has loved a man; when that happens in the right way she is happy in other people's love as well as her own . . . . You might say that she knows completeness." (2:1966, p. 103)

It is clear from these passages that romance occupies a key position in heroines' development; romance is not only credited with their maturation, but it is the single experience that gives their lives meaning. The pattern established in an early romance novel like *Seventeenth Summer* is repeated throughout the sample, even dominating current romance fiction such as *California Girl* (3:1981). Although Angie is an accomplished student and will be attending a prestigious midwestern college in the fall, all this pales before romance. Similarly, Jennie Webster's (*California Girl*) long years of swimming practice and subsequent success as a junior olympic competitor contributes less to forming her gender identity than does her brief romance with Mark Waverly. Both novels make it clear that romance opens up new vistas, and feelings, and provides experiences that make heroines feel more alive, with newly acquired strength and purpose. Nothing else in their lives can quite match this.[8]

This aspect of the code of *romance* points to its complexity as a social process. On the one hand, romance can elevate people and make them feel more human. On the other hand, romance contains dynamics through which adolescent heroines negotiate their own subordination for romance's hidden agenda is power.

Romance is about power

Romantic relationships feature heroines' attempts to try to negotiate better terms for themselves—to seek ways to be influential and powerful, and to participate in decisions that may affect their relationships. This process of negotiation or absence thereof reveals romance to be an important experience for learning about the power relations between women and men.

At the outset, the structure of romance works against heroines having any "formal" power and authority. By the latter I mean the right to make overt decisions that are publicly recognized as legitimate. I have previously noted that boys have much "cultural capital" in the novels. This ranges from the popularity of a Jack Duluth (*Seventeenth Summer*) to the respected position in the community of Manuel Silva (*Paintbox Summer*). Boys control the terms of romance by making heroines their exclusive property. This subtly occurs during the moment of specialness when heroines' are convinced of boys' commitment to them, when the heroine becomes the girlfriend. Contained within this specialness is a dynamic of power and control that circumscribe the form and expression of heroines' authority while celebrating male prerogative. In becoming "his girl," the girlfriend takes up a position within the nexus of male power and control in which she literally is his. That boyfriends do consider girlfriends their property underlies the many textual references to ownership. Mark Waverly's arm on Jennie Webster's shoulder is a signal to all the world that "this girl belongs to [him]" (*California Girl*, 3:1981, p. 71). Calling Ludell (B. Wilkinson *Ludell and Willie*, 2:1977) "his girl" is only one manifestation of Willie's perception of Ludell as his property. This also extends to dismissing Ludell's desire to work when they marry.[9]

Lest anyone think that heroines are passive here, the novels demonstrate that heroines actively seek ways to influence boys and shape the course of their romances. However, the code of romance sets strong limits on the form of heroines' power. For a girlfriend, feminine power is confined to an "informal" system of covert action and subterfuge. A typical form of feminine power involves "scanning." Girlfriends constantly search boyfriends' remarks for hidden meanings and intentions in order to acquire the information they need to act in a manner befitting the situation. In *My First Love and Other Disasters* Victoria Martin feels constraints on directly asking Jim the meaning of his actions. Instead she is confined to "second guessing" the content of his remarks. "Jim shows David [the child Victoria babysits] how to hold on to the board and I feel super because he picked my kid. That must mean something" (2:1979, p. 82). In *Jean and Johnny*, Jean ponders the significance of Johnny's smile and the fact that he has called her a "cute girl" (Cleary 1:1959, p. 50). After some thought she decides that this reveals Johnny's interest in her. Heroines also "just happen" to be near boys' lockers in E. Conford's *Seven Days to a Brand-New Me* (3:1982) and have other heroines spy on boyfriends in Du Jardin's *Practically Seventeen* (1:1943), *Sister of the Bride* (2:1963), and S. Pevsner's *Cute is a Four-Letter Word* (3:1980). These informal demonstrations of power are not given formal recognition in the novels and are often censured in cases where discretion and moderation have not been exercised.

There are stiff penalties for heroines who dare to be assertive. A case in point is Kentucky Jackson of *Practically Seventeen* (1:1943) who openly flirts with boys and takes the initiative in romance. In *California Girl*, Mark Waverly objects to Jennie Webster's request to see his art work (and by implication get to know him better) by telling her that "it was the man who was supposed to invite the lady to his room to see his etchings. She's not meant to invite herself!" (3:1981, p.71). This rebuke prevents Jennie from taking any further direct initiative; instead, she employs subterfuge where Mark is concerned. Other heroines such as Victoria Martin of *My First Love and Other Disasters* (2:1979) and Finn Rousseau of *Up in Seth's Room* (2:1979) do try to manage gender relations so that they can secure a role in shaping the power structure of their romances—these actions cause the breakup of their romances. This fictional device and others I have discussed serve to maintain the power structure of romance.

Romance involves learning to relate to males

In *Paintbox Summer* heroine Kate Vale utters a truism of these novels when she announces that "getting along with men was important . . . [It] was one of the things [she] knew she must learn to do" (1:1949, p. 42). "Getting along" means establishing a romantic relationship with a boy and trying to preserve it at all cost. The novels convey to the reader that any other type of relationship, such as friendship is an impossibility. Two cases in point are *Very Far Away From Anywhere Else* (2:1976) and *Up in Seth's Room* (2:1979). In the first story, the novel ends with the impossibility of any relationship between Owen Griffith and Natalie Fields because of Owen's difficulty with envisioning a friendship rather than a romance with Natalie Fields. In the second novel, the impossibility of friendship between the sexes is clearly indicated when Finn Rousseau's father exclaims "Friends?" . . . "Since when are boys and heroines friends?" (2: 1979, p. 93) Indeed, not in romance novels!

This "getting along" also means accepting the idea that boys will be in charge. One of the basic lessons that Kate Vale and other heroines learn from romance is that the ability to "get along" is primarily worked out within a set of power relations that do not favor feminine initiative as the previous section has clearly indicated. The novels on the whole contain no relationships, adult or adolescent structured around female and male parity. The latter relates to the other lesson heroines learn: that heroines are the ones who must continually compromise and adapt themselves to boys' needs.

Romance is a personal experience

In general, in these novels romance is never presented as a form of social experience that involves many people. Each romance is presented as entirely unique as if it is happening for the first time ever. As Angie Morrow notes, "People can't tell you about things like that, you have to find them out for yourself" (Daly 1:1942, p. 3). Because romance is situated in personal life, whatever problems heroines have are considered to be individual and not characteristic of romance itself. Heroines look to deficits in themselves, not in romance, whenever problems occur. They rarely "compare notes"—their friends are just as inexperienced romantically and can be of little help. This "privatization" of romance is further encouraged by placing it outside of public life and into the realm of private life, a realm that often involves individualistic solutions.[10] This privatization is yet another mechanism for cloaking the true nature of the power relations in romance, keeping them from public scrutiny and forestalling the possibility of change.

Summary

The common vision of romance—girl meets boy and it's all hearts, flowers and sweetness—confronts us with the innocence and specialness of love. Romance may be many things, but it is neither simple nor innocent. This chapter has shown that romance is a highly contradictory experience for heroines and interacts with their subordination in complex ways. Wexler (1983) argues that self, intimacy, and interaction mask fundamental tensions in a social order and are important mechanisms for incorporating individuals into that order. Romance channels heroines' hopes and dreams for intimacy and connectedness into a relationship with a special boy. The self-transformation that romance effects is presented in the novels as the key to personal and social happiness. Although romance bestows recognition and importance on heroines, it ultimately constructs feminine subjectivity in terms of a significant other, the boyfriend. This dynamic of specialness is a key ingredient in securing heroines' gender subordination.

The special recognition that scores of heroines experience links up with another contradictory aspect of romance: romance creates young woman as terms in a circuit of exchange where their value is acquired through affiliation with boys. This once again points to economics as a basic component of all romantic relationships. Although the novels present emotion and feeling as romance's foundation, the exchange relationship is the true basis of romantic attachments. The emotional and sexual favors girlfriends exchange for prestige and the feeling they "belong" foreshadow the kinds of bargains adult women strike as wives and mothers. In these novels romance has all the hallmarks of a training camp for marriage, where heart and hearth become bound together and the wifely qualities of self-sacrifice and fidelity are instilled. As such, romance is an important social dynamic for the learning of gendered relations of subordination and domination.

Although the code of romance involves certain conventions and constraints, heroines do not automatically obey all the rules. At best, they seek to balance delicately their need to have some say in their romances, avoiding at all costs the appearance of seeming too pushy. That they are not entirely successful comes as no surprise when one considers the tremendous constraints the novels place on feminine initiative. All this points to the fact that even though romance is important in securing heroines' social subordination, their consent is not easily won.

This is especially the case when it comes to sexuality. I have suggested that heroines use romance to transform the coarser aspects of sexuality in favor of a diffused sensuality and gentleness. However, this practice acts back on heroines. Romance not only centers heroines' sexuality around heterosexuality, but also becomes a powerful way of controlling the range of their sexual pleasure. Hence, the code of romance is ultimately about power: who has it and who may legitimately exercise it. Sexuality emerges as a thorny issue in teen romance fiction. The next chapter elaborates on this theme, and discusses the role of families in regulating heroines' sexuality.

3
Sealed with a Kiss: The Code of Sexuality

Romance colors the ways in which sexuality is presented in adolescent romance fiction. It promotes sexuality as something magical, mystical, and loving that happens to girls. However, sexuality is about more than magic, love, and commitment. For, as Foucault claims in his *History of Sexuality* (1980), sexuality also concerns knowledge, power, the body, and the sets of relationships that solidify definitions of sexual conduct.[1] According to Vance (1984), sexuality also has elements of danger amid the possibilities of pleasure.

Foucault's important contribution lies in the insight that sexuality is not so much a system of prohibition and constraint; rather, it involves the incorporation of increasingly wide areas of knowledge. This knowledge concerns definitions of "proper" sexuality and the regulation of sexual practices. Of prime importance is the "deployment of sexuality," which refers to the position sexuality occupies within the network of institutions where sexual behavior occurs. For Foucault, the primary elements in this network are the husband–wife and the parent–child relationship. Both of these are based in the family relationship whose purpose is to "anchor sexuality and provide it with a permanent support" (Foucault, 1980, p. 108). The family and other institutional networks such as the church play a role in regulating sexuality by defining legitimate sexuality and marking out the sites where it may or may not occur. Power is central to Foucault's views on sexuality: "Power is not an institution, and not a structure; neither is it a certain strength we are endowed with; it is the name that one attributes to a complex strategical situation in a particular society" (Foucault, 1980, p. 93). Power relations can take the form of defining what is legitimate or secret knowledge and what is illicit sexual behavior. Power mostly operates by designating sites of pleasure and "appropriate" objects of desire. Hence, power operates at the very fundamental levels of identity and meaning.

Sealed with a kiss

Foucault's work has much to reccomend it for the analysis of sexuality in teen romance fiction. Despite this, it is necessary to extend his analysis in several directions.[2] Although his concept of power unseats the idea of men's absolute power and women's total submissiveness, it does not shed light on the particular power relations between and among the sexes or on the everyday experience of sexuality within relationships. This level is where power relations in teen romance fiction are most visible.

Another limitation involves the absence of romance in his construction of the deployment of sexuality. In romance fiction, romance is where sexual meanings are established; it is the primary way in which heroines are prepared for their positions in heterosexuality. Furthermore, Foucault's model of sexuality may be too general to explain the nuances of adolescent sexuality. A way around this limitation is to use the concept "forms of sexual expression." This heuristic device can then be used to account for the many practices that constitute adolescent sexuality. It also permits the realization that textual representations of sexuality can change as a literary form evolves over a number of years. One can then group teen romance fiction according to the forms of sexual expression found in individual novels and the ways in which sexuality is treated over time.

Foucault has little to say about what Vance calls the "tension between sexual danger and sexual pleasure" (Vance, 1984, p. 1) and how this dynamic can be powerful in structuring women's sexual experiences. Both pleasure and danger emerge as key critical issues in investigating feminine sexuality along with the more traditional concerns with restriction and oppression (Coward, 1985; Snitow, Stansell & Thompson, 1983). Pleasure and danger are important categories of analysis for sexuality in adolescent romance novels. For heroines, sexuality involves a great deal of repression, very little pleasure, and considerable danger.

This discussion provides a backdrop for how sexual meanings are constructed in romance fiction. In the context of the novels, sexuality refers to girls' acquisition of knowledge about their bodies as well as about their relation to them. Closely connected to this relation are the rules surrounding the use of the body, rules that involve not only prohibitions and constraints, but also pleasure and desire. Power enters the picture in the form of girls' struggles to control their bodies and define what sexuality means to them. Together these factors constitute how sexuality is deployed and generate the code of sexuality in the novels. The key elements of this code are:

1. Romance is the only proper context for sexuality.
2. Genital sexuality is mostly reserved for adults.
3. Girls respond to boys' sexual overtures but do not initiate any of their own.
4. Resistance to genital practices is encouraged.
5. Sexual definitions reside within a network of power based in romance and the family.

With this overview in mind, I will now examine the romance novels as to how sexuality contributes to the discourse on femininity.

Romance and sexuality

Although each period contributes to establishing the connections between romance and sexuality, the novels of period 1 shape the contours of the code of sexuality in the entire sample. Here, sexuality is signified by the occasional hug and kiss. The kiss becomes the dominant form of sexual expression in period 1 novels and remains so throughout the novels of other periods.

Like Sleeping Beauty, heroines' romances are sealed with the kiss. In *Practically Seventeen* (1:1943) the sometime romance of Tobey Heydon and Brose Gilman is finally confirmed when Brose gives Tobey his class ring and cements their relationship with a kiss on the hand. Halfway through *Seventeenth Summer* Angie Morrow experiences her first kiss: "In the movies they always shut their eyes but I didn't. In the loveliness of the next moment I think I grew up . . . . Jack kissed me and his lips were as smooth and babysoft as a new raspberry" (1:1942, p. 59). The first kiss signals growing up: it facilitates the awakening of girls' sexual feelings and gives them a particular form.

The kiss becomes the symbol of love in these period 1 novels and remains so in period 2 fiction. In *Up in Seth's Room* (2:1979), Seth's kiss signifies for Finn Seth's commitment even though the text is very clear that Seth does not love her. Similarly, in *Drop-Out* (2:1963) the first kiss of Mitch Donelson and Donnie Muller is interpreted by Donnie as a token of Mitch's love and is therefore welcomed. This linking of sexuality with love is especially strong when sexuality includes intercourse.

Genital relationships do not occur with any frequency in the novels, and nowhere are they sanctioned between adolescents. However, they find reluctant recognition in some novels from period 1 and 3 such as *My Darling, My Hamburger* (2:1971) and *I'll Always Remember You . . . Maybe* (3:1981).[3] What somewhat legitimates intercourse is that it is the outcome of long-term relationships that have all the hallmarks of "trial marriages." However, the novels as a whole favor a "wait until we are married" attitude reinforcing this attitude through their treatment of sexuality. First, sexual intercourse is presented as a dangerous practice that must be strictly controlled.[4] In *Drop Out* Donnie's neighbor Mrs. O'Meara warns her that "sex is like a kitten they can take out of a little box to play with, then put back when they're through. Too late they discover they've got a tiger on their hands" (2:1963, p. 68). Sex is compared to "dynamite" that "you don't turn . . . on and off like a radio" in *Mr. and Mrs. Bo Jo Jones* (2:1967, p. 62).[5] The latter novel and *My Darling, My Hamburger* (2:1971) use the stock device of the heroine's pregnancy as a consequence of intercourse. In both novels, July Greher and Liz Carstensen feel guilty and see their pregnancies as a punishment for teen intercourse.

Girls respond to boys

Although some interest and knowledge of sex is allowed in later romance fiction, in the end the novels define girls' sexuality as distinctly nongenital. Another thread running through the novels is that girls should follow boys' cues and not take the lead. Heroines' lives are marked by continuous waiting. They wait to be asked for dates and, most important, they wait to be kissed. These heroines have good reasons for their concern over being perceived as too forward, for in their world proper femininity requires a certain passiveness with their ability to take the initiative restricted to carefully defined situations.

This pattern is evident in all periods. Jean Jarrett of *Jean and Johnny* (1:1959) is chastised by her sister Sue for telephoning a boy and appearing to be "too eager and too available" to him. Similarly, in *Paintbox Summer* Kate Vale (1:1949) accuses her friend Misty of "throwing herself" at boys and behaving in an "improper" manner. In *Up a Road Slowly* (2:1966) Julie Trilling is very attracted to her childhood friend, Danny Trevort, but is reluctant to show him how she feels. Not until Danny has kissed her and confessed his love is Julie able to share her feelings. "Coming on too strong" is a prime concern of Jennie Webster in *California Girl* (3:1981). For over a hundred pages the reader waits along with Jennie for that first kiss, which finally happens toward the end of the novel.[6]

Furthermore, the topic of heroines' sexual pleasure is rarely discussed in specifically sexual terms. Heroines' sexuality is presented as expressive and responsive to boys. The language used avoids the concrete and specific in favor of the vague and evocative:

> Jane's heart began to hammer curiously, and she felt almost frightened. (*The Boy Next Door*, 1:1956, p. 26)

> Something deep within me stirred and a throbbing warmth surged through my whole body until the very tips of my fingers tingled. (*Seventeenth Summer*, 1:1942, p. 53)

> I felt the warmth of his hand . . . The touch had created a tingy tingle of electricity that reached the insides of my heart . . . (*P.S. I Love You*, 3:1981, p. 34)

The novels avoid the distinctly physical aspects of heroines' sexuality, primarily dwelling on psychological aspects. *My First Love and Other Disasters* (2:1979) which is the only novel analyzed that directly discusses male erection, has nothing to say about any accompanying genital responses in heroines. Although it is certainly true that the psychological is an important aspect of sexual response, downplaying physiological components removes this dimension as a legitimate aspect of heroines' sexuality.

The silence surrounding heroines' sexual pleasure is especially apparent in novels where intercourse occurs. In *Mr. and Mrs. Bo Jo Jones* (2:1967, p. 9) all the reader learns is that July is "humiliated," "shattered," and "furious" with herself and Bo Jo afterwards. When Paul Leonard (*I'll Always Remember You . . . Maybe*, 3:1981) goes off to college, he decides to sever the relationship with his steady girlfriend Darien Holmes. Darien is reluctant to agree to this, holding onto the hope that Paul will change his mind. During a Christmas visit, Paul sees Darien and they renew the sexual side of their relationship. The way in which this episode is treated once again shows a reluctance to treat girls as active in their own sexual pleasure:

As he began kissing me again, the word *savagely* that Genie [Darien's friend] and I used to howl over when we read gothics aloud went through my mind. It didn't seem funny at all now. And if Paul's love-making was more urgent this time, that was only natural, considering that we'd been separated for so long. The important thing was that we were back together. The next time or the next he'd be more relaxed and tender . . . the way he used to be. (3:1981, p. 113).

Darien's responses are lost through the focus on Paul's actions and the passive character of the heroine is once again reinforced.

My Darling, My Hamburger is one of the few novels where a heroine expresses her desire for a boy. Liz's note to Sean saying "I want you" is the most direct statement of feminine desire in the entire sample (2:1971, p. 44). The sexual tension between Liz Carstensen and Sean Collins supposedly culminates the night of the Winter Starlight Dance when Liz and Sean are stranded with a flat tire at Marine Park. I say "supposedly," since Liz's oblique remark to Sean that she is "not in a hurry to go home anymore" stands as the only textual clue as to what may transpire (2:1971, p. 68). That intercourse has occurred is confirmed some chapters later when Liz finds herself pregnant. By leaving out Liz's actions, the text silences Liz at an important point in the novel. Liz here assumes a certain passivity, seemingly worn down by another of her fights with her parents and Sean's continual sexual pressure. Hence, the power of her initial desire for Sean has been totally lost by the time this episode occurs. An important aspect of heroines' sexuality is subverted by a common convention of romance fiction: the weary capitulation of the heroine to the masterful hero.

Families and girls' sexuality

Another vital element in the deployment of the heroine's sexuality is the family. Fathers and brothers, and to a lesser extent, mothers and sisters are the source of authority and power over teenage girls' sexuality. Moreover, families do not represent a community of interest in the novels; rather, they are places where the unique and often oppositional interests of the each sex manifest themselves.[7]

Familial control of sexuality takes a number of forms in these romance novels. In period 1 it appears as an all-encompassing cloud over girls' activities. It manifests itself in the ever-present differential curfews for girls and boys in *Seventeenth Summer* (1:1942), *Practically Seventeen* (1:1943), *Wait for Marcy* (1:1950), and *Sorority Girl* (1:1952). In these novels, heroines are constantly interrogated as to where they are going, what they doing, and when they will be home. Boys' movements are not subject to such scrutiny.[8] That sexuality is the latent content of this surveillance is evident in *Wait for Marcy*. When Marcy returns late from the big school dance with Jerry Bonner, her family's boarder and her father's employee, alarm sweeps her family. The cause of panic is not so much Marcy's lateness, but the fact that she is out with someone older than herself. An atmosphere of possible sexual transgression hangs over the entire episode and clouds the reaction of both Marcy's father and brother. When the family finally learns that Jerry had to pick up his wife (a secret kept from the Rhodes's) from the train station in the next town and that Marcy accompanied him to supply directions, everyone is relieved. Marcy's reputation remains unblemished, and Jerry's sexuality is restored to the proper confines of marriage.

The family assumes a very visible mode of control over heroines' sexuality in period 2 as well. The "double standard" so prevalent in Period 1 is carried over in several period 2 novels. It is depicted as a "natural" consequence of being female in *Ludell and Willie* (2:1977, 1981) through Willie's comments that his "Mama don't never say nothing bout when I come or go," "I'm a boy!" (2:1977, 1981, p. 90). Willie voices the rationale for this gender difference as "a boy can take care of hisself out there" (2:1977, 1981, p. 91). However, more than girls' seeming helplessness is a foot here. Mis Lizzie's words to Ludell indicate the social sanctions that back up this double standard:

"When young men get ready to pick themselves someone to marry, they don't pick the ones who've been pawed over. They go get themselves a LADY!! . . ."

"[Y]ou have to understand that it's different for a boy. They don't have anything to lose. Nobody'll talk about them, but it's another story for the girl." (2:1977, 1981, p. 82).

Fear of sexual intercourse underlies these admonishments. Heroines' real and imagined involvement in sexual intercourse creates a series of "moral panics" in families. The constant arguments between Finn

Rousseau (*Up in Seth's Room*, 2:1979) and her parents regarding her relationship with Seth Warnecke are generated by a single question: "Were she and Seth having sex?" (2:1979, p. 143). The dominant atmosphere in this and other period 2 novels is that of adults' suspicion about the extent of girls' sexual activities. In *Ludell and Willie* (2:1977, 1981) young black women are the object of adults'—especially brothers'—constant watchfulness. If they date a number of boys, as is the case with Ruthie Mae Johnson, they are dubbed "fast-behinds" by their brothers and become the subject of wild rumor and innuendo. In the case of Ludell, merely holding hands with boyfriend Willie is enough for a report to her grandmother that the two were "brazenly locked up" while walking along the street (2:1977, 1981, p. 49).

Where romances were unconditionally approved by families in period 1 fiction, they are now suspect in period 2. Victoria Martin of *My First Love and Other Disasters* sums up the dominant sentiment of fathers towards boys: "they're all out to steal his precious baby" (2:1979, p. 13). This is echoed in *Drop-Out* where Donnie Muller lives in a climate of suspicion and accusations whenever a new boy enters the picture. Her father carefully scrutinizes her manner for any evidence of sexual involvement with boys. Even heroines' simple actions can entice boys. Mrs. O'Meara, Donnie's neighbor, warns that "a boy takes his cue from the girl—you just remember that" (2:1963, p. 44). *My Darling, My Hamburger* (2:1971) rivals *Drop-Out* in the total atmosphere of wrongdoing that surrounds every move of heroine Liz Carstensen. Another father figure—Liz's stepfather—continuously interrogates her about her actions. His constant innuendos regarding Liz's presumed sexual involvement with Sean culminates in him calling Liz a "little tramp" (2:1971, p. 67).

These novels demonstrate the contradictory position that sexuality occupies in heroines' lives. Heroines may have desires, but their desires are to be held in check. Otherwise, they run the risk of familial censure and all the consequences that implies. Sexual desire has another consequence for heroines not yet discussed: it makes them vulnerable to sexual exploitation.

Genital relationships and girls' resistances

In all of the novels, sexuality is confined to clearly defined life stages. When girl meets boy and falls in love the occasional chaste kiss and hug is permitted; beyond this, however, girls' sexuality creates alarm in the world of the romance novel. The first kiss stands as the sign of a heroine passing from girl to woman; sexual intercourse is not afforded an equal status. Despite this, intercourse plays an important role in consolidating heroines' sexual identities through the stands they must take, especially in period 2.

As I have indicated, genital sexuality poses great difficulty for heroines. They find themselves caught between adherence to a dominant sexual code forbidding teenage intercourse and the new sexual demands placed on them by boyfriends. Parents who subscribe to traditional forms of sexual expression apply additional pressure. This pressure culminates in heroines' resistance to both boyfriends and parents. A good example is found in U. Le Guin's *Very Far Away From Anywhere Else* (2:1976) where the romance between Owen Griffiths and Natalie Field takes an unexpected turn. On an outing to the beach, a kiss threatens to turn into something else. Owen's decision that intercourse should be the next logical step in their relationship results from media representations of proper gender relations and peer pressure: "Man Plus Woman Equals Sex. Nothing else. No unknowns in the equation. Who needs unknowns?" (2:1976, p. 43). For Natalie, just being with Owen is enough, and she is quick to remind him of this to forestall any further sexual advances. The stand that Natalie takes confirms her belief that sexuality has no role in her life at this time, and that a sexual relationship may jeopardize her future plans for a professional musical career.

Sexual conflict has a hidden dimension in romance fiction. *My First Love and Other Disasters* (2:1979) and *Up in Seth's Room* (2:1979) demonstrate its actual content: control of heroines' bodies and definition of their sexual pleasure. In the first novel, Jim Freeman is the boy of Victoria Martin's dreams—blond, tan, and an athlete. Victoria's summer job as a mother's helper on Fire Island allows her to realize her dreams for Jim will be working there as well. Her fantasies are, however, shattered when Jim applies tremendous pressure for a sexual relationship on the very first date. Victoria immediately interprets the conflict as involving power and control: " 'I don't want you to do that,' I say, and it's really crazy because here it is, my body, and he's annoyed that he can't do what he wants to it. Unreal. And he really is annoyed, like it was his" (2:1979, p. 102). Victoria's remarks have little effect on Jim. As they leave the beach, Jim continues to kiss her and only stops when they part for the night. The next evening at The Monkey (the local teen club), Jim wastes no time inviting Victoria to go out and sit with him on the pier. At her refusal, Jim flares up, remarking, "You have a lot of growing up to do" (2:1979, p. 137), and turns to dance with another girl. Jim infantilizes Victoria in an attempt to instill doubt in her mind regarding the validity of her actions. This discrediting of the heroine's feelings and right to control her body is also evident in *Up in Seth's Room*.

Seth Warnecke also pressures Finn Rousseau to sleep with him. This shatters Finn's feelings regarding the special quality of their romance and reveals Seth's lack of respect for her opinions. Finn's resistance only makes matters worse, causing a breach in their relationship. Some time later, Seth explains that his relentless pressure was a male tactic to counteract what he interpreted to be Finn's empty and meaningless protestations:

"I always figured the thing to do was try, just keep trying. You know. If at first you don't succeed . . . that's the male creed."

"That's a poem," she said. "I don't understand. What does it mean?"

"It means that the macho thing to do with a girl is never take no for an answer. Just keep trying. Wear her down one way or other." (2:1979, p. 190)

Although Finn is finally able to convince Seth of the validity of her position, the novel leaves the reader with the implication that at some future date Finn will be involved in a genital relationship. There has never been any question regarding Finn's or any other heroine's eventual incorporation into this form of sexuality. Finn's decision to forego intercourse represents a stage in her sexual development and is not viewed as a legitimate perspective to guide the remainder of her life. Timing has been the issue in this and other novels. This points to how the novels link sexuality with power, control, and knowledge.

Sexuality, power, control and knowledge

The novels establish connections by privileging romance as the set of relations in which heroines' sense of their own sexuality arises and where their knowledge of sexuality is acquired. Heroines' heads throb (*My First*

Love and Other Disasters, 2:1979), stomaches feel fluttery (*Practically Seventeen*, 1:1943), faces burn, palms sweat, (*Princess Amy*, 3:1981), and the girls feel tingly all over (*P.S. I Love You*, 3:1981) only after that special boy has sealed his love with a kiss. I have already discussed the importance of the dynamic of individual specialness as it pertains to romance. This dynamic exists within the context of sexuality and knits together questions of power, control, and knowledge in adolescent romance fiction.

In all the novels, girls' sexuality is dormant up to the moment of romantic specialness. Sexual pleasure begins with romance and is ultimately shaped and controlled by this same set of relations. At the juncture of the moments of romance and specialness, the heroine becomes both sexually aware and subjected to the male power and control underlying sexuality. This represents the heroine's incorporation into the power relations underlying heterosexuality. The formal control of romance by boyfriends is consolidated through their positions as definers of girls' sexuality. This control is buttressed by the books' insistence that boys are the only legitimate objects of girls' desires.

The resistances of heroines in so many period 2 novels provides a clear glimpse of the systems of power and control implicit in the code of sexuality within the entire sample. Prior to this period, questions of power and control were not directly addressed. During period 3 they are once again submerged below the text's surface. At the outset, genital relationships are an intrusive element in period 2 novels. However, this particular form of sexuality is contained within traditional sexuality through its contextualization within romance. This is most apparent in the novels *Mr. and Mrs. Bo Jo Jones* (2:1967), *Up in Seth's Room* (2:1979), *My Darling, My Hamburger* (2:1971), and *Very Far Away From Anywhere Else* (2:1976). Intercourse puts heroines in the position of reacting to boys either responding to their sexual advances or having to fight them off. Both constrain female sexuality, molding it as response rather than action.[9] The control of sexual meanings is also achieved through the absence of a discussion of the full range of sexual responses. By emphasizing the psychological and excluding the physical, the texts legitimate a passive female sexuality.

The subject of teenage intercourse and heroines' resistance are important developments within the code of sexuality in the sample because they clearly set up a dichotomy between male and female sexuality, defining a heroine's sexuality in relation to that of her boyfriend. Boys initiate all sexual encounters. Tom Kitchell hugs Jean Burnaby (*Sorority*

Girl, 1:1952), Tootie Bodger kisses Barbara MacLane (*Sister of the Bride,* 2:1963), Paul Leonard has intercourse with Darien Holmes (*I'll Always Remember You. . . . Maybe,* 3:1981). In these novels and scores of others, male sexuality is understood as active, spontaneous, and most important, genital in nature. The novels of period 2 take male sexuality one step further by portraying it as rampant and dangerous through the characters of Brett Kingsman (*Up a Road Slowly,* 2:1966), Sean Collins (*My Darling, My Hamburger,* 2:1971), Ed Brooks (*Ruby,* 2:1976), and Seth Warnecke (*Up in Seth's Room,* 2:1979).

Heroines' sexuality is also portrayed as dangerous, but in a different way. The linking of biological reproduction with sexuality renders heroines' sexuality as dangerous and makes families show an interest in preventing heroines from being "out of control." The resistances of heroines to boys' sexual overtures tends both to defuse the danger of their sexuality and cement that sexuality into patterns the very opposite of boys': passive, controlled, and nongenital in nature. Through this process, sexual desire is held in check, leaving love as its substitute. Sex then becomes the domain of masculinity, a domain to which girls have access, but legitimately only through a romance with a boy.

Summary

Heroines and young women readers learn several things about sexuality. They learn that feminine sexuality is dangerous, that sexual desire must be properly channeled, and that the proper channel is heterosexual romance. Other lessons heroines learn by heart concern their roles as enforcers of the traditional code of sexuality that limits sexual expression to chaste kissing. Heroines also learn that their bodies are the site of many struggles for control—boyfriends, parents, and the girls themselves all contend for ultimate control. Another aspect of sexual knowledge relates to the relation between sexuality and procreation. Heroines learn that this relation is much closer for women than it is for men because almost every instance of intercourse results in pregnancy. They learn that biology is destiny. The novels deliver a strong ideological message that once again reinforces the old double standard that is rooted in a rigid gender division. Heroines learn that heterosexuality means sexuality. The emphasis on a single sexual orientation perpetuates the idea that sexuality is a unitary phenomenon rather than a process marked by a plurality of definitions as Caplan (1987) observes. Another important lesson concerns feminine sexual identity as characterized by a low level of sexual desire and action. This is quite similiar to Victorian perspectives on adult women's sexuality as "passionless" (Cott, 1978). However, romance fiction contains strong undercurrents: heroines strain against this passionlessness, where they endeavor to control their own sexuality.

Barrett (1980) contends that sexuality has a political character in that it involves the unequal power relations between women and men. The romance novels I have analyzed certainly exemplify this. Becoming a woman involves a complex process through which the limitations on female power and initiative are learned as well as how to transcend those boundaries. The novels show that a tremendous struggle surrounds the securing of young women's subordination and that in the end they accommodate themselves to whatever autonomy they can secure.

There is another important aspect of romance fiction that I have not yet discussed. The ways in which beautification centers heroines' consciousness in their bodies are discussed in Chapter 4.

4
Mirror, Mirror on the Wall: The Code of Beautification

In the folktale "Snow White and the Seven Dwarfs," the Queen stands before her mirror repeatedly asking who is the fairest woman of all. This question is likewise posed by the heroines of teen romance fiction as they gaze into their mirrors. In the tale, the mirror answers that it is not the Queen who is the fairest, but another woman. Heroines also learn that they are not fair enough and look to beauty products and fashion to transform themselves into a vision of beauty. Unlike the Queen, the heroine has other mirrors. One mirror is her boyfriend, who is the reason a heroine primps. Another mirror is society, which holds up to heroines a standard of beauty that is almost impossible to attain.

In romance fiction, beauty is the ticket to romantic success, power, and prestige. While interest in beautification and fashion is a way of securing and attracting boys' attention, it also constructs sets of gender meanings around pleasure, bodily comportment, and self.[1] Before discussing the code of *beautification*, I would like to address several of the tensions inherent in beautification and fashion for women.

The politics of beauty

Spelman points out that women have been historically viewed as body, as bound to their own bodies or responsible for the bodily aspects of life (Spelman, 1982, p. 125). This ranges from women's relation to childbirth and child-rearing to the spectacle of women as beautiful objects to be looked at. These represent women's experience of their bodies under both patriarchy and capitalism.[2] Each has helped to alienate women from their physical selves. Rich (1976) sums up the prevailing sentiment: to be a woman today means either being imprisoned in the body or denying it in favor of an engaging personality and intelligence as the marks of femininity. Neither of these by itself is a satisfying way of conceptualizing femininity. To deny the body in favor of the intellect is to fail to recognize an important aspect of women's identity. To glorify the body solely for another, particularly, for a man, is to participate in one's own oppression.

Hence a heavy weight hangs over women when it comes to beauty. Women who devote much of their time and energy to attaining a beautiful body are castigated as vain and narcissistic. Those who refuse to primp and paint are regarded as "plain Janes," as somehow not fulfilling their social obligation to be beautiful for men. Beauty is certainly in the eye of the beholder, but when it comes to women, the eye that stares back to them from their mirrors is not their own, but a man's. For as Chapkis (1986) notes, women beautify themselves for the recognition and life opportunities that beauty affords, particularly those that men offer. Lakoff and Scherr (1984) further observe that women can "trade" their beauty for strength, influence, power, and security. Hence beauty is not for women's own pleasure, but is rather a commodity to be bartered for romance and power (Chapkis, 1986, p. 95). A woman is not on her own here; she has much help from the "beauty/fashion complex."

The cosmetics and fashion industry occupies a strategic position as the origin of many of these ideologies of beauty for today's women. Bartky explains that this "beauty/fashion complex" often offers a single vision of beauty: small nose, flawless complexion, blond hair, and slim figure (Bartky, 1982, p. 135). Cosmetic firms use this vision of glorified women's bodies to ingrain the habit of repeated use of beauty products. Their hidden agenda is the deprecation of women's bodies. This occurs through the implication that women's bodies are lacking in beauty in the first place, thus requiring the technology of cosmetics to approach the visions of perfection that this industry offers.

There is a central irony here in the current ideal of the "natural" beauty. One is to become beautiful using techniques that conceal the use of cosmetics in the first place. For as Chapkis reminds us, "a 'real woman' would be naturally feminine while she [the inferior woman] is only in disguise" (Chapkis, 1986, pp. 5–6). The current emphasis on blending cosmetics and the return to "natural" shades of foundation, eye shadow, and lipstick are ways of reconciling the irreconcilable. This is further complicated by the fact that despite tremendous outlays in time and money, most women can never attain this beauty ideal, thus condemning them to the relentless pursuit of an elusive ideal.

This attention to cosmetics has the effect of fragmenting the body into its various parts, which are then regarded as problem areas to be worked on. As the ideal image is attainable only through makeup for the face, and creams and lotions for the legs, women can regard their bodies as separate areas, having—according to Coward—a "life of their own" (Coward, 1984, p. 43). This fragmentation is doubly reinforced by the fashion industry. Coward explains that fashion "implies a mode of dress, or overall style, which is accepted as representing up-to-dateness" (Coward, 1984, p. 29). Clothing is central to one's body image, achieving its effect through its ability to define or camouflage body parts. Waists are emphasized through tight belts; straight or full skirts define or conceal legs and hips. Hence, through fashion and cosmetics, the notion of woman as body comes full circle in the fragmentation of women's sense of self.

Chapkis (1986) notes that appearance "talks," that its message concerns not only gender but race and class as well. Lakoff and Scherr contend that beauty is always connected to class (Lakoff & Scherr, 1984, pp. 251–280). The dominant class defines what constitutes beauty through its ownership of the beauty/fashion complex and ability to consume on an immense scale. This elite class also serves as the model of success and glamor for the other classes, presenting just one vision of beauty. That standard of beauty—blond, slim, and small-featured—is not only class-based, but stands in contrast to nonwhite ethnic looks. Beauty becomes political when it is used to support the power of one class and race to dominate other sectors of society, instilling in them doubt and feelings of inferiority. Not only does beauty divide women, but it also creates barriers along class and racial lines.

Many of these features are found in teen romance fiction where they form the central elements of the code of *beautification:*

1. Heroines are plain before beauty routines.
2. Heroines must disguise the use of beauty products and appear naturally beautiful.
3. Beauty is the precondition to romance.
4. Heroines are recognized for their beauty.
5. Beauty routines develop a consciousness of physical appearance as a dominant characteristic of femininity.
6. Heroines' bodies are gradually sexualized.
7. Heroines resist sexual objectification.
8. Beauty models are class-and-race specific.

I now trace the development of the code of *beautification*, starting with how heroines become beautiful.

Plain Janes and painted ladies

When white heroines look into their mirrors, the reflection they see does not please them. They see freckles, drab hair, chubby cheeks, or a general unattractiveness. Their reaction is not self-acceptance, but a decision to alter their appearance. Although beautification is important in each of the three periods, the novels of periods 1 and 3 provide the best glimpses of how the "plain girl" becomes a beauty who wins the admiration of all and the affection of that special boy.

Heroines derive their models of feminine beauty from magazines. In period 1, heroines devour movie-fan magazines in a conscious effort to copy the special look of the stars. Dyer (1979) explains that women stars of the 1940s and 1950s were considered to be fashion leaders and beauty models for women, and were often photographed in fashions specifically designed for them. In *Motion Picture Magazine* (1953, April, p. 10) June Haver, a Twentieth Century-Fox Star, acts as a beauty consultant to readers. Here she imparts the secrets of lovely skin while cultivating a camaraderie between fan and star. Never mind that she is also promoting Lux soap! The idea of the "natural beauty" is also evident in a beauty column in *Screen Stories:* "Want the lads to think you're just 'naturally pretty,' don't you? Use make-up, of course, but apply it the smart way!" (Herrick, 1952, p. 48).

In period 3 fashion magazines and models still provide heroines with standards of beauty. Today's models sell commodities through their special look. The faces of supermodels such as Clotilde and Patti Hansen look out from the covers of *Glamour* and *Vogue* as examples of what women should look like. The fact that artificiality is at the center of this look is evident in Clotilde's observation that she is "an optical illusion" (Lakoff & Scherr, 1984, p. 111) created by the camera and makeup. The fact that this look is the result of hours of work and the orchestration of legions of beauty specialists is suppressed in the final product: the natural look.

Several novels provide excellent glimpses into the dynamics underlying heroines' transformation from plain to pretty. In *Seven Days to a Brand-New Me* (3:1982), heroine Maddy Kemper concludes that she is

"Drab Person of the Year" from face to personality. The novel takes its name from Maddy's quick self-improvement program that features an entire makeover. Clara Conrad's dreams of becoming a popular girl revolve around being "as cute as possible" (Pevsner, 1980, p. 62). Like Maddy, Clara has her own improvement- and popularity-plan based on a new "look." When Kate Vale (*Paintbox Summer*, 3:1949) sees her image in the mirror, she frowns, remarking that her freckles and wide mouth make her unattractive. Kate immerses herself in a self-improvement project during her summer at the artist colony in Provincetown.

Other novels convey the idea that heroines' bodies are inferior in their un-madeup state. In *Practically Seventeen* Tobey Heydon remarks that her sister Alicia looks "ghastly in the morning, being so pale and washed out without her makeup" (1:1943, p. 22). Similarily, in *Wait for Marcy* (1:1950), Marcy and her friends are lounging in old clothes without makeup and set hair, enjoying themselves and the freedom that this "natural" state affords them, and suddenly the doorbell rings. The heroines must hide, fearing that their boyfriends might glimpse them in their natural state. Although the novels are clear that this natural state is unattractive and that they need cosmetics, heroines who do use makeup are caught in a central contradiction: their beauty must appear natural and not show the traces of the work of beautification.

Beauty is the disguise that many heroines uneasily wear. Heroines such as Kentucky Jackson (*Practically Seventeen*, 1:1943) and Devon Merriott (*Wait for Marcy*, 1:1950) are censured as "painted ladies" because of their obvious use of cosmetics. Cass Canfield's experimentation with an old rinse goes awry (*Blueberry Summer*, 1:1956), leaving her hair a rainbow of golds and yellows. Heroines spend so much time on bodily transformation because they understand the close connection between beauty and romance.

The girl of his dreams

Heroines feel that no boy could possibly care for them as they are. As soon as they meet a potential boyfriend, they immerse themselves in rigorous beauty routines.[3] These images dominate many period 1 and 3 novels,[4] but E. Ogilvie's *Blueberry Summer* contains the most sustained treatment of the topic. Heroine Cass Canfield initially appears as a "plump girl with a round, sulky face and brown hair scraped back into an untidy pony tail," whose "shapeless sweatshirt . . . made her look not only plumper but as shapeless as the garment itself" (1:1956, p. 7). All her mother's efforts to teach Cass poise and a sense of fashion have no effect until Cass makes up her mind that she is going to become the beautiful self she imagines. Essential to her transformation is a boy and involvement in a fairy-tale romance that would bring out the "fine and unique under the ugly-duckling exterior" (1:1956, p. 46). The desire to please Adam Ross proves to be this kind of experience, although the romance is far from a fairy tale. Cass's dreams of a slim self are realized through her dieting. Where she formerly would pay scant attention to her hair and clothes, these become her preoccupations once Adam is part of the picture. The novel ends with a slim and confident Cass, and the promise of not only a firm romance with Adam, but also with other boys as well. This novel sends a strong message to readers: beauty efforts are rewarded by the devotion of the boy of your dreams.

Feeling pretty

This romance fiction outlines both the process of becoming beautiful and the result, the picture-pretty girl. Beautification is one of the ways in which women's consciousness becomes centered in the body, with a focus on the physical self as a defining feature of femininity. Women's consciousness is constructed with every stroke of the hairbrush and twist of the curl. Julie Connors of M. Stolz's *The Day and the Way We Met* notes that all this beauty activity is natural, "as much as part of a girl as her heartbeat" (1:1956, p. 159). Other heroines concur. Clara Conrad (*Cute is a Four-Letter Word*, 3:1980) feels that her self-improvement program was worth it all when she secures the attention and affection of the popular Skip Svoboda. Beautification only achieves its effect when heroines receive the recognition and approval of their second pair of eyes, boys.

Heroines' femininity is constructed during the moments of special recognition that bind together romance, sexuality, and beautification. Such a moment is captured in *Wait for Marcy* when Marcy debuts in party dress in front of her family and boyfriend Steve (1:1950, pp. 65–66).[5] Marcy "floats" in layers of white netting flecked with silver swirling about her. Steve conveys his reaction through an appreciative "Wow," likening Marcy's appearance to that of a Hollywood star on her way to a premiere. In *P.S. I Love You* Mariah Johnson comments on the effect her romance with Paul Slade has on her appearance:

> In one short day, I had turned pretty . . . Just the night before I'd been practicing my smile, and it had been just as rigid as it had always been. But Paul had said my smile was beautiful—sure enough, now it was (3:1981, 60).

Contained in this observation is the idea of women's bodies as the legitimate object of the male gaze. Bartky (1979, p. 36) notes that this look sexually objectifies women and separates their bodies into parts, which then become emblematic of the total person. This is well illustrated in *Up in Seth's Room* where Finn Rousseau's father signifies his appreciation of her party attire by a whistle and calling her a "knockout" (2:1979, p. 26).[6] This moment of recognition contains the dynamic through which heroines are sexually objectified and participate in their own objectification; they enjoy being recognized by boys and looking pretty for them.

Period 1 novels represent the beginning of a theme that runs through all the novels and connects the elements of the code of beautification. Here young women come to be represented by and to see themselves as body. In this period heroines are drawn into this perspective through the recognition they receive when specially attired in party clothes. When it comes to period 2 novels, heroines are recognized as sexy bodies no matter what they are wearing.

In the eye of the beholder

The most noticeable thing about the treatment of beautification in the novels of period 2 is that there is little indication as to how heroines get this way. The many pages devoted to applying makeup, setting the hair, and choosing clothing which are so characteristic of period 1 are replaced by the fact that heroines appear to be naturally beautiful without any visible work.[7] A case in point is Liz Carstensen (*My Darling, My Hamburger*, 2:1971) whose beauty and grace simply exist. There are no indications that she spends any time before the mirror. The same may be said for Gloria (*My First Love and Other Disasters*, 2:1979), who always looks as if she just emerged from the beauty salon. How does one make sense of this? Girls' faces become less important in defining their prettiness in period 2. Consequently, there are fewer allusions to cosmetics. However, other aspects of heroines' bodies—breasts and hips—now define their attractiveness. Heroines' bodies are now sexualized, a new development in the novels.

This coincides with increased sexual tensions in period 2 novels and represents another way of sexually objectifying heroines. Styles of dress such as the low-cut neckline of Liz Carstensen's prom dress and Maggie Tobin's clinging jeans (*My Darling, My Hamburger*, 2:1971) reveal bodily areas previously concealed.[8] The abundant wolf-whistles and catcalling that greet heroines in public places are other indications of this objectification.[9] Where boys would gaze longingly at heroines' faces in period 1 novels, heroines' bosoms, hips, and thighs now are objects of their gaze and desire. One of the best examples of this fragmentation of the heroine's body occurs in *Up in Seth's Room*, when Jerry Demas meets Finn Rousseau. Jerry "sizes up" Finn with a head-to-toe look that is sexual in intent (2:1979, p. 22).

Jerry's "roaming hands" at the party signify that he regards Finn as just another body. In *My Darling, My Hamburger*, Liz Carstensen and Maggie Tobin accept a ride from two boys, Rod and Don. The heroines thank the boys for the ride. Don frames his pleasure in this manner:

> "It was really a pleasure meeting you," Don said.
> His voice was deep and sincere.
> "Thank you," Maggie smiled.
> "Yes, indeed." Then he added with an innocent smile, "And you've got a nice pair of knockers" (1:1971, p. 35).

What is pleasurable is not Maggie's personality or her company, but the sight of her breasts. Don's look has the effect of reducing Maggie's entire sense of self to body and its individual parts.

The reclassification of the heroine as sexy body is highly contradictory in period 2. In Chapter 3, I indicated that heroines may look somewhat sexy but should not be sexually experienced. Style and fashion are intricately implicated not only in attracting a boyfriend, but also in sexualizing heroines' bodies, whether they are aware of it or not. Although, certain styles may gain boys' recognition, it is now a recognition that not only objectifies heroines, but also makes them vulnerable to sexual exploitation.

Through the looking glass

Although, many heroines accept beautification as an important part of femininity, some, like Julie Connors (*The Day and the Way We Met*, 1:1956), Judy Graves (*Junior Miss*, 1:1942), Jane Howard (*The Boy Next Door*, 1:1956), and Amy Painter (*Princess Amy*, 3:1981) question these practices. These novels constitute a distinct minority of the books, but they nevertheless merit discussion as they represent additional tensions within the novels' ideology of femininity.

The most direct statement of this resistance is found in *The Day and the Way We Met* when Julie Connors calls into question what she terms this feminine "glossing and burnishing, this daily and nightly coddling of your good points, subduing of your bad" (1:1956, p. 159). However, Julie never gives up her own beauty routines as she is not convinced that she can realize her long-held dream of a romance with Geoff Miller without this glossing and burnishing. The reader becomes acquainted with Judy Graves through her struggles with her mother and sister to remain unchanged. Although it is true that Judy is physically and psychologically transformed at the prospect of romance near the end of the novel, she resists beautification longer than any other heroine. Likewise, in *Princess Amy* Amy Painter declines to go along with the "you can never be too slim" (3:1982, p. 52) philosophy of her aunt Marcella and cousin Candace. She also refuses to sit about like Candace and her friends when she could be swimming and sailing. Like Judy, Amy feels satisfied with her physical self until Aunt Marcella sends Amy's confidence into a tailspin by buying her a jumpsuit one size too small. Despite this, Amy's self-confidence is restored once she leaves Mackinac Island. In *The Boy Next Door*, Jane Howard is baffled by her younger sister Linda's continual attention to her appearance. Although Jane is disappointed by her "plain face . . . and . . . no color hair" (1:1956, p. 10), she does not become a slave to the mirror or consider self-improvement programs as do other heroines.[10]

I have already discussed how boys' approval acts as a second mirror for heroines to test the effects of their beauty efforts. Gazing in both mirrors, heroines like Cass Canfield, Maddy Kemper, Kate Vale, Clara

Conrad, and Judy Graves see the results of beautification in the form of a new identity. Although heroines like what they see, they are convinced of their acceptability only after a boy has given his approval. Boys are the only ones allowed to derive pleasure from girls' looks.

There are sanctions against heroines who consciously bask in the sunlight of self-admiration. In *Practically Seventeen* (1:1943) Kentucky Jackson arrives at Green Lake at the beginning of summer vacation. Kentucky is quickly christened the "southern menace" by heroine Tobey Heydon and her friends because of Kentucky's impact on their boyfriends. Kentucky gathers all the boys into an admiring entourage that spends days "gazing up solefully" at Kentucky's "absolute perfection" (1943, p. 142). Kentucky is criticized for her devastating effect on the boys and the fact that she knows she is beautiful. Kentucky clearly derives a conscious pleasure from looking beautiful, and, although she enjoys the boys' compliments, her sense of self is not dependent on the boys' approval. Similarly, Devon Merriott of *Wait for Marcy* (1:1950) visits her cousin Liz Kendall, who happens to be Marcy's close friend. All the boys are enthusiastic about Devon's beauty and dream of spending time with her. The other girls christen Devon a "steamroller" whose purpose in life is to get boys in "her clutches" (1:1950, pp. 93–94). Like Kentucky, Devon savors her beauty, not for the effect it has on others, but because it makes her feel good. Both of these characters partially subvert the dominant relationships between beauty, power, and gender in romance fiction. Their self-confirmation does not take place totally within traditional patterns of male power and authority. Although these subversions appear in a minority of the novels, their presence is important because they point once again to the fact that romance fiction is not a seamless text[11] when it comes to representing femininity.

These novels reveal the strains within the code of beautification and its relation to femininity. It is interesting that those novels that question beautification and its patterns of power are most concentrated within period 1 where there is also the greatest endorsement of beautification. One explanation for this apparent contradiction lies in the fact that when cultural practices are represented in literature they are not of one fabric. Although there is overwhelming agreement as to the necessity and value of beautification, other interpretations enter through the back door, so to speak. However, the questioning of various aspects of femininity that appear in the novels from time to time are just that—questions and not fundamental changes.

Skin-deep

In the world of romance fiction, when women of color peer into the mirror, the vision confronting them is a perplexing one. The chocolate complexions, prominent lips, and curly hair of black heroines stimulate pride in some and are a source of self-loathing for others. While all heroines have misgivings about their physical selves, no white heroines experience self-consciousness over skin color to the degree manifested by black heroines. It would be a mistake to assume that the heroines of color in *Ruby* (2:1976), *The Friends* (2:1973) and *Ludell and Willie* (2:1977, 1981) automatically internalize white models of beauty. Rather, these novels show the rarely disclosed dimension of beautification and femininity: the pain involved in accommodating someone else's definitions of self. *Ludell and Willie* contains the best discussion of the impact white models of beauty on poor black heroines. Ludell laments the double standard of appearance for women and men:

> "Wish I could be natural with him, like he is with me. He'll come right out on the front proch in the morning wearing a stocking cap and don't be the least bit shame—but me? I be running for a scarf if I just come outside to see and my hair's not combed. I'm always worried he might see me less than perfect and it's so stupid!" (2:1977, 1981, p. 42)

In *The Friends* Phyllisia Cathy sees herself as "plain and tall . . . and without shape" (2:1973, p. 27). These misgivings about feminine appearance hold regardless of race and class differences. A white middle-class heroine like Marcy Rhodes (*Wait for Marcy*) and the white working class Jean Jarrett (*Jean and Johnny*) have expressed the same sentiments. However, specific race dimensions of beauty are revealed in *Ludell and Willie* when Ludell and her friends are discussing the results of the cheerleading tryouts. All have mixed feelings about Edwina, who uses bleaching cream to meet the preference for lighter skinned girls. Further indication of the considerable pressure to conform to white beauty standards is provided by Ruthie Mae, who speaks of a boy who would not date her because she was "jes too dark!" (2:1977, 1981, p. 57). Underlying these discussions is the pain involved in adjusting oneself to standards beyond one's control. Daphne Duprey of *Ruby* stands out as one of the only heroines black or white content with herself. Daphne's obliviousness to her appearance and concentration on developing a keen mind make her a rare heroine in romance fiction. These three novels constitute a small fraction of the sample of romance fiction, but their power to expose the false foundations of beauty and the pain it entails is considerable.

Summary

The image of the heroine standing before the mirror with her mascara as the magic wand that promises to transform her into someone beautiful and desirable is a key component in the feminine discourse developed in romance fiction. According to Winship (1978), becoming beautiful is a means through which women acquire "creative individuality" and experience a sense of personal success. That this success is purchased at the expense of developing an integrated sense of body and mind is downplayed in romance fiction. Another aspect of beautification that must be teased from the texts is that heroines become sexually objectified in their quest for the ideal boy. Heroines' utter conviction that the only way to attract a boy is to maximize the visual effect they have intimately involves them in their own subordination because of the connections between looking and power. Romance fiction is an exemplification of Coward's important observation that "women's inability to return such a critical and aggressive look is a sign of subordination, of being recipients of another's assessment" (Coward, 1984, p. 76).

The code of beautification continues the theme of heroines' consciousness developed in relation to boys. What the novels say about heroines' physical selves is bounded within that larger configuration of power and control inhabited by both romance and sexuality. In becoming the girl of a boy's dreams, the heroine accepts another's version of reality as her own: how she should behave, think, and look. The ability to define reality for another is certainly one of the more important forms of social power. However, it is important to reiterate the fact that beautification especially exemplifies, in the final analysis how gender relations in romance fiction exist in a kind of "teeth-gritting harmony."

Thus far I have dwelt on the gender dimensions of romance, focusing on how the codes of romance, sexuality, and beautification contribute to the developing discourse on femininity. The introduction of class and racial aspects of the code of beautification serve as a reminder that femininity is shaped by these social processes as well. Chapter 5 will examine the class and racial aspects of femininity in romance fiction.

5
Keepers of Heart and Hearth: Gender, Class, and Race in Romance Fiction

Thus far, romance, beautification, and sexuality have been central components of femininity in romance fiction. However, these are only part of the picture. Femininity arises through the "material" aspects of life such as babysitting, housework, shopping, and the consumption of goods and services. Moreover, women's and girls' experiences in these areas are not of one piece. Femininity cannot be understood without accounting for the ways that class and race differentially structure women's and girls' experiences in romance fiction and everyday life.[1] Before analyzing class and race in adolescent romance fiction, I want to turn to recent accounts of the relation between gender, class, and race in modern society.

Women, race and class

Women are placed differently within the class structure partly as a result of gender and race (Davis, 1982; Hartmann, 1981; Hooks, 1984). Women do not easily fit into traditional definitions of class based exclusively on the wage and on work struggles, because of the ways that women's paid work is differentiated according to class and race.[2] Traditional accounts of women's class position are based on the wage-earning spouse and family (Wright, 1978) or leave women out of the picture altogether (Poulantzas, 1975). These accounts are often oblivious to the fact that many white working-class women and women of color have long been wage earners in their own right (Kessler-Harris, 1982).[3]

Traditional class theory also glosses over the differences between women's and men's experiences in families and the real economic dependence of some working and nonworking women. Moreover, it ignores the fact that even when women are in the workforce, they still work in two sectors: one where they are paid and the other where they are not. Moreover, traditional theory does not pay attention to women's work as housewives and consumers as important aspects of their class position. In order to conceptualize women's class locations in a way that takes into account their varied social positions, I will draw from recent research on housework, wage work, and consumption, starting with Wright's (1978) notion of "contradictory class location."

Contradictory class location

From a Marxist view, class has been defined as the relationship of the individual to the means of production. The means of production involves the patterns of social relations that arise when women and men work on and change nature. Under capitalism, some people produce what Burawoy calls life's necessities while others control the surplus, that is, the gap between wages received and the actual value of workers' labor power (Burawoy, 1979, pp. 13–16). What results is a set of tensions between owners (capitalists) and workers (the working and middle classes). Production is the central element in these definitions of class. Because housewives and managerial, supervisory, and technologically oriented occupations do not fit these traditional class definitions, there has been a movement away from production as the basis of class membership (Ehrenreich & Ehrenreich, 1977).

Wright explains that the middle class and women have "contradictory class locations": they simultaneously occupy several class positions depending upon the criteria used.[4] The recent research on American class structure revealed that one-half of the class positions were either working-class or contradictory class locations (Wright et al., 1982, p. 724). When looking at the working class from the perspectives of gender and race, they found that this class was composed mostly of women and minorities (Wright et al., 1982, p. 745).[5] While this study illuminates the class position of many working women from various races, it leaves out how housework and consumption patterns impact on women's class locations.[6] Nevertheless, the notion of contradictory class location is useful once the domestic sides of women's lives are taken into account.

Housework

For the past fifteen years, housework has been identified as an important element in women's class position. By concentrating on the continuities and differences between housework and paid work, "domestic labor" theory provided a way of accounting for the class location of nonwage earning women. Dalla Costa (1972) treats housework as "productive" work that contributes to surplus value. Under capitalism, the gap between wages received and the actual value of workers' labor power creates "surplus value" or profit, which belongs to capital. In the case of domestic labor, the profit is not in dollars and cents. As the housewife feeds and clothes her family, she performs work necessary to the maintenance of capitalism by readying them for another day of work. Coulson, Magas, and Wainwright (1975) view housework as "unproductive" because the housewife is not in a direct relation to wage-earning; her work mainly benefits her family. According to Delphy (1976), domestic labor is a separate economic form, with its own organization of work and it's own relations of power and control.[7]

Although interest in the domestic-labor debate has waned of late, the importance of this research should not be underestimated. It was the first to demonstrate that women's class position is in part rooted in their work at home, and that this work has linkages to the larger economy. But in uniformly considering the home as the main source of women's oppression, domestic labor research overlooked the tensions inherent in the domestic setting. For women of color involved in domestic-service work, their own work at home and in others' homes may give housework a different meaning.[8] As Hooks (1984) observes, the long involvement of white and black working-class women in the world of work can at times make the prospect of spending more time at home more inviting. This observation does not downplay the oppressiveness of household tasks, but rather serves as a reminder that lumping women together in a common category simply ignores how their experiences vary. Housework once again figures prominently in current explanations of the class position of both wage and non wage-earning women, particularly in the work of Hunt and Starrs (1983), who argue that the traditional productive/nonproductive distinction may no longer be tenable given both the present tendency in capitalism to take away worker control and the rise in importance of service-sector work. Drawing an analogy between housewives and domestic workers, Hunt and Starrs emphasize that only the existence of the wage contract as opposed to the marriage contract distinguishes between paid and unpaid domestic service (Hunt & Starrs, 1983, p. 96). Both types of workers perform work that is outside commodity production; their production is for immediate use and not for exchange. If housewives received pay for their work as domestic workers do, they would occupy an intermediate position within the working class, one termed the "semi-working class." This analysis by Hunt and Starrs provides a way of accounting for housewives' class position without recourse to defining their location through the wage-earning spouse or family.

Out to work

Gardiner argues (1977) that examining women's wage work still does not markedly clarify their class position. Even when women work, they are likely to be dependent on a wage earning spouse or other forms of financial assistance because of the ways that gender, class and race structure wages.[9] According to Amott (1985), the workforce is internally stratified according to race, gender, and class. White women still earn only seventy-three percent as much as white men ("Employment in Perspective: Women in the Labor Force," 1988, p. 1); black women earn sixty-five percent of white men's wages and other women of color receive even less. ("Employment In Perspective: Minority Workers," 1988, p. 1). Women's relationship to wage work is further mediated by family responsibilities, housework, economic dependency on men, and the phenomenon of single women heading households. These mesh together to form a complex pattern that conditions the kinds of wage work women perform.

Although there are more women than ever in the workforce, they continue to be clustered within the traditionally feminine work of the nursing, teaching, clerical, and the service industries. Between 1970 and 1980 the service sector grew by fourteen million jobs, with women new to the workforce filling seventy-five percent of the jobs (J. Smith, 1984, p. 302). Keeran (1985) estimates that by 1990 service industries will employ almost three-quarters of the labor force, mostly women. These developments are very significant for women in view of the nature of service sector work. For as Castells notes, this work involves the production of benefit or the well-being of the recepient and is primarily interpersonal and relational in nature (Castells, 1980, p. 169).

Housework and the paid work of women have historically interpersonal and relational. Current service-sector work is making women's work inside the home more similar to that outside. However, the real and imagined control that women have sometimes experienced as homemakers (Oakley, 1974) rarely extends to service work, especially in traditionally feminine work (Apple, 1988; Castells, 1980). The features of low pay and little control are characteristic of working-class jobs in general. The developments I have outlined spell trouble for many women, especially for working-class women and women of color, who have historically occupied the lowest-paying echelons of service occupations (Davis, 1982).[10] Service work for many women means taking positions within the working class or the working poor.

Although wage work and housework are important determinants of women's class position, there is yet another important area that has been given little recognition to date. Consumption conditions women's class position as surely as these other factors.

The opposite side of the paycheck

Whenever we eat, put on clothing, or walk through the door of our home, we are involved in a complex set of economic and social relations that have strong gender dimensions. The act of eating a bowl of soup is a case in point. If the soup is homemade, the ingredients must be grown, assembled, processed, and served. Women of all races and classes occupy a strategic position within this cycle, often as worker inside and outside of the home.[11]

Weinbaum and Bridges define consumption as "the work of acquiring goods and services" (Weinbaum & Bridges, 1979, p. 194). To this definition I would add the fact that there is an accompanying transformation of goods and rendering of services mainly performed by women for household use. Historically, women have done the shopping and arranged for services on the part of the household (Howe, 1978). Women have also worked on the raw materials that goods represent, refashioning them into the kinds of things that not only maintain life, but enhance it as well. These activities represent what Weinbaum and Bridges term "the other side of the paycheck" (Weinbaum & Bridges, 1979, p. 190).

This other side has economic dimensions that may not be readily apparent. Kyrk (1923) claims that consumption has strong ties to the economy, and is the aim and culmination of production. Goods are produced to be used and to turn a profit; when used up they are purchased anew, thus continuing this economic process. I have previously argued that women are closely linked to the economy through their centrality within housework and their historical association with nurturance (if they work for pay, this is doubly the case). Consumption is another aspect of this nurturance which is anchored in a family structure where women are the ones who stretch the paycheck to buy more or just get by.

Women occupy contradictory class locations through consumption depending on whether if they combine their own wage work with domestic duties and have access to spouses' wages. For example, a woman may be working class from the vantage point of a service-sector job, semi-working-class as a housewife, but have a spouse of the working or middle class. The combination of two working-class incomes or the addition of a middle class income may allow consumption on a much grander scale than would be the case if a woman's consumption were limited by her own pay.[12] The significance of a spouse's income or lack there of is evident in the case of single female heads of families. If previously married, these women may lose access to spouses' consuming power, thereby becoming working-class from the perspective of housework, wage work and consumption (Scott, 1985).

Consumption has cultural dimensions as well. Barthes (1978) observes that commodities such as clothing carry cultural messages. A cotton as opposed to a silk dress can signify not only occassion (everyday versus dress-up) and gender, but mark out class boundaries. Carter's (1984) historical study of the consumption practices of young West German women demonstrates the existence of consumption practices characterized by class differences. The notions of "getting by" and "buying more" are useful to identify further these differences. Middle-class consumption features quality and quantity, buying finer and more goods that can be put on display. Emphasis is placed on buying goods ready for immediate use. Clothing is ready to wear, and food may be precooked. Working-class consumption involves purchasing necessities and few luxuries. Goods often require considerable transformation to make them usable. Fabric can be turned into clothing; flour and shortening are essential for bread. With paychecks stretched to get by, the life of commodities is also stretched to the limit.

Keepers of heart and hearth

Teenage girls and class

An area I have not yet discussed is that of class and adolescent girls. Most are neither full-time paid workers nor homemakers, but are partly involved in both kinds of work. They do paid and unpaid work as babysitters, domestics, and mother's helpers in their own or others' homes. As with adult women, consumption figures prominently in their lives. In teen romance fiction, girls' consumption in the middle class is mainly for personal enhancement and is tied to their own earning power and to that of fathers. Working-class white girls have a limited personal consumption while black girls manage family consumption as one of their domestic responsibilities. Bertaux provides a way of clarifying girls' class position through the concept of "class trajectories" (as discussed in Wright, 1979, p. 93). Such trajectories are a series of positions through which individuals move in the course of work and overall life experience. In romance fiction, most adolescent girls are strongly situated within a domestic context and some form of casual service work, both of which are working-class positions. From the point of view of consumption, girls may be either working- or middle-class, depending on their own and their parents' earning power.

In the preceding sections I have shown that class position is shaped by gender and race in complex ways and that women's and girls' class positions are defined through consumption, paid work, and domesticity. It is time to place this discussion in the context of adolescent romance fiction, looking at how together gender, class, and race shape the novels' version of femininity.

Housework: a labor of love?

By and large the lives of women and girls revolve around the home, although the kind and degree of involvement in domestic tasks varies by period, class, and race. A dominant pattern emerges, that of a white middle-class father, a working-class homemaker mother, and several children. This pattern is strongest in period 1 and 3. Although period 2 introduces the topic of wage-earning white women, this aspect of white femininity is largely underrepresented in the fiction as a whole. Another gap in romance fiction is the few references to races other than white.

The occasional black, hispanic or Native American character may be found in period 1 fiction, but it is not until period 2 novels that any women of color take centerstage. Even though black women and girls are the focus of only three out of fifteen novels in this period, these novels reveal much about the continuities and differences of women's and girls' social experiences by race and class.

White women

A single image dominates housework in romance fiction: housework is a labor of love performed by white women with little complaint. Although domesticity shapes white women's lives in most of the novels, it is especially the case in period 1. Adam Wentworth's statement in *Blueberry Summer*, "What is a home without a woman?" (1:1956, p. 63) is emblematic of how white women are associated with home and family in this period. In *The Boy Next Door* (1:1956), Mrs. Howard constantly cooks; her neighbor Mrs. Sanderson is described as a "maternal figure." Mrs. Morrow of *Seventeenth Summer* (1:1942) dusts and polishes from dawn to dusk; in *Practically Seventeen* (1:1943), the Christmas Eve dinner concludes with the women doing the dishes and the men nowhere in sight. In *Paintbox Summer* (1:1949), the big party at Manuel Silva's home depicts women not only cooking the meal but also cleaning up while the men relax and sing songs. Newlywed Morgan Miller's definitions of being a good wife in *The Day and the Way we Met* (1:1956) have to do with shopping, cleaning, and greeting her husband "at the door with a smile and a good dinner waiting and all the things it says in the magazines" (1:1956, p. 209).

Period 2 novels contain the beginning of paid work for some white women. However, paid work does not change these women's status as full-time homemakers, but simply adds more hours to their already full days. Readers are introduced to Mrs. MacLane (*Sister of the Bride*) returning home from a full day of teaching weighted down with heavy bags of groceries. Mrs. MacLane begins her "real" work—cooking, cleaning, and shopping assisted only by her daughter Barbara, and young Gordy MacLane's comment that housework is "women's work" (2:1963, p. 174) sums up men's and boy's aversion to housework. There is a measure of truth here, as women rarely receive help from men when it comes to housework. Another "wonderwoman" is Aunt Cordelia of *Up a Road Slowly* (2:1966). Cordelia teaches school, supervises a working farm, cares for an aged mother, two spinster aunts, a niece, and a "helpless" brother Haskell.[13] Haskell views men as above such mundane matters and tries to counsel his niece Julia that it's "a man's world" and she should "learn to play the game gracefully" (1966, p. 32). Although the novel contains strong statements and examples of male privilege, it also gives voice to the resentment and bitterness of women toward this double load which surfaces in Aunt Cordelia's determination that Julia will not meet a similar fate.

In period 3 novels, domestic themes persist, although the number of direct references to housework decreases. What occurs in their place is an increased emphasis on women as nurturers responsible for the psychological well-being of families. This is quite evident in *California Girl* (3:1981), where Mrs. Webster's life centers on maintaining daughter Jennie's emotional equilibrium so that she can be successful in junior olympic competition. Somehow household work is magically done without anyone lifting a finger. Similarly, Mrs. Holmes in *I'll Always Remember You . . . Maybe* (3:1981) comforts and supports daughter Darien after the breakup of her romance. Although Mrs. Johnson of *P.S. I Love You* (3:1981) does some housework, her primary responsibility is to dispense large quantities of sympathy and understanding to daughter Mariah.

Black women

Black women are key figures in their homes in three period 2 novels. *The Friends* (2:1973) centers on the Cathys, a West Indian family whose affluence stands out amid the general poverty of Harlem. The father, Calvin Cathy, owns a small restaurant; Ramona Cathy sews and keeps house with the aid of daughters Phyllisia and Ruby. *Ruby* (2:1976) and *Ludell and Willie* (2:1977, 1981), also place black women in a domestic context. The former, the sequel to *The Friends,* opens some time after the death of Ramona Cathy. Calvin invites a woman acquaintance to keep an eye on Ruby and Phyllisia and to do the housework. Miss Effie is first described as going "straight to the kitchen like a homing pigeon" (2:1976, p. 109). From that point on she becomes increasing defined in domestic terms: joyfully cooks and cleans because she thinks this is the way to Calvin's heart.

Housework assumes a labor-intensive quality in the second novel, *Ludell and Willie*, which is set in rural Waycross, Georgia. This novel provides many glimpses of women in poor black families, which are epitomized by the Ludell's family, the Wilson's. This novel is unique, in that it is the only one that has elderly women performing all the household tasks. Housework is backbreaking for Ludell's grandmother Mis Wilson, as she must work in the absence of running water, electricity, and convenience appliances. Clothes are ironed using an old-fashioned flatiron that must be heated repeatedly. Mis Wilson has a double relation to housework because she takes in washing and ironing, thereby converting her home to a place where she also works for pay. Other black women such as Mis Toosweet and Sissie White, experience continuities between working in and out of their homes through their work as paid domestics. At a later point I will return to this theme of how all women's work in these novels is continuous across class and race distinctions.

White girls

Housework is high on the agenda for white girls as well. When adult women are not present, housework falls squarely on their shoulders. Period 1 novels present many scenes in which girls have ample opportunities to hone their domestic skills, although at times they do so reluctantly. In Period 1 Angie Morrow (*Seventeenth Summer*, 1:1942) has specific household responsibilities that include dusting, doing dishes, and caring for her younger sister. It seems like all Angie does is one domestic task after another. Like Angie, Cass Canfield of *Blueberry Summer* (1:1946) assumes total responsibility for running the household and caring for her young brother during her mother's absence one summer. Although Cass protests the intrusion of these unwanted tasks on her dreams of a leisurely summer, she nevertheless complies and even comes to enjoy them. Washing, ironing, and preparing supper have been the responsibility of Julie Ferguson (*Going on Sixteen*, 1:1946) as long as she can remember. The home became Julie's domain after her mother's death. In *The Day and the Way We Met* (1:1956), teenage Julie Connor continues her sister Morgan's legacy of domestic responsibility after Morgan's marriage. As in the previous novel, the heroine's mother is dead. Morgan's cheerful domesticity is contrasted to Julie's dislike of housework. Although Julie's father is ablebodied, he renders no assistance. Instead, Julie must order brother Ned to help out.

In period 2 (1963–1979) heroines continue their involvement in housework, although references to housework itself have markedly decreased in comparison to the novels of period 1. On one level, *Sister of the Bride* (2:1963) harkens back to a 1950s domesticity. On another, it questions traditional femininity. For Barbara MacLane domesticity is the way to Bill Cunningham's heart. Barbara's actions stem from Bill's disclosure of his lack of domestic comforts at home because of his mother's career. The cookie jar is empty, and clothes go unmended. Only a woman can perform these duties, in Bill's eyes. Barbara obliges by baking batch after batch of cookies, which Bill promptly consumes. However, Barbara eventually realizes that Bill has been only looking for "a domestic little wren" (2:1963, p. 179) and not a girlfriend. Barbara explodes at being manipulated:

> Suddenly she was mad. Just plain mad. Who did Bill think he was, anyway, eating her cookies day after day and then coming around taking it for granted she would do his mending? She was not his mother. Or his wife . . . . [S]he did not want to mend his shirt, and she was not going to mend it. (2:1963, p. 178)

After this initial rage, Barbara blames herself, and eventually recants her anger. Such ferociousness, she reasons, will not help her "to get along better with boys" (2:1963, p. 180). Other period 2 novels such as *Drop-Out* (2:1963), *Up a Road Slowly* (2:1966) and *I Will Go Barefoot All Summer For You* (2:1973) depict heroines doing the dishes, cleaning, and washing. In general, white heroines are involved in fewer domestic tasks since domesticity itself is not an overriding theme in period 2 fiction. The shift to romantic and familial conflicts overshadows other aspects of heroines' lives.

Period 3 novels do not approach the 1950s in their focus on housework although *Princess Amy* (3:1981) comes close. Helping with household tasks is portrayed as being as natural as breathing to Amy Painter. Amy is a fictional "Miss Mom" as she automatically clears the supper table and volunteers to help with the dishes despite the presence of a maid. Denied the opportunity to pursue these interests because of the presence of paid domestics, Amy manages to keep her skills honed by helping out at a friend's home. In *P.S. I Love You* (3:1981), Mariah Johnson assists her mother in the daily maintenance of a posh Palm Springs Abbott estate, where they are housesitting. Mariah automatically falls into domesticity, uncomplainingly performing her tasks even when it comes to the tedium of polishing the silver.

Black girls

Black girls are caught between the two worlds of school and home, and much of their time is spent fulfilling large domestic responsibilites. This is evident in three period 2 novels, *The Friends* (2:1973), *Ruby* (2:1976) and *Ludell and Willie* (2:1977, 1981). After Ruby and Phyllisia (*Ruby*) have played a prank on Miss Effie and thus caused Calvin Cathy to decide to force Miss Effie to leave, the girls are left with all the housework. Although they clearly despise housework and protest to Calvin, he makes it clear that the housework is now their job. He continually chastises them whenever his meals are not on the table when he returns home (2:1976, p. 24). Edith Jackson (*The Friends*) leads a double life as schoolgirl and as mother to her sisters and brother. Her mother is dead, so she must clean, cook and look after the household despite the presence of two male family members. Edith's internalization of housework as women's exclusive work is evident in her automatic trade of textbooks for pots and pans upon returning home. In *Ludell and Willie*, Ludell does all the cleaning and cooking after her grandmother's stroke. Ludell must also care for her paralyzed grandmother, and receives help only from neighborhood women.

Romance fiction presents readers with one view of housework: a labor of love. This dawn-to-dusk work is rarely questioned by white women and girls. Although *Ludell and Willie*, *The Friends*, and *The Day and the Way We Met* expose the drudgery concealed by the "labor of love" ideology, this is a minority opinion. By placing white women and girls within an all-encompassing domestic context, the novels are able to only not establish a division of labor based on gender, class and race, but to present it as an ideal toward which all women and girls should aspire. One sees the class and race dimensions of this ideal in *Ruby* and *The Friends* are revealed in Ramona Cathy's status as full-time homemaker. Because so many girls also do housework, it is not age that is the determining factor, but rather gender and class. Through the constant association of all women and girls with housework, the novels send readers strong messages that home is where they belong and should stay.

Consumption: Getting by and buying more

In romance fiction, consumption is anchored in families, and it becomes yet another labor of love. The novels show differences along class lines concerning the kinds of commodities purchased, how they are used, and the meanings that accrue to them. Consumption especially demonstrates the ways that women's and men's wages, along with women's ingenuity, make the difference between getting by and buying more. Girls' consumption is largely personal in nature and is directed toward maintaining their prospects for romance, whereas adult women "consume" on the part of families. Periods 1 and 2 provide the best glimpses of the class basis of consumption.

Shopping is a major form of consumption for white women and girls; it is also a mechanism for reinforcing these girls' positions within traditional femininity. Shopping serves another function: it strengthens the bond between white women and girls, and is the activity through which women pass on their accumulated domestic knowledge. In *Going on Sixteen* (1:1946) homemaker Ella Sawyer and daughter Anne delight in shopping for clothes in order to maintain their fashionableness and social position as trendsetters in the community. Their ability to buy more and more emanates from Ella's prudent consumption practices and the substantial income of her businessman spouse. This novel provides evidence of differences in consumption practices and meanings by social class through the "party dress" episode.

A new party dress is an absolute necessity for Anne Sawyer. Shopping for it is a routine although exciting matter. For Anne's close friend, Julie Ferguson, however, shopping is an auspicious event that is dreamed about and anticipated with great relish. Limited funds mean that she must spend a great deal of time calculating how to stretch her fifteen dollars to cover a dress and shoes. Where Anne's generous budget allows her to purchase a sumptuous gown, Julie must settle for gingham. Gingham serves as a reminder of Julie's social class: "[T]he fact that it was gingham bothered Julie. It didn't make it seem like a party dress. Gingham was something she had worn half her life" (1:1946, p. 26).

Here a commodity both stands as a cultural marker of the working class and throws up boundaries between classes.

Another period 1 novel, *Jean and Johnny* (1:1959), provides additional evidence for class differences in consumption. Even with two paychecks, the Jarretts barely get by. Shopping for food becomes the occasion for penny-pinching as Mrs. Jarrett must buy cheaper carton milk and whole pound butter in order to stretch her dollars (1:1959, p. 58). Clothes are made at home or purchased on sale. This continual need to transform goods into a usable form creates additional work. Daughters Jean and Sue Jarrett come to view this continual frugality and effort as the model for their own consumption. Although Jean and Sue lament the lack of money to purchase little extras, each learns to be resourceful in stretching her dollars.

Another shopping episode illustrates how "making do" is central to working-class consumption. The big dance and Jean's need of a special dress results in a debate, with the first thought being how the old can be made again usable. Because Jean thinks her romantic future with Johnny is riding on a dazzling appearance, she insists on using her twenty-dollar savings on a store bought dress. However, the need to transcend the moment of the dance and to consider the future persuades Jean to buy a "sensible" dress of polished cotton. Like Julie Ferguson, Jean also has a friend who has the financial resources to do more than just window shop. Elaine Munday always has plenty of money. Thanks to her executive father, she never has to agonize over how to spend it. While Jean ponders how to buy a dress for twenty dollars, Elaine is already planning to have shoes tinted to match her dress.

A similar tension is maintained between working-and middle-class consumption in period 2. In *Camilla* (2:1965), two friends Camilla Dickinson and Luisa Rowen represent opposing class views. Camilla's Park Avenue apartment with cook and maid is a strong contrast to Luisa's Greenwich Village loft. Although both girls attend the same private school, Luisa's tuition comes from the food budget. One episode serves to signal the class differences that underlie consumption. Camilla's mother impulsively buys several cashmere sweaters with matching skirts for Camilla. No sooner do Camilla and Luisa arrive at the Dickinson's apartment than Camilla's mother commands Camilla to try them on. Luisa's downcast demeanor bespeaks the class differences between the girls which here is symbolized by Luisa's worn sweater and Camilla's cashmere. Later on Luisa's mother rails at Camilla, citing the social inequalities that allow the Dickinson's to "wrap you up in cotton wool and guard you from life" while no one protects her own children (2:1965, p. 113). Other class differences emerge when Camilla is prevented from dating Frank Rowen, Luisa's brother, because of "the way they live." People are judged by their consumption styles in *Mr. and Mrs. Bo Jo Jones* (1967), where the disapproval July Greher's parents show toward her romance with Bo Jo has class dimensions. The Jones's servicable clothing and the "plainness" of their home mark them as unfit for association with the Grehers. Mrs. Jones's "making-do" consumption is contrasted with the conspicuous consumption practiced by the old-money Grehers.

In *Ludell and Willie* (2:1977, 1981) and *The Friends* (2:1973), where black women figure prominently, other views of consumption emerge. Consumption takes the form of a pooling of resources across households and generations. In *Ludell and Willie* the household is a productive unit. Making clothing and having gardens are vital to the survival of these poor black women and their families. Ready-made clothing is a luxury. The many scenes of Ludell's grandma fitting Ludell's home-made clothing while Ludell dreams of being able to buy clothes that fit well emerges as a class perspective on consumption. With food in short supply and utilities rarely paid, consumption as practiced by poor black women features collaboration. A telephone is shared among several families as is running water. This kind of consumption is found nowhere else in the sample and may be associated with class, race, and rural living. Working-class black women in urban settings are in worse straits than their white counterparts. In *The Friends,* Edith Jackson's worn clothing is a sign of no money even for limited personal consumption. Edith holds in check her desires for personal commodities because, as breadwinner, she must use her money for food and housing. Unlike the women in *Ludell and Willie,* Edith has no extended family or community to help her get by.

These novels reveal how commodities mark out and maintain class boundaries. Commodities not only sustain life, but also embellish it as well. Commodities become a symbol of individual and family status and wealth through the ability of women to manage their own and spouses' incomes and to consume more or make do. Young women become consumers primarily within a domestic-romantic context, with romance fiction chronicling how the home becomes their place in the world. Girls' consumption also acts as practice for the kinds of consumption that they as adult women are expected to perform for families. Although women's and girls' consumption appears as noneconomic, it actually completes the economic process when purchases are made. It is directly responsible for the profits companies make. For women who work for pay, connections to the economy are even stronger because a part of their wages is returned directly to business through consumption. In the following section, I discuss the meaning of women's and girls' involvement in yet another world, that of work.

The world of work

Although some novels of all three periods introduce the topic of white women's paid work, this aspect of their lives is underrepresented. Women of color, however, are no strangers to the world of work. In each novel where women of color are present wage work is as much a part of their identities as housework. For both groups, wage work becomes an extension of their duties at home. Women's occupations mentioned in this romance fiction—domestic service, nursing, teaching, clerical, advertising, and the law—is service sector work based on the ideas of helping and caring. Although most white teenage girls do casual paid work such as babysitting, the work of many black girls is necessary to the well-being of their families. Their long-term part-time domestic service helps put food on the table and pay the rent. Like that of their adult counterparts, their work also forms a continuum to the home. In this section, I will trace women's and girls' involvement in the world of work as one aspect of their class position.

White women

Over and over again, the novels reinforce the traditional wisdom that work is a man's world and a woman's place is in the home. This most often applies to the white-middle class woman who is portrayed as the "little woman with the apron." This perspective is supported in period 1 fiction by the fact that in two novels white middle-class women give up their careers after marriage. Lila Rhodes of *Wait for Marcy* (1:1950) uses her nursing skills to repair the scraped knees and elbows of the neighborhood children. Ellen Sawyer of *Going on Sixteen* (1:1946) draws on her training as a professional artist to decorate her home and coordinate family clothing. The career skills of both women have been redefined as primarily domestic through years of work in the home. *Jean and Johnny* (1:1959) is the only period 1 novel in which a white woman of any class works outside of the home. Mrs. Jarrett works part-time as a sales clerk in a fabric shop. The novel makes it clear, however, that Mrs. Jarrett works only out of necessity, to supplement the family income. The fact that she is always depicted in her home and never at work provides additional support for this view.

Period 2 provides glimpses of white women whose jobs in the workforce are mostly pink-collar service jobs or the traditionally feminine professions of teaching and nursing. Of the fifteen period 2 novels in which occupations are discernible, seven married white middle- and working-class women are employed. These jobs range from supermarket checker in *Drop-Out* (2:1963) to nursing in *Up in Seth's Room* (2:1979), teaching in *Sister of the Bride* (2:1963) and *Up a Road Slowly* (2:1966), advertising in *Fridays* (2:1979), and law in *Hey, Dollface* (2:1978) and *Fridays* (2:1979). Mrs. Rousseau (*Up in Seth's Room*) combines her full-time nursing career with fulltime responsibility for the home. *Hey, Dollface* gives the best example of the "supermom" who effortlessly puts in a whole day's work as a high-profile attorney and then returns home to domestic tasks. However, period 2 novels are silent as to the dark side of carrying a full load on two fronts. Although close to half of the novels contain working women, readers only come to know about this aspect of their lives through scattered references in the text. Like period 1, period 2 women are never represented at their jobs. Rather, readers are bombarded with so many domestic references that this work becomes the reality while paid work seems remote and an addition to their "real" work at home.

In period 3, half of the white women hold down jobs. In *Cute is a Four-Letter Word* (3:1980) Mrs. Conrad's work as an elementary-school principal is a result of being widowed with a daughter to support. Similarly, newly divorced Mrs. Johnson (*P.S. I Love You* (3:1981) teaches at a day school to support her daughters. Readers are left to wonder if both women would be working if their life histories had been different. As in period 1, two women have forsaken their careers for marriage. Mrs. Holmes's career of interior design (*I'll Always Remember You . . . Maybe,* 3:1981) and Mrs. Webster's status as a championship swimmer (*California Girl,* 3:1981) ended at the altar. Their decision to forego careers was a direct response to the husband's refusal to "allow" them to work. As in other periods, domesticity becomes white women's real work.

Black Women

The white middle-class model of a male breadwinner and economically dependent wife does not apply to the lives of black women. Although black women are situated in the world of work, their ties to domesticity are equally strong because of the kind of work they perform. These women experience continuities between working in the home and working out of the home as paid domestics. The glimpses of black women's work demonstrates how the division of labor in the workforce is stratified by race as well as by gender and class.

In all periods most black women work as paid domestics or maids. In *Sorority Girl* (1:1952) there is mention of a "colored maid" who serves as a dressing-room attendant in the large hotel where Jan Burnaby attends a sorority dance. The Vales employ a black maid in *Paintbox Summer* (1:1949) as do the Dickinsons (*Camilla,* 2:1965) and Painters in *Princess Amy* (2:1981). The stereotype of the nurturing self-effacing black woman looks out from the text in the first two novels. In *Princess Amy,* Letty's disgust over demanding household members periodically surfaces through her pointed humor. *Ludell and Willie* (2:1977, 1981) provides the best glimpse of black women and girls as paid domestics. Women such as Mis Toosweet, Sissie White, Mrs. Johnson, and Mis Wilson all work long and hard hours in the homes of white families with little complaint. In order to endure the five to six days a week of hard work the women create fantasies about "glo-o-rious white ladies" (2:1977, 1981, p. 2) who pay well and treat them kindly.

These attitudes and traditional forms of black women's work are called into question in the same novel by Ludell's mother Dessa. That Dessa clearly sees the dead-end quality of domestic work is evident in her response to Ludell: "I have to work, and I'm not about to stay down here scratching for a living in no white person's kitchen" (2:1977, 1981, p. 117). Dessa sees low wages as the result of how race conditions black women's work. She has moved north to obtain better work and a better life. Her subsequent insistence that Ludell come to live with her emanates from Dessa's wish that Ludell not experience the fate of black women in the rural South.

White girls

In general, most girls do not work for pay. When they do, their paid work acts as an extension of the domestic side of their lives, although its exact meaning varies according to the class and race of the person intepreting it. In all periods, girls' centrality to housekeeping is reinforced by their service-related jobs of babysitting and domestic work. This work furthers their domestic ties because their own or others' homes are most often the sites of their work.

In period 1 three white girls work parttime in service occupations. Misty Seaton (*Paintbox Summer*, 1:1949) works as a salesclerk in a small gift shop and art gallery. Jean Burnaby (*Sorority Girl*, 1:1952) packs candy into boxes. Julie Connor (*The Day and the Way we Met*, 1:1956) does clerical work in a library. Sue Jarrett (*Jean and Johnny*, 1:1959) does occasional sewing to earn extra money. In each novel, the extra money goes for personal consumption. In other period 1 novels girls perform much unpaid housework and babysitting work that foreshadows their paid work in period 2.

If white girls work for pay, it is not apparent from period 2 novels. Rather, they do much unpaid babysitting and housework in their own homes and depend on parents for their spending money. This absence of white girls from paid work may coincide with the shift in focus in period 2 novels discussed in Chapter 3, where I argued that the warfare between girls and parents regarding romance and sexuality resulted in the careful monitoring of their whereabouts. Confining heroines to the home gives them little opportunity to do paid work. Although in their resistance to dominant gender relations heroines attempt to transcend traditional femininity, the lack of opportunity to have many experiences beyond the home reinforces the femininity they oppose.

Period 3 contains only two heroines who work for pay. In *Cute is a Four-Letter Word* (3:1980) Clara Conrad babysits a neighboring child after school. Clara undertakes this work mainly out of concern for Jay Frank. Clara believes that Jay is too small to be doing many domestic tasks for himself (3:1980, p. 26) and that he needs guidance. There is a brief reference to Amy Painter's work in her parents' restaurant (*Princess*

Amy, 3:1981). These representations of girls' paid work once again place them within the service-domestic context. Additional reinforcement for this view comes from the fact that other period 3 heroines do not do paid work, as well as from their strong presence as helpers at home.

Black girls

Like their adult counterparts, girls of color experience the world of work from a young age in period 1 and 2 fiction. This is not the casual housework and babysitting of white heroines. Rather, it is continuing heavy domestic work. Race interacts with gender and class to create the economic and social conditions requiring these girls to be economically contributing members of families.

The only period 1 novel where these young women work for pay is *Mrs. Mike* (1:1947). Katherine Flannigan takes a young Indian girl, Anne, from the local mission school to work in her home as a domestic. This work must be seen in the larger context of the school's attempt to make Anne into a "proper" young woman. One aspect is the mission's refusal to call Anne by her Cree name Mamanowatum and the obliteration of any traces of Anne's Cree culture. Mamanouwatum's work in the Flannigan household has all the hallmarks of a domestic apprenticeship to prepare Mamanouwatum for future work in her own home. However, the militant Jonathan Forquet, Mamanouwatum's future spouse, pulls her towards Cree culture and the eventual refusal of a white domestic femininity.

The Friends (2:1973) and *Ludell and Willie* (2:1977, 1981) are the only two period 2 novels that feature black girls working for pay. In the first novel, Edith Jackson takes on paid domestic work to support her family after her father's death. Another critique of the racial division of labor in *Ludell and Willie* is supplied by Ludell Wilson, who works for the white Seaman family. In throwing the children's vomit- and urine-soaked sheets and towels into the garbage instead of cleaning them, Ludell rejects the notion of the submissive black woman who unquestioningly performs her work no matter how distasteful it is. In another telling episode after Ludell cleans and polishes the Seaman's pink bathtub, she takes a bath for the first time in a real tub. While luxuriating, Ludell contemplates what Mrs. Seaman would do if she knew that Ludell's "behind [was] all spread out in their tub" (2:1977, 1981, p. 11). Ludell continues to experiment with Mrs. Seaman's makeup as she cleans her dressing table. Such actions represent Ludell's awareness of a complex dialectic: although black women are routinely situated in the realm of domestic work in the homes of white people, this work is also an expression of the barriers between black and white women along class and racial lines. Black women must take jobs that white women no longer have to perform.

These novels depict women's and girls' involvement in the world of work mostly as an economic necessity, rarely as a matter of choice. The "supermom" ideology in periods 2–3 prevents the dark side of emotional and physical burn-out from the double load from surfacing, even in the novels of the 1980s. Because women's paid work is characterized by service to others, it is no respite from the home, but rather replicates many of the features of domestic work. In this way, wage work and domesticity come together to draw most women into the working class. Girls are initiated into this model of femininity through their own paid work; they also are on working-class trajectories. However, there are some fractures in this domestic model, which become apparent when the question of the girls' futures is examined.

Future worlds

Along with the domestic focus is an emerging discourse on education beyond high school. In each period there are heroines whose educational goals include college and even specific career plans. However, as my discussion will show, romance fiction presents a particular view of heroines' education and careers.

A college education is considered to be a source of accomplishment and the vehicle to enhanced personal value in several novels. Period 1 heroines, such as Angie Morrow (*Seventeenth Summer,1:* 1942), Kate Vale (*Paintbox Summer,* 1:1949) and Julie Ferguson (*Going on Sixteen,* 1:1946) may spend a number of years pursuing a course of study; the novels make it clear, however, that college is a "finishing school" and is not supposed to lead to strong career interests. The emphasis is on a general curriculum that will allow girls to mark time before marriage. Kate Vale voices this position: "Oh, I suppose I'll do what all the other girls do—go away to school for four years, get a job somewhere and work for a while until I get maried. Isn't that the routine?" (1:1949, p.

23). Kate's Aunt Dot provides a role model as a career woman: she encourages Kate to pursue a career in art. However, this perspective has little force in the novel as Dot herself is single and viewed as an anomaly.[14] Although it is true that Kate will attend art school at the end of the novel, the reader is left with the sense that her art studies will be of secondary importance compared to her romance with Bill Cunningham.

College also figures prominently in the plans of period 2 heroine Julie Trilling (*Up a Road Slowly*, 2:1966). This is an outcome of her father's position as a college professor and her Aunt Cordelia's example of a career teacher. However, Julie's romantic involvement with Danny Trevort limits the direction of her education. Julie's ambivalence towards her future is very evident the day of her high school graduation: her foremost desire is to "marry Danny the next day and move into a cottage" (2:1966, p. 183). The constant references to Danny leaves the reader with the strong impression that marriage and family may take precedence over any career. College as finishing school is also evident in *Sister of the Bride* (2:1963): Rosemary MacLane decides to continue her education after marriage. Rosemary's decision is an outcome of an idea of her spouse Greg and her mother that college means being a better wife and mother. Both novels focus on education for personal edification and how it will contribute to better domestic skills.

These patterns continue to structure period 3 novels. Mariah Johnson (*P.S. I Love You*, 3:1981) wants to write romance novels. However, there is no mention of how writers train and the work involved in getting published. In *I'll Always Remember You . . . Maybe* (3:1981) Darien Holmes's decision to go to college is a way to transcend the paralyzing influence of her failed romance. Darien's decision is not tied to any firm career plans other than to someday perhaps work in a museum. In *Princess Amy* and *California Girl*, romance once again conditions the decisions heroines make about their futures to the extent that they are willing to change plans for boyfriends.

There are only two novels in which heroines have strong career orientations and both occur in period 2. Natalie Fields of *Very Far Away from Anywhere Else* (2:1976) aspires to be a professional musician and composer. She has taken many steps toward realizing her dream, including winning a summer scholarship to study at Tanglewood. However, Natalie's must choose between career and romance with Owen. There is no suggestion that romance, marriage, and career could possibly coexist. In *Ruby* (2:1976) higher education holds the possibility of a better life for young black women.[15] Although both Ruby Cathy and

Daphne Duprey have college plans, Daphne links college with her personal and political vision of black power. Going to an Ivy League college is a way for Daphne to learn the white system of power and then to work within it to effect change. This is also the only novel to give a forceful representation of college as instrumental in helping young women to break out of the cocoon that domesticity winds around their futures. Yet the legitimacy of this vision is limited because Daphne's being a black lesbian has already marginalized her. Hence, her career aspirations are made to seem outside of the traditional and legitimate femininity the novels promote.

This discussion shows how romance novels manage the challenges to traditional femininity inherent in college and careers for white girls. As Sharpe (1978) notes, the matrimonial-bureau ideology is a middle-class perspective on girls' higher education. Work and college simply put the finishing touches on heroines to enhance their value as future wives and mothers. The possibility of white heroines reworking this finishing-school ideology to develop a lifelong career with or without marriage is not yet realized in this romance fiction. However, the subject of black heroines' education reveals a different dynamic. Here, race works through gender and class to render college a way out of dead-end work and the key to social mobility and power. Nevertheless, the adventures of black women in the world of college and work should not compete with the home.

Summary

In this chapter I have argued that heart and hearth are central to the vision of femininity offered by these romance novels. Despite the fact that these novels span forty years, from 1942 to 1982, one thing remains constant: women and girls' lives begin and should end at home. Heroines of all races and classes are offered this version of femininity as an ideal toward which they should aspire. It is presented to readers as the truth about women. Although the novels allow wage work as a part of the picture, it must not supplant or compete with the domestic side of life. The fact that this ideology of domestic femininity is a class and race perspective, and not an immutable truth, never surfaces in the novels. It has often been noted (Kuhn & Wolpe, 1978; Oakley, 1972) that domestic femininity has its roots in the rise of the white middle class in the nineteenth century when women found themselves increasingly removed from the world of commerce and ensconced in their homes as managers of the domestic economy. In romance fiction, this perspective is at the center of both middle- and working-class gender identities. Although some working-class women lead a double life, their domesticity still counts the most towards their gender identity. However, it would be erroneous to conclude that there are no tensions within this gender ideology. I have discussed how several white heroines resisted the idea of a life totally centered around domestic concerns in order to carve out their own futures. However, the power of domesticity is so great that these heroines are pulled toward a domestic future. In the case of black heroines, especially those from the working class, this white domestic femininity still looms large in the background. In the final analysis, heroines can never step out of their present and future gender, class, and race positions as keepers of heart and hearth.

The previous chapters have indicated how femininity is constructed through the content of romance fiction in the form of the codes of *romance, sexuality,* and *beautification*. However, content is not the only source of gender meanings. Chapter 6 will discuss the contribution narrative form makes to the particular version of femininity that the novels offer to readers.

6
Becoming a Woman: Narrative and Femininity

People of all ages delight in telling stories as well as in reading the well-told tale. What began as a way to fix memories and convey knowledge in oral cultures is now the dominant structure of almost every Western cultural form, particularly the novel. Narrative form almost seems universal with its beginning, middle, and end despite the fact that it is the product of particular historical circumstances (Davis, 1987). Indeed, there are those that argue that we make sense of the world through the very stories we tell and read (White, 1981).[1] Like many readers, I have been fascinated by written stories since childhood. Stories can captivate readers, transporting them to different times and places, thereby enriching their own lives. However, stories can captivate also in the sense of ensnaring readers through their content and form in ways that are not altogether salutary. According to Eagleton (1979), narrative can reinforce existing patterns of social interaction at the same time as it goes against the grain of convention.[2] However, teen romance novels more often go with the grain, containing traditional gender sentiments largely because of the very form that fiction takes.

Story is a particular type of narrative featuring characters, events, and the resolutions of conflicts. Characters perform actions that create a problem, which eventually is solved. According to Hodge and Kress (1988, p. 229) narrative refers to "the organization of the world as constructed by a text." Narrative also indicates the kinds of actions that involve characters along with the form those actions take. The narrative structure of the romance novels I studied was organized through two pairs of binary opposites, the Good/Bad and Strong/Weak.[3] These oppositions generated virtually all of the characters in the sample. The notion of binary opposites for characters and actions specifically allows for the analysis of the tensions within the romance stories, a dimension that has often been excluded in the analysis of popular fiction. In teen romance fiction a particular theme or leitmotif encapsulates the dominant traits of the heroine and connect form (the binary opposites) with content (the codes of *romance, beautification,* and *sexuality*). Narrative form in romance fiction is more complex than that of most folk tales. In addition to one main narrative pattern, this romance fiction also contains two variations, which together describe all the heroine's actions in the novels. With this overview in mind, I now consider the role form plays in constructing once again an almost seamless representation of femininity over forty years.[4]

The girl next door

In each period the heroine's character is established through comparing her actions and attitudes to those of other characters. This is especially the case in Periods 1 and 3. The dominant character is "the good girl," who strongly adheres to the components of the codes of *romance, beautification,* and *sexuality* discussed in the previous chapters. She is the quintessential "girl next door,"—meek, kind, and pure of heart. In contrast to this good girl is another female character that I have termed the "other girl" modifying the category of "the other woman" used by Mussell (1975) in her analysis of gothic romance fiction. This girl is assertive with boys, and has beauty, poise, and self-confidence. She knows what she wants and how to go about realizing her desires.[5] At this point, I have described characters that seem on the surface to be almost stereotypical. This is far from the case. The novels contain tensions within these characters and within the femininity they represent. To exemplify the workings of this Good/Bad opposition, I will first discuss four representative novels from period 1 and period 3. I will then look at period 2 fiction in isolation, as the Good/Bad opposition here involves changes in meaning that merit special consideration.

Good girls

Both Angie Morrow (*Seventeenth Summer*, 1:1942) and Jane Howard (*The Boy Next Door*, 1:1956) fit the description of the "good girl" in almost every respect. Both heroines are totally naive when it comes to attracting boys and are continually embarassed at the mere mention of dating. Of the two heroines, Angie is the most reserved and lacking in self-confidence. Angie's naivete lays the groundwork for her first love experience with Jack Duluth. Through observation of other girls and her older sister Lorraine, Angie gradually learns the "really useful knowledge" of romantic attraction. Angie is most conscious of the code of romance as it it relates to overt attempts to secure Jack's attention.[6] Several times, Angie directly addresses the reader noting, "You can't ask a boy, 'When will I see you again?' . . . A girl just can't say that sort of thing to a boy" (1:1942, p. 21). Angie's passivity is evident in her interactions with Jack, which are limited to listening and responding to his actions. However, Angie is not at all content with her image as a quiet girl. She laments her inability to be talkative and considers herself boring. Angie's continual speechlessness acts as the symbolic accompaniment to her passivity. Much of her behavior emanates from her family's emphasis on decorum and reserve. However, it is precisely these qualities that win Jack's love.

Angie has had few experiences with boys. Jane Howard, on the other hand, has grown up with Ken Sanderson, the boy next door. Like Angie, Jane is also shy and reserved. When Ken's friendship assumes romantic overtones that Jane is not prepared for, she panics. Jane's confusion over the nature of her feelings for Ken causes a breach in their relationship that leaves the door open for her sister Linda. Later on, when Ken incurs a financial debt that can be eradicated only through taking on an after-school job, he is forced to quit the football team in midseason. Almost all of Ken's acquaintances, including Linda, desert him; Jane remains open and understanding. As a good girl, Jane receives her reward. By the end of the novel, Jane and Ken renew their friendship with a romance in the offing.

Good girls appear in period 3 as well. Two representatives are Clara Conrad of *Cute is a Four-Letter Word* (3:1980) and Maddy Kemper of *Seven Days to a Brand-New Me* (3:1982). The tradition of the quiet reserved heroine continues in these novels. Both Clara and Maddy are witty and outgoing with their female friends, but very insecure where boys are concerned. Clara's and Maddy's shyness is symbolized by the fact that they continually blush whenever boys are mentioned. Both intensely desire romance with the boys of their dreams—Skip Svoboda for Clara and Adam Holmquist for Maddy. No matter how strong these desires are, each nevertheless abides by the unwritten guidelines regarding girls' role in romance. Their goodness and niceness is clearly established through their ability to appear passive.[7] Where Jane Howard and Angie Morrow simply wait for boys to make the first move, Maddy hangs about Adam's locker at school or just happens to be in the vicinity of his route to classes. She appears to have a plausible reason for being in both places. However, she stops short of any formal actions such as initiating a conversation or telephoning him. Like Angie Morrow, Maddy plays a waiting game; she waits for Adam to call (3:1982, p. 1), to notice her (3:1982, p. 9) and ask her for a date (3:1982, p. 101).

Clara Conrad admires Skip Svoboda from afar. Her method of facilitating romance involves popularity and joining the Pom Pom team. As Skip is the most popular boy in the school and captain of the basketball team, Clara reasons that it is inevitable that their paths cross. The following conversation between Clara and her best friend Angel, however, demonstrates how closely she adheres to male prerogative in matters of romance, despite the measures she has taken:

> I had just to mention his name when Angel and I were having lunch. She didn't react, so that gave me the courage to tell her he had called me last night.
>
> "Oh, I'm glad." She actually did look pleased. "I hope you two can get together. That is, if you want to."
>
> If I want to! I couldn't believe Angel. "Isn't that up to him?" I said. (3:1980, p. 78).

Clara carefully allows Skip to take the initiative and complies with his wishes even though Angel encourages her to be more assertive. When Clara asserts herself, Skip interprets this as disloyalty and selfishness. Clara is not able to remain Pom Pom team captain because of her sense of responsibility to Jay Frank, the child for whom she babysits. Skip interprets her actions as disloyalty both to the Pom Poms and to the basketball team. As Skip had rigged the Pom Pom captain election so that Clara would win, he expects Clara to make a continuous show of gratitude. The text is very clear that Clara is acting from a sense of honor that is entirely appropriate given the dishonesty of Skip's actions. Clara maintains her status as a good girl because it is Skip's sense of values that is in question.

Becoming a woman

Other girls

Several other girls are presented as the exact opposite of the good girl: Jane Rady (*Seventeenth Summer*, 1:1942), Linda Howard (*The Boy Next Door*, 1:1956) and Mary Louise Dryden (*Seven Days to a Brand-New Me*, 3:1982).[8] Angie Morrow views Jane, Jack Duluth's former girlfriend, as a distinct threat to her developing romance. Jane's unrestrained and happy manner form a counterpoint to Angie's timidity and reserve. Angie admires Jane's ability to play up to boys and her general worldliness. However, the novel does not present Jane as an admirable character let alone a model of femininity. Her carefree manner is judged to be excessive and in violation of women's expected demeanor. Jane monopolizes Jack's attention even though it is apparent to all that Jack and Angie are on a date. Jane's violation of the private-property relationship underlying romance is severely censured.

Whereas Jane Howard was reluctant to begin dating, Linda Howard of *The Boy Next Door* has been waiting for this moment for years, as is apparent in this dinner-table conversation:

> "I mean," said Belinda, with astonishing firmness, "that you made me a promise. You said when I was in high school—and now I'm in high school. So there!"
>
> "Belinda!" said her mother sharply.
>
> "I'm sorry, Daddy." Linda's eyes lost their momentary glint and her lashes fluttered. "But you can't break a promise. You *must* remember. And I've waited and waited." (1:1956, pp. 28–29)

Linda's intentions are later revealed to be not about romance with a single boy, but with attracting boys in general. In no time at all she has won over most of the boys in her school, including the boy next door, Ken Sanderson. When Jane's relationship with Ken becomes strained, Linda openly seeks Ken's attention: "Belinda laughed a lot and kept batting her eyelashes at him, in a way she had just acquired. Why, she's playing up to him Jane realized" (1:1956, p. 38). Once Linda becomes Ken's girlfriend, she becomes well known via Ken's own popularity. The text gives no indication that Linda has any strong emotional attachment to Ken. Rather, she regards Ken as a challenge, and as a way of furthering her own social status. This is clearly seen through Linda's reaction to Ken's decision to quit the basketball team in mid-season.

"Why it's a dreadful thing! . . . If he's not careful he'll wake up and find he's the most unpopular boy in the senior class." She spread her hands in dismay. "And then where will I be?" she wailed. (1:1956, p. 124).

Soon Linda becomes restless and begins to "play the field"—a clear violation of a girl's role in romance. This lack of emotional investment is what differentiates Linda from Jane and ultimately results in Linda's textual censure.

Although the character of Mary Louise Dryden in *Seven Days to a Brand-New Me* does not have the force of a Linda Howard or Jane Rady, she nevertheless is Maddy Kemper's dark counterpart. Like her predecessors, Mary Louise is presented as a teenage *femme fatale* who exists to thwart Maddy's romantic efforts with Adam Holmquist. Maddy characterizes Mary Louise as a sorceress who has "enchanted him; *entranced him*. Put a spell on him" (1:1981, p. 63). Maddy construes Mary Louise's interest in Adam as evidence that she is a romantic opportunist. When the true reasons for Mary Louise's and Adam's companionship are revealed to be nonromantic, Mary Louise's character undergoes a conversion in Maddy's eyes.

In these period 1 and 3 novels, the Good/Bad opposition structure remains unchanged despite the nearly forty years separating the two periods. What gives this opposition its meaning is the distinction between the heroine and the other girl in terms of their motivations for romance and the methods used to attract a boy. However, this Good/Bad opposition hinges on a more subtle interpretation of heroines' actions. Jane Rady and Linda Howard introduce a set of codings within the Good/Bad opposition: the active/passive and selfless/mercenary codings. These codings represent the fundamental characteristics that determine which characters are presented to readers as positive models of femininity. The best examples of how these codings function can be found in *Practically Seventeen* (1:1943) and *California Girl* (3:1981).

In the first novel, heroine Tobey Heydon comments that she is "not at all the mercenary type and [has] never liked a man according to how much he could do for me in the way of entertainment" (1:1943, p. 12). This passage prepares the reader for Kentucky Jackson who is portrayed as the opposite of Tobey. Kentucky immediately surrounds herself with boys, including Brose Gilman, Tobey's boyfriend. Some time later, readers learn that Kentucky has used the boys to pass the time until a boy of her own age arrives. Tobey and her friends are totally passive in the face of these circumstances and patiently await the day when Kentucky tires of the boys. Luanne Chapman of *California Girl* (3:1981) resembles Kentucky Jackson in several respects. Luanne is a popular girl whose position as school beauty queen and head cheerleader gives her considerable recognition. She was once the girlfriend of Mark Waverly, and thus makes her a potential rival for the heroine, Jennie Webster. Luanne's actions after Mark's automobile accident are conveyed to the reader in this manner: "They said when she heard that Mark would never walk again, she said she was too young to be tied down to a cripple. She walked right out of that hospital and got into Chuck's car and drove off" (3:1981, p. 47). Mark's friends interpret her actions as desertion and callousness, something a good girl would never do. Jennie's subsequent attempts to help Mark regain his confidence are presented to readers as evidence of her selflessness as opposed to Luanne's self-interest. Once Luanne becomes aware that Mark is approaching complete recovery, she decides to reclaim Mark, although he is now interested in Jenny. She launches an active campaign that includes telephoning Mark and talking to him whenever possible. Her active quest for Mark fails in the face of the less assertive Jennie Webster.

Once again the goodness of the heroine is demonstrated through her forbearance in the face of romantic difficulties. The other girl makes her intentions obvious and vigorously pursues her goals through any means available. She suffers the ultimate penalty of not experiencing romance with the boy of her dreams.

Out of control

The novels of the 1960s and 1970s have fewer characters who leap from the page as the extremes of the good girl and other girl. This obscuring of sharp distinctions between the heroine and other characters is accompanied by the decreasing importance of the other girl. This may be due in part to the fact that some heroines' actions are now similar to those of the other girls of periods 1 and 3. No longer a dichotomy, the Good/Bad opposition becomes a continuum along which the character of the heroine develops. As heroines themselves move towards positions that were formerly occupied only by the other girl, they become reclassified in the eyes of parents, especially fathers, as wayward and "out of control." The many conflicts that characterize period 2 fiction are responsible for heroines simultaneously occupying both positions on the Good/Bad continuum, depending on whether the vantage point is that of the parents or boyfriend. What constitutes a good girlfriend and good daughter are by no means synonymous in this period.

I have discussed previously how the codes of romance and sexuality contain tensions stemming from conflicts of interest between parents and daughters. Although there are some disputes with mothers, these take on secondary status in comparison with the primary importance of conflict with fathers.[9] *Camilla* (2:1965) features the clash between Camilla Dickinson and her father Rafferty over Camilla's choice of the poor but honest Frank Rowen as her boyfriend. Up to this point, Camilla has lived the sheltered life of a Park Avenue rich girl. Her romance has given her the courage to begin to express her opinions, which causes Rafferty alarm. Camilla's refusal to obey Rafferty's ban on dating Frank results in her being banished to boarding school.

Ruby (2:1976) and *Up in Seth's Room* (2:1979) form companion pieces by virtue of continuing father-daughter disagreements. In the first novel, power is the hidden agenda of the open warfare between Ruby and her father, Calvin:

> No . . . the issue is not obedience or disobedience . . . the issue is me! My love! the needs of my body . . . of my mind . . . you must know that I am not a child . . . that I do not want innocence. I want to live. . . . (1:1976, p. 169)

As Ruby openly challenges Calvin's authority, she is reclassified as rebellious just as Finn Rousseau changes to a stranger in her father's estimation. In *Up in Seth's Room,* Finn's refusal to stop seeing Seth is interpreted as defiance. Like Ruby, Finn sees the conflict hinging on paternal power:

> For the first time she felt his vulnerability. Felt that he was hanging onto his position . . . but that he was no more secure than she was . . . . She had always thought of him as so . . . *powerful, all powerful,* and now . . . he was doubtful of his own power. (2:1976, p. 163)

Finn later argues that she is not only a daughter, but also a person who is entitled to some control over her life. However, all three novels disguise the power component of these struggles by presenting them as questions of respect for parents.

The struggle with fathers has its parallel in the tremendous tension characterizing the romantic relationships of this period. Conflicts with boyfriends are another aspect of the resistance of heroines to male authority and dominance. The conflicts within romantic relationships cause heroines to view their boyfriends as exploitive, untrustworthy and domineering.[10] This dissension translates into the ambivalence heroines feel towards romance in *My Darling, My Hamburger* (2:1971), *Up in Seth's Room* (2:1979), and *Mr. and Mrs. Bo Jo Jones* (2:1967). Although the heroines of these novels may desire romance, their actual experiences do not fulfill their expectations of emotional satisfaction. For example, in *Drop-Out* Donnie Mueller's growing intimacy with Mitch Donaldson moves from initial warmth and fulfillment to tension, and finally to a loss of love. Heroines are consequently reevaluated by boyfriends as cruel in light of girls' bids to compel boys to deliver on promises to love and cherish.

Heroines are further involved in actions that cause them to be regarded as both good and bad at the same time. This refers to heroines' growing stance as active and sexual. In Chapter 3 I discussed the double-edged quality of sexuality for heroines. To become sexually active means incurring the wrath of families. To remain sexually inactive means conflicts in romance and possible loss of romantic prospects. Heroines are caught in a bind which makes it extremely difficult to maintain a "nice girl" image without risking the disfavor of someone. However, sexuality becomes more contentious when pregnancy is the outcome as exemplified by *Mr. and Mrs. Bo Jo Jones* (2:1967) and *My Darling, My Hamburger* (2:1971).

Both novels turn on the dilemma that pregnancy poses for three characters: July Greher, Lou Consuelo and Liz Carstensen. In *Mr. and Mrs. Bo Jo Jones*, July's pregnancy as evidence of sexual activity heightens the tension with her parents that originally developed from their disapproval of Bo Jo. The pregnancy forces July and Bo Jo into a marriage that neither wants. Although the pregnancy distresses July's parents, this reaction is mild in comparison to the moral outrage that the hint of a contemplated abortion brings. July's censure by friends and family continues throughout the novel. In the same novel, Lou Consuelo's pregnancy and subsequent abortion turns Lou into the incarnation of evil. Lou has ambitions to become a professional singer despite her marriage. Lou's experience raising most of her brothers and sisters while a child herself has made her wary of becoming a mother. The novel presents Lou's refusal to remain pregnant as a more serious transgression than July's unwed pregnancy.[11] Lou's situation reveals the strong operation of the selfless/mercenary coding in the construction of her character. Her desire to determine her future hinges on the exercise of control over her body which is interpreted by all as an expression of selfishness (2:1967, pp. 145–146). At this point, July becomes converted to a "nice girl" because of her willingness to continue the pregnancy. July's position as transgressor has been erased as she is transformed into a dutiful wife and mother while Lou becomes more villified.

In *My Darling, My Hamburger* Liz Carstensen's pregnancy does not receive any approval, but it does not receive the strong censure directed at Lou Consuelo. Lou is vilified because she refuses the "natural" outcome of sexuality within marriage. However, both pregnancies terminate in abortion. Because of this, both characters are punished. Liz feels very guilty and loses Sean Collins. Lou's marriage dissolves when she refuses to have another baby as a "replacement."

This discussion of the Good/Bad opposition shows the boundaries around the heroine's character in this romance fiction. Although forty years separate an Angie Morrow from a Maddy Kemper, there is a thread that connects them. Their ability to maintain the "nice girl" image means living within a carefully circumscribed description of femininity, one that extols caution, selflessness, and seeming passivity. However, the Good/Bad opposition also reveals many tensions for certain heroines straining against these boundaries. In the following section, I discuss the Strong/Weak opposition, which is also important in generating characters.

Cinderella in a corner

A continuing thread throughout teen romance fiction involves the power of romance to transform the character of the heroine. The heroine is the lone Cinderella sitting in a corner, dreaming of her prince. By the end of each novel, a large change in personality has occurred; the heroine feels more confident and desirable as a girlfriend. Prince Charming in the guise of the boyfriend is responsible for this wondrous transformation. This pattern of a *weak* heroine who becomes *strong* is mostly found in the novels of period 1 and period 3. In these two periods, heroines eagerly anticipate romance and unquestioningly commit themselves to boyfriends. This acceptance of romance as inevitable and desirable characterizes the narrative structure of the majority of the novels. In the *acceptance* pattern, heroines rarely question the desirability of romance. Because period 2 fiction departs from the acceptance pattern in important ways, it will be discussed separately.

In period 1, heroines such as Angie Morrow (*Seventeenth Summer* 1:1942) and Kate Vale (*Paintbox Summer* 1:1949) are initially presented as having little confidence in themselves; they feel a sense of aimlessness after high school and are uncertain as to their future. This lack of purpose is seen as a sign of weakness. Angie credits her first date with Jack Duluth as bringing about certain personal changes:

> And if I looked at myself in the mirror that morning I would see something different. My face would be the same but yet something had changed, and I would try not to look straight at my family all day in case they might see it too, and smile at each other and say, "Angie's growing up." (1:1942, p. 25)

These changes involve Angie's becoming recognized as "somebody" by virtue of her association with Jack. At Pete's, the local teenage-gathering place, Angie makes her public debut as Jack's girlfriend. This creates quite a stir among the other boys, like Swede, who had scarcely given Angie a thought before this. In this moment of social triumph Angie is reminded of her weaknesses: her lack of self-confidence and general naivete. Yet as Angie's romance develops, she becomes more aware of things happening before her very eyes. This is evident in her ability to empathize with her older sister's romantic problems.[12]

In *Paintbox Summer* Kate Vale's romance with Manuel Silva, as later with Bill Edmond, is responsible for her maturity at the end of the novel. The novel opens with a very unconfident Kate who greatly desires to "acquire some sense of security within herself" (1:1949, p. 46). This unsureness is revealed in a certain awkwardness with boys. Kate envies the poise and sense of social accomplishment of her mother and sister Valerie. Rather than spending the summer loafing about Haddonfield as she had always done, Kate's Aunt Dot arranges for her to be an apprentice painter for the artist Peter Hunt in Provincetown. This provides the context for her first romance with Manuel Silva. Manuel Silva effects a sudden change that results in a new Kate: "She had never felt so sure of herself, so self-assertive. One short month had given her more than she could evaluate" (1:1949, p. 118). Later on, this more assertive Kate even ventures a retort to friend Bill Edmond's usual teasing, something she would have never done before. These changes in Kate are most evident to Aunt Dot during a trip to New York City. Without a second thought, Dot attributes the changes to romance. A changed Kate even stands up to her parents regarding her education. Whereas the Vales expect Kate to pursue a liberal arts degree, Kate secretly longs to attend art school. Through Bill's intercession, Kate is finally able to summon the courage to disclose her plans to her parents.

Several period 3 novels continue the theme of the transformative powers of romance. *Seven Days to a Brand-New Me* (3:1982) especially plays on the theme of transformation through heroine Maddy Kemper. The novel opens as Maddy takes stock of herself, locating her problems as "shyness, lack of confidence, and feeling plain" (3:1982, p. 47). The goal of Maddy's self-improvement program is to project a "New Maddy" the epitome of charm and grace, and capable of attracting the attention of Adam Holmquist. The program works wonders; Maddy becomes more friendly and outgoing. Her inability to hold a conversation with Adam slowly disappears as she gains confidence from his interest in her. As the novel closes, Maddy and Adam are well on they way to romance.

Another period 3 novel, *California Girl* (3:1981), presents heroine Jennie Webster as an outsider. She is outside the high school social community. As a new student from California, her rigorous schedule of swimming practice affords little free time. Despite the honors she wins for her swimming, Jennie still feels like a "great big zero" (3:1981, p. 9) because she has never been out with a boy. From the moment that Mark Waverly asks Jennie to the homecoming game and dance, a noticeable change occurs. Jennie's anonymity gradually gives way to popularity once she becomes Mark's girlfriend. Mark's support and encouragement give Jennie the courage to confront her parents and swimming coach over certain matters of paramount importance to her (3:1981, p. 90). It is only after meeting Mark that Jennie is able to inform her coach, Tod, that she is "sensible" and capable of making her own decisions. Her swimming competitiveness takes on a new edge with Mark at her side. The new Jennie is more self-confident because of romance.

The contestation and reluctance variant

Although this acceptance pattern is the dominant narrative form, there are novels in which heroines are indifferent to or question romance. The *contestation* variant spotlights the heroine's conflicts in romance as important experiences in constructing her femininity. This variant occurs in almost every novel of period 2. The reluctance variant centers around the heroine's hesitation to become romantically involved because she feels that romance is simply unimportant. Here the heroine is happy just as she is. Nonetheless, the heroine eventually commits herself to romance and experiences a delayed transformation from girl to woman through it.

The contestation variant

Once again romance looms large as responsible for heroines' gender identity formation. Love is not the only factor that changes the heroine. Strength is gathered from the particular positions heroines assume regarding their adherence to expected romantic behavior. Two period 2 novels *My Darling, My Hamburger* (2:1971) and *Ruby* (2:1976) best illustrate the contestation variant.[13]

Although I have discussed Liz Carstensen as the focus of *My Darling, My Hamburger*, the novel is also concerned with Liz's friend, Maggie Tobin. From the outset, Maggie's characteristics are similar to those of so many heroines—shy, lacking in confidence and ill at ease with boys. Sean Collins' friend Dennis Horowitz is equally shy, but summons up the courage to ask Maggie for a date. Maggie's discomfort stems from concerns over the kinds of sexual behavior that may be expected of her. Maggie's strict adherence to a particular interpretation of permissible sexuality causes her to interpret Dennis's kiss on their first date as a prelude to "going all the way."[14] Maggie continues to interpret Dennis's every move as sexual in intent. Their rocky romance finally founders when Maggie decides to help Liz in securing an abortion. The novel closes with Maggie's high school graduation. In a moment of reflection, Maggie notes that she has progressed from being a "silly and foolish" girl (2:1971, p. 110). Nevertheless, Maggie does not exude the tremendous self-assurance of period 1 and period 3 heroines. Both the romance with Dennis and the resulting conflicts have brought Maggie to the point where she is no longer terribly frightened, but she is still not confident enough to be optimistic about her future.[15]

In *Ruby* (1976), Ruby Cathy experiences a similar transformation in personality through romance and its attendant conflicts. Initially, Ruby is presented as unable to change her circumstances, even though she bitterly resents her father's control over her life. Daphne Duprey's assertiveness and drive act as a model for Ruby's emerging sense of self-worth. However, Daphne's demands for a show of strength from Ruby place severe strains of their relationship: "[They] had lost—were losing—their closeness. They worked more, touched less, were less affectionate, unable to relax (2:1976, p. 98). In the wake of escalating conflicts with Daphne, Ruby vows to be decisive with her father.

> I will . . . I will take a stand . . . as soon as I am secure . . . secure. I will talk to him . . . I will tell him that I am of age . . . that I shall go where I choose . . . do what I will (2:1976, p. 98).

Ruby does indeed develop strength in ways that are not so apparent to Daphne. When Calvin and Ruby's cousin Frank are discussing politics, Ruby intelligently discusses the Black Power movement, to the amazement of all (2:1976, p. 113). This event signals a change in her demeanor; in the past she would have been silent and fearful of expressing her opinions. Ruby's strength is also demonstrated in her forbearance when dealing with her abusive, crippled teacher Miss Gottlieb, who returns Ruby's kindness with racial slurs. As important as each of these strides are, Ruby is still unable to stand up to Calvin. This creates so much dissension in her relationship with Daphne that Daphne distances herself from Ruby. Their relationship, like so many others in period 2 collapses under these continual stresses.

Without a doubt Ruby's romance has played a key role in her self-development. Slowly she has gained a self-reliance that culminates in her decision to relate to Calvin the exact nature of her relationship with Daphne. At this point, the road she has traveled converges with that of Maggie Tobin. Both are in the process of becoming women, both have been disappointed in romance, and both stand at the crossroads of their young lives. Yet Ruby remains well within the private world of emotions as the end of the novel intimates that her romance with her former boyfriend Orlando will be renewed.

In the contestation variant the "they lived happily ever after" motif does not hold sway. The future is one of uncertainty for girls. The individual strength and poise of a Maggie Tobin or Ruby Cathy are not for participation in the larger social world. The trials they have endured and the strength they have gained prepare them for yet another Dennis or Orlando, for many romances to come.

The reluctance variant

In four novels the action turns on heroines' reluctance to become girlfriends.[16] This is due either to the presence of consuming special interests or to the presence of a close friendship with another girl.[17] This continues until the "right" boy comes along, and then the heroine becomes converted to the virtues of romance. Two novels, *I will Go Barefoot All Summer for You* (2:1973) and *Junior Miss* (1:1942) nicely display this variant.

As the first novel begins, Jessie Preston is totally oblivious to romance. She prides herself on a certain toughness, which is signified by the callouses on her feet. Jessie has lived with her aunt and cousin since the death of her guardian. Jessie and her cousin Frances are close friends until Frances begins to behave "strangely": she uses lipstick, wears dresses, and notices boys. The arrival of a distant cousin, Toby Bright, turns Jessie's life topsy-turvy. At first Jessie dislikes Toby, calling him "the ugliest boy" she has ever seen (2:1973, p. 24). However, Jessie's toughness dissipates as her interactions with Toby increase, and he is reclassified as a "nice boy." A turning point occurs on a bicycle trip when Jessie falls and Toby kisses her to confort her. After her initial embarassment, Jessie begins to take great care with her appearance and even fantasizes about a romantic future with Toby. Toby returns to his home in Baltimore, and Jessie decides to run away so that she can be with him. Jessie's journey becomes one of self-enlightenment as she is forced to confront certain questions surrounding her birth. Romance has given Jessie the strength to face the fact that her mother and father were never married. The text signals Jessie's considerable maturity by her desire to continue interacting with boys, and by the fact that she accepts an invitation to attend the homecoming dance.

For Judy Graves of *Junior Miss* and her best friend boys are the furthest things from their minds.[18] Like Jessie, Judy has certain qualities that cause her family to consider her as a tomboy. Judy's mother expends considerable effort to teach Judy not to be clumsy and loud and to instill in her a sense of demureness and poise. All these efforts fail until Judy is invited to a dance at the home of one of her friends. The day of the dance Judy immerses herself in a rigorous beauty routine. When Judy's date, Haskell Cummings, arrives, she is poised, speaks in carefully modulated tones. and is an altogether different girl. Judy's request that Haskell keep her cosmetics in a handkerchief for fear of loss is in direct contrast to the formerly self-sufficient Judy. That this change has been the result of a possible romance with Haskell is abundantly clear. The novel ends with a father proud of his daughter's ability to mesmerize a boy.

The reluctance and contestation variants clearly show how the Strong/Weak opposition generates characters who, despite various factors, achieve selfhood through romance. Although Judy Graves and Jessie Preston are strong young women before their romantic experiences, their virtues go largely unacknowledged until they have experienced romance. The contestation variant interjects the idea that romance can serve as a crucible for self-development through the stand heroines must take on various issues. Although heroines are empowered, there are many limits to their power and authority.

Becoming a woman through romance

This analysis of the narrative structure of romance fiction shows its remarkable stability despite the forty years between the first and last novel of the sample. Even though there are two narrative variants, each is organized through the central motif of "becoming a woman through romance." The narrative structure in the form of the Good/Bad and Strong/Weak oppositions remained very constant over time despite the introduction of conflict in period 2 novels. This narrative structure was linked to the codes of romance, beautification and sexuality through the novels' central motif. This intertwining of form and content is one way in which romance fiction reconciles several sets of contradictions. It reconciles the dark side of romance with its self-confirming aspect. Although heroines develop from weak and uncertain individuals into strong and confident young women, they are prepared not for the whole world, but for the relational aspects of life, especially romance. Although heroines transform themselves into beauties, their beauty is not for themselves but for others. Even though romance has a sexual component, heroines are not permitted to act on their sexual feelings.

Davis (1987, p. 18) argues that certain elements of narrative structure such as character and action can work to defuse the many tensions within a text. Although I cannot fully relate Davis's important argument about narrative form, I do want to sketch it here. Briefly, the forces of patriarchy, capital, and colonialism have left their marks all over the pages of realist fiction, particularly through the insistence that novels have settings, characters, plots, and dialogue. Each of these have developed historically in Western society in relation to gender, class, and race so that narrative form, like content itself, is not neutral but ideological. For example, for a character to be constructed, a writer must select traits, place the character in a location, and give the character something to say. Each of these processes involve the selection and simplification of the potential range of possibilities so that characters become carriers of ideology. However, readers do become caught up with characters, and the story takes on a life of its own.

Romance novels present readers with a certain version of gender relations, where girls' first love experiences set the tone for their lives. These novels attempt to present this highly ideological version of social relations as the truth about women. I say ideological because what the novels speak are only half-truths regarding women, their lives, and their capabilities. Like Davis, I argue that novels are removed from lived experience through the very processes involved in their construction. I am not claiming that stories have no relation to lived experience, but that when readers think novels are life, ideology is achieving one of its goals. A product of the imagination and literary convention assumes the aura of reality.

Summary

Narrative has an important role in making sense of one aspect of experience that pertains to gender relations. The novels hold up to readers one exemplar of proper femininity in the guise of the Angie Morrow character which is the focus of period 1 and 3 novels and hovers about the margins in period 2. She is the standard by which all characters are measured. However, this character embodies a very conservative version of gender relations. Through characters such as this and the codes of romance, sexuality, and beautification, readers are presented with a partial version of gender relations. Together they constitute an almost seamless gender text. I say almost, because the dynamics of reading are quite complex and can only be fully understood in reference to actual readers of the romance who form the topic of the next chapter.

7
Romancing Girls: Romance Fiction and Its Readers

Up to this point I have discussed teen romance fiction from the view of language and narrative. In this chapter I connect the world of adolescent romance fiction with that of actual readers. Precisely how this story version of gender relations relates to the lived experience of readers cannot be intimated from the texts alone. To understand the impact of these novels on readers, it is necessary to enter the world of those who mostly read this fiction, teenage girls and where they read romances, the schools.[1] In this chapter, I discuss aspects of my recent study of teenage girls' romance novel reading in schools. I explore how middle- and working-class girls from diverse racial backgrounds constructed their subject positions within heterosexual femininity through reading romances. I also consider how romance-reading related to girls' schooling and their future expectations as women. I contend that these gender positions are highly contradictory and that romance fiction both reinforces traditional gender ideologies and allows girls to reflect on these ideologies. Before doing this, I provide a context for romance novels in schools by reference to recent research on the school text.

The authority of school texts

The question of where instructional materials derive their power and authority to speak to students must underlie any account of reading in school. Does the authority come from the text? From the structure of schooling? From the interactions between students and teachers? Luke, de Castell, and Luke (1989)contend that each of these is implicated in textual authority. Olson suggests that texts often contain the "authorized version of society's valid knowledge" and that textual features endow textbooks with their authority (Olson, 1980, p. 192). This may be true in the case of texts like basal readers, which have a long history as legitimate school texts. However, texts like romance fiction hover on the fringes of respectibility. This is evident in the concerns voiced by parents and teachers about the appropriateness of such books in schools. Yet one sees many students reading teen romance fiction that has been secured in school libraries or ordered through school bookclubs.

To understand romance fiction's power to speak to readers, one must look to the readers themselves and the text in use in classrooms. Fetterly (1978) and Morely (1986) argue that textual meaning is shaped through the knowledge and resistance that readers bring to reading. Such reading can become an act of opposition to dominant curricular arrangements by those who feel most oppressed and powerless. On the other hand, Luke, de Castell, and Luke (1989) note that power relations in classrooms often place teachers in positions of authority through their ability to select texts and to shape through their own interpretations, what students learn from texts. Teachers themselves do not teach in a vacuum. School administration pressures towards student achievement and good discipline can play an important role as to which texts are ultimately used in classrooms and how they are used. Each of these dynamics contributes to the authority and power of romance texts in classrooms.

Thus far, I have spoken of students, teachers, and texts in a generic sense. I now want to look at text use within reading classes for reluctant readers. Much paper and ink has been devoted to strategies for teaching reluctant readers and a publishing industry empire has been built on materials specifically written for these readers. According to Otto, Peters, and Peters reluctant readers are often students who may be able to read, but refuse to do so out of disinterest in reading materials or schooling (Otto, Peters, & Peters, 1977, p. 313). Or their refusal to read may mask some actual reading difficulties. The literature on reluctant readers argues that students can best be taught to read through the use of Hi-Low books, materials that are highly motivating, but control vocabulary complexity and general text difficulty (Estes & Vaugh, 1973; Fader & McNeil, 1968).[2]

Since the 1970s, paperbacks have been specifically written and marketed for the reluctant reader as "classroom libraries" claiming to capture students' interests while facilitating growth in reading. Enter almost any middle or junior high school remedial reading classroom and you will see books from Scholastic's *Action, Double Action,* and *Sprint* series, as well as the paperbacks of Quercus and Sundance for reluctant readers.

A newcomer to the Hi-Low field is the teen romance novel. Series romance fiction shares all the characteristics of other Hi-Lows, especially in the differentiation of content on the basis of gender. For example, the *Action* books feature mystery and adventure for boys and romance, dating, and problem novels for girls. As I will now show, teenage female reluctant readers have enthusiastically taken up the reading of romance fiction within their reading classes, often over teachers' objections. The authority of these texts to speak to students emanates precisely from the interaction between specific readers, teachers, texts, and context.

The research context

During an eight-month period in 1985–86, I studied teen-romance-fiction readers in three schools in a large American midwestern city, "Lakeview." Once dominated by automobile, farm equipment, and the alcoholic beverage industries, the economic crisis of the late 1970s has left its imprint on the city and its surrounding communities. Plant closings have transformed Lakeview from a smokestack city to one of empty factories and glittering strip malls. Most new businesses are in the service sector such as fast food and insurance companies and these employ the bulk of working- and middle-class women and men. Lakeview School District is a large district drawing students from the inner city and some of the outlying areas that were annexed to the city thirty years ago. The sites for my research were Jefferson and Sherwood Park, two outlying 7–8 middle schools, and Kominsky, an inner-city 7–9 junior high school. At the time of the study, Lakeview was in the process of converting the junior high schools into middle schools. Jefferson and Sherwood Park each had about three hundred students. Sherwood Park's student population was mostly white. Like Sherwood Park, Jefferson was predominately white, but had three Chinese students as well. Kominsky's 700+ student body was composed of about one-half white, one-quarter black and one-quarter hispanic, with a small Vietnamese and Asian Indian population. Both Jefferson and Sherwood Park arrange their students into three tracks (low, medium, and high) for reading instruction.[3] Reading placement was based on the results of: district-wide and individual school standardized reading test scores, teacher recommendations, and students' previous grades. Kominsky and Sherwood Park also had additional reading support service through the federally funded Chapter

I program that enrolled one-half and one-quarter, respectively, of their students.[4]

In order to study readers and their romances I used a variety of methods (See Appendix A). An initial sample of seventy-five girls from the three schools was assembled through interviewing teachers and librarians as to who were heavy romance-fiction readers and by personally examining school and classroom library checkout cards and book-club order forms. A reading survey (see Appendix D) was given to all seventy-five girls. I interviewed, individually and in small group settings, twenty-nine girls of the seventy-five—the heaviest romance-fiction readers. These twenty-nine girls had five teachers for reading in the three schools. I observed in these classrooms and interviewed these teachers as well. What I discuss in this chapter stems from the written reading survey of the seventy-five girls, from observation, and from interviews of the twenty-nine girls and their five teachers.

Romance novels in classrooms

Who reads teen romance fiction? My reading survey showed that the novels tended to be read by white middle-class girls aged twelve through fifteen at Jefferson and Sherwood Park[5] and to a lesser degree, by black, Hispanic and Asian girls at the three schools.[6] At Jefferson and Sherwood Park, romance novels accounted for thirty-six percent of all books checked out from school libraries and ordered through bookclubs as compared to twenty-five percent at Kominsky. This is in keeping with recent Book Industry Study Group surveys that have placed romance fiction within the top three kinds of books adolescents read that include adventure novels and mysteries (Market Facts, 1984). Another characteristic of readership besides class, race, and age has to do with how readers are grouped for reading instruction. The twenty-nine girls were identified by school personnel as "reluctant" or "slow" readers and were tracked into remedial or low-ability reading classes. This pattern was repeated in their math and English classes as well. These girls were characterized by counselors and teachers as girls who would have difficulty completing the remainder of their schooling, who were more interested in boys than in academics, and who would, in all probability, marry early and be young mothers.

The five reading teachers of these twenty-nine girls provided much insight into the complexity of teen romance fiction in schools. Three teachers were aware of the nationwide controversy surrounding these books, and all felt some degree of apprehension regarding their use. The contradictory position of teachers is nicely illustrated first through the observations of Mrs. M. (Kominsky) and then Mrs. K. (Sherwood Park), both white middle-class teachers:[7]

> I feel guilty about letting the girls order these books through TAB [a school bookclub]. I read a couple of them once. They are so simple and the characters in the novels are stereotypes. You know, mom at home in her apron, dad reading the paper with his feet up. But the girls seem to like the books and the classroom sure is quiet when they're reading them.
>
> The girls just love them [romances]. I see them reading their books in study hall and even in lunch. Can you believe that! I'm just happy that they are reading, period.

The romance-reading occurring in these teachers' classrooms was the outcome of several factors, ones that indicate the delicate interplay of readers, teachers, texts, and context. The overwhelming desire of teachers to see students reading and reasonably interested in books generated the notion in Mrs. K.'s mind that "any reading was better than no reading." Teachers were also under tremendous pressure by the administration to improve students' measured reading scores. In the case of Chapter I teachers Mrs. K. and Mrs. M., those scores were key ingredients in retaining the annual federal funding of their programs and, by implication, their jobs. All five teachers conceded the difficulty in keeping order in classrooms in which students were resisting instruction. Securing students' consent to read voluntarily made the teachers' lives in the classroom "tolerable."

Most romance-novel reading occurred during "independent study," which was in great abundance as instruction was mostly organized around individual learning models to provide for the specific needs and interests of each student. This was especially the case in Sherwood Park and Kominsky. During the usual classroom period in each school, students read or worked on skill sheets after administrative matters concluded. Student and teacher interactions were mostly limited to the correcting of skill sheets, updating reading folders, giving directions, and answering procedural questions. Students mostly read privately and rarely shared their reading with their teachers or others students.

Although most books were student-selected, teachers attempted to influence book choice by categorizing books into "quality" award-winning books[8] and "fluff" books like series romances. That students did not automatically accept teachers' authority regarding book choice was illustrated by Mrs. B., a white middle-class Kominsky Chapter I teacher, and five of her students. As a strong advocate of "quality" teen literature, Mrs. B.'s room was crammed with an array of quality paperbacks, magazines, and newspapers.[9] No romance fiction was found in this classroom library. The girls brought romances from home, libraries, or mail-order bookclubs. Mrs. B. more or less tolerated the romances in her classroom. This tolerance was the result of administrative pressure to show reading gains and the protest of five girls.

Of all the teachers, Mrs. B. felt most apprehensive about granting any legitimacy to the romances. She fitted the romances into her "quality literature" perspective by striking this bargain with her students: for every romance read, the girls must read other types of books. The reality was that Mrs. B. hoped to make the girls lose interest in the romances so that they would expand their reading to the quality books. This tension was revealed in Mrs. B.'s exhortation during weekly library visits to "choose something good, something you'll want to stick with." When students inquired into the reasons behind Mrs. B's. dislike of romances, she neither offered any explanation nor encouraged any critical dialogue with the romance-fiction readers about their reading.

Five of Mrs. B.'s students took matters into their own hands by fiercely championing their romance-novel reading. Tina, a white working-class student, used Mrs. B.'s words "read something interesting," to defend her choices. Tomeika and Jan, a black student from the middle class and a white student from the working class respectively, supported their reading tastes by citing their mothers' devotion to the books as proof of the worthiness of romance-reading. White middle-class Carol saw romance fiction as something truly pleasurable to read in comparison with her other schoolbooks. Finally, all five girls would languish over teacher-selected books, mutilating the pages and cover, while complaining how boring the books were. Or they would retire to the "book nook" to read covertly their favorite romances they had stashed away among the floor cushions.

This discussion demonstrates how some girls reinterpreted school policy regarding which texts had legitimacy and authority in classrooms.

A teacher's attempts to impose her authority to choose texts had the effect of hardening these girls' resolve to continue their reading. By resisting this authority, the girls wrested some control over the reading curriculum. However, as I will later show, this practice had consequences for their schooling and femininity.

Readers and romances

An amazing amount of romance-fiction reading was apparent among the twenty-nine girls. Allowing for the fact that some girls were more avid readers than others, the girls as a whole read an average of six romances a month at home and school.[10] However, these girls did not read romances indiscriminately—that is not just any romance novel would do (for a list of the most popular books, see Appendix E).

Most of the girls were loyal to certain individual authors like Stella Pevsner, Ellen Conford, Norma Fox Mazer, and Francine Pascal. High on their lists were also romance lines like Silhouette's "First Love" and "Blossom Valley," Scholastic's "Wildfire," and Bantam's "Sweet Dreams" and "Sweet Valley High." The latter were favored because they provided an easy and cheap way of securing books through their bookclubs. More important for Silhouette readers was the fact that Silhouette publishes a newletter soliciting letters from readers. The girls viewed the newsletter as important because in the words of Val, a working-class Hispanic student at Kominsky,

> They [Silhouette] care about what we want in books. . . . I wrote once about a book I hated. I even got a letter back from Mrs. Jackson [an editor]. Funny thing, nobody ever asks us our opinions about nothing.

That these opinion polls are part of Silhouette's sophisticated marketing program does not detract from the positive impact they have on the girls. The overall effect was to provide them with the experience of having their voices heard.

Why girls read romance novels

In many ways, the girls in my study gave reasons for reading romances that were comparable to those of the adult romance readers in Radway (1984). In both studies the reasons combined elements of fantasy, knowledge, and pleasure. The seventy-five girls in my study read romance fiction for the following reasons:

1. Escape, a way to get away from problems at home and school.
2. Better reading than dreary textbooks.
3. Enjoyment and pleasure.
4. To learn what romance and dating are about.

The theme of escape from problems emerged over and over again as some girls recounted how the romances provided them with glimpses of a world quite different from their own: no family problems and always a solution to any conflict. Mary Jo, a fourteen year-old white middle-class student at Sherwood Park, commented that the romances portrayed the world as "I would like it to be." The happy resolution of family problems in the romances of Francine Pascal was especially appealing to twelve year-old Carrie, a black middle-class student at Kominsky:

> In her books things get all mixed up like fights and other stuff, but basically people still love each other. I'd love to have a family like the Martin's [in *My First Love and Other Disasters*]. Sometimes when I read I kind of pretend that the family in the story is my family.

Precisely why romance-novel reading was highly valued in school is evident from the words of Claire, a white working-class student at Sherwood Park: "It's really a bore 'round here. Readin' Sweet Valley turns the worst day into something special." Furthermore, romance-novel reading provided the girls with the space to engage in something truly pleasurable and personal during the school day. The books left them with the same good feelings as meeting with their friends at lunch and in the halls. The companionship of other students and romance-reading sustained them through an otherwise tedious school day.

There was yet another aspect of the pleasure of the text. This involved the positive feelings that derived from identifying with romance-fiction heroines. Without exception, these heroines were smart, funny, and resourceful. Being recognized as someone special, as nice, intelligent, and humorous was important to the girls. They were all aware of the social and academic significance of their placement in low-ability reading classes, and many felt that their teachers did not see them as intelligent or nice people. This desire to identify with a smart heroine coincided with the girls' desire to have teachers and other adults regard them as nice and capable despite their academic placement.

The girls derived pleasure from imagining themselves as the heroine of romance novels. Through their reading, they lived out much of the specialness and excitement associated with being the object of a boy's affection. Much of this desire seemed to hinge on their perception of romantic relationships in fiction as eminently satisfying, with all minor misunderstandings eventually resolved. However, few of the girls envisioned romance in everyday life as anything like romance fiction. Pam, a fifteen year-old white working-class student at Jefferson, summed up the feelings of several of the girls:

> Nobody has these neat boyfriends. I mean, most of the guys boss you around . . . and bash you if you look at somebody else. But it's fun to read the books and think that maybe someday you'll meet a really nice guy who'll be good to you.

The novels operated at a distance from girls' own lives and provided a comfort zone where there were no consequences for risking all for love.

This process of identification was also evident when there was a mismatch between the girls' own lived romances and those they encountered in fiction. Marge, a black working-class student at Kominsky. claimed that most of the romances she read did not accurately portray romantic relationships as she encountered them in everyday life.[11] Like Pam, Marge wished that the boys she knew were more like the boys in the novels: "treatin' you good. Not bossin' you 'round and tryin' to hit on you all the time." Marge went on to note that girls would probably always have to "fight off boys," but that it was nice to dream that things could be otherwise. The romance novels provided Marge and Pam with the dream of an ideal romance. Romance-reading allowed them to transform present and future romantic relations in imagination according to their aspirations.

The romances gave the girls who were not dating and some of the shyer girls, the opportunity to take romantic risks without consequences. Trina, a thirteen year-old Chinese middle-class Jefferson student, noted that "sometimes the way guys are in the books helps us girls understand them a lot better." This "primer" quality found favor with thirteen year old Marita, a working-class Hispanic Kominsky student. Marita's reading provided a valuable source of information on romance. Marita's family strictly controlled her whereabouts. None of her sisters were permitted to date until they were seventeen and they did not speak openly about their experiences. Marita related that several of her friends were in similar situations and depended on romance novels for their knowledge of dating.

The good romance novel

The girls had very definite ideas about what made for a good romance novel. These centered on textual characteristics of the heroine and hero. The good romance has the following characteristics:

1. Is easy to read.
2. Does not drag.
3. Is one where the heroine and hero are cute, popular, nice, and have money.
4. Has a happy ending.
5. Is one where girls are strong and get the best of boys.

The appeal of many of the series romances was that they were 150 to 175 action packed pages of easy reading. The girls placed a premium on these structural characteristics and the relevance of the books to their lives. Pat, a white middle-class student at Jefferson, explained that the novels "Are sure easy to read. I know all the words and don't have to skip any of 'em." This preference for easy reading had unexpected consequences for the girls, however. Mrs. T., a white middle-class Jefferson reading teacher, saw a mutually reinforcing relationship between romance-reading and the girls' status in the schools:

> Some of the girls show great impatience at reading books that are long or contain a great deal of exposition. That's why they like romance novels. Sure, they like to read about boys—that's all

they have on their minds. But they do like anything that's easy and doesn't make them think. The romances are mindless drivel.

Other teachers commented that the girls "only do what they have to to get by." In the eyes of teachers and school officials, the structural characteristics of romance fiction had become emblematic of the girls' identities as reluctant readers. Stated another way, the girls' preference for easy reading cemented their identities in teachers' minds as pupils who seek "the easy route" in school and life.

The girls also had definite ideas about what constituted an ideal heroine and hero. The former should be "pretty, smart, and popular." The preference for a popular heroine was closely correlated with the girls' own desires to be liked by both girls and boys in their everyday life. Another priority was to be cherished and treated well by a nice boy. Those characteristics that helped heroines attract boys were precisely the ones they wished for in their own lives. The ideal hero had some similarities to the heroine. He should be "cute," "funny," "strong," "nice," "have money," and "come from a good home." Although cuteness was certainly important, niceness and strength were indispensable. Strength did not so much connote physical prowess but rather stood for an array of attributes such as courage, initiative, and protectiveness. The girls as a whole were repelled by teenage versions of the "macho man" in books and everyday experience. As Karen, a white middle-class Sherwood Park student, explained, "When I read a book, the guy has to be nice, has to be, he has to treat his girlfriend and everybody with respect." This notion of respect had especially to do with being attuned to the heroine's needs and feelings. When girls compared the hero to boys they knew, there was the occasional boy reminiscent of the hero, but mostly the boys they knew did not measure up to this ideal.

According to several girls, stories should end happily—that is, the heroine and hero should have ironed out their difficulties and become once again a couple. The overwhelming preference for the happy ending was closely related to the romance novel's power to involve the girls vicariously in the developing romance. Several of the older girls who were romantically involved looked to romance fiction to provide in fantasy the hoped-for outcome of their own relationships. Patty, a fifteen year-old white working-class Kominsky student, exemplified this position: "It would be nice to think that Tommy and me would end up like Janine and Craig [the couple from the popular *Blossom Valley* series], you know, married with kids and having a nice home, car and money."

The saga of this couple's romance, separation and final marriage held out to this reader the possibility of living happily ever after.

The final quality of a good romance involved a strong assertive heroine, especially in relation to boys. May, a black working-class Kominsky student, strongly expresses this sentiment: I've got no patience with girls who let boys walk all over them. Believe you me, no boy mess with me or he be sorry." Linked with this preference for assertive heroines was a distinct pleasure in reading about heroines who "got the best of boys." In this regard, Victoria Martin of F. Pascal's *My First Love and Other Disasters* was mentioned by several girls as a heroine whose courage and forthrightness they admired. This notion of "besting boys" and "keeping them in line" was most often applied to situations where the heroine knew best and when boys tried to compel the heroine to do things against her beliefs.

I have thus far indicated the fluid and often contradictory quality of these readers' interactions with texts, where story-world and lived experience meet. An underlying theme is how readers' gender subjectivity is shaped through their reading. I will now discuss the dynamics at work during reading that not only helps create girls' femininity, but also provides the occasion for pondering that femininity.

Creating and pondering femininity

I want to return to earlier observations regarding the role of the text in shaping gender meanings. Although readers' life experiences are important in constructing meaning when reading, the text still exerts a measure of control over those meanings. In this regard, Iser (1974, 1980) claims that this happens through "blanks" or gaps in the text. Many times the threads of the plot are suddenly broken off, as happens between chapters for example. Or they continue in unexpected directions. These textual features prompt readers to "read between the lines." The blanks call for combining what has previously been read with readers' life experiences and expectations. Although teen romance novels are not characterized by many unexpected twists and turns, they nevertheless require a certain amount of constitutive activity on the part of readers. When female readers encounter textual blanks that involve matters of femininity, two things occur. Readers are offered models of femininity, but are also given opportunities to ponder femininity. I will exemplify this dynamic by recounting three girls' readings of *Against the Odds* (Marshall, 1985).

Annie, Marcy, and Nancy, three white middle-class eighth-grade Sherwood Park students in Mrs. J.'s reading class, had recently read *Against the Odds*. The story focuses on the struggles of four girls, Trina, Laurie, Joyce, and Marsha who are among a group of twenty-five girls registering as new students at the all male-Whitman High School. The four girls decide on Whitman because it has the strong math and computer science curriculum their old school lacks. The school's ninety-year history as an elite all-male college-preparatory institution is about to change under court-mandated affirmative action. The girls are initially greeted with protest signs of "No Girls at Whitman High!" catcalling, and continual harrassment. The girls confront the troublemakers and establish themselves as serious students. Trina, in particular, wins the respect, admiration, and affection of the most hardboiled of all the boys, Chris Edwards. The novel ends with the vision of a romantically involved Trina and Chris and the promise of a more gentle "battle of the sexes."

All the girls agreed that heroine Trina Singleton caused them to think about themselves as young women. Nancy clearly expressed this in her comments on her favorite romance heroine: "That's gotta be Trina Singleton in *Against the Odds*. Trina is the kind of person I want to be 'cause she's not afraid to fight for her rights, while another girl might chicken out." This novel has certain blanks that invite completion as part of the developing story and characterization. At one point, Trina and her friends have a plan to revenge themselves for all that they have endured and to put a stop to the harrassment once and for all. Readers are left to contemplate what this plan might be for several pages and even then it is only gradually unfolded. Annie filled the blanks in this manner:

> A: It was fun trying to figure out what Trina and the other girls would do to get back at those boys. I thought that they would sneak into the boys' locker room and do something to their sports equipment. Marsha had the guts to do something like that.
>
> LKCS: Was that something you might have done?
>
> A: Are you kidding? No way! I'd never have the guts. Well, you'd have to do something that's for sure. Hmm, I'd probably start a rumor about the guys or every time me and my friends would see them we

would make like we were talking about them. They can't stand that!

Marcy's reactions to the same passage also set up a confrontation between who she is and who she would like to be:

M: I figured Trina and Laurie would come up with something fantastic. I never thought in a million years that they would stuff confetti drenched in cheap perfume into the boys' lockers.

LKCS: Would you do that, get even in this way?

M: Well, I'd like to do something like that, to get even with some of the boys in my math class who are real pains. But I'd get chicken and probably just fume.

LKCS: Can you tell me more?

M: It's kinda difficult, I mean, well, I guess I don't want to be seen as a girl who's too pushy with boys. You have to be careful about that. But then you can't let the boys push you around. I don't know.

Annie's and Marcy's hypothesizing revealed several things about the reader-text-context relation. For both girls, the blanks allowed them to imagine a course of action that tred a line between what was possible given the story they had constructed and what they thought would be possible given their imagination and femininity. The way Annie filled in the unwritten portions of the text acknowledged that gender tensions exist and that girls are not passive victims. Her predicted plan and subsequent response showed a femininity that allows for collective action against boys, but sets limits on how forceful that action may be. In relation to the text, Marcy adopts a position that sharpened a tension within her femininity when she admired the characters' plan, but was doubtful of her own ability to act in a similar manner. Like Annie, she drew on her femininity and the previous portions of the text to use the blanks as an opportunity to imagine a more assertive femininity. For both girls, filling the blanks had set in motion reflections on their femininity.

As the twenty-nine girls read their romances, they constructed a story that put their own hopes for and fears of romance in center stage. While reading the romance text, they brought to bear their past and present

Romancing girls

positions within the school as they become the subject of the romance text. The girls' school identities as reluctant readers and their desires to be seen as capable influenced their reading of the romances. Equally important was the girls' ability to become the heroine and experience being an assertive and cherished girl. Each of these constituted the contradictory and at times fragmenting gender positions girls constructed in the course of their reading.

The girls' romance-novel reading had strong oppositional overtones. The girls' identification with the assertive heroines they read about fueled their attempts to continue their reading at all costs. The girls' vision of the romance novel as a vehicle for instilling a certain vitality into their reading classes was in one sense a bid to have some power and control over their schooling. They attempted to legitimate a text that operated on the fringes of accepted instructional materials. In view of the fact that written texts form the mainstay of instruction in America, the girls' actions carry much significance.

The girls brought a certain pleasure in femininity into classrooms, with romance-novel reading becoming a symbol of their femininity. McRobbie (1978a) claims that girls' pleasure has always been problematic in schools. whether it takes the form of their flirting, wearing sexy clothes or openly primping in classrooms. In a manner similar to Radway's Smithton readers (1984), the girls took pleasure in their ability to make sense of the novels and to articulate what these stories were about. This feeling of competence was not one that they usually experienced in school. The girls' reading of romance fiction refuted in their own minds judgments of their competence by school personnel. The act of creating meaning allowed them to refuse, if only momentarily, their identities as reluctant readers.

The girls continually used the romance novels to make a temporary escape from the problems and unhappiness associated with school and life difficulties. In general, the girls were barely passing their courses. Many experienced the strain and uncertainty of the downward economic trend gripping Lakeview. Their glimpses of an economy in trouble did not prevent many of the girls from dreaming of a secure and comfortable future through a good marriage combined with their own employment. Although many of the girls were aware of the disjuncture between that world and their own, the novels provided the space for them to dream and construct reality as they would like it to be. The novels therefore played on many girls' desires and yearnings for a different present and future.

Romance-fiction reading positioned girls within heterosexuality through their identification with heroines. That girls become the heroine through imagination was clearly indicated by twelve year-old Annie, a white middle-class student at Sherwood Park: "It's just when you're reading you're in some other world, well, not really physically, I mean, but you imagine you are. Sometimes I feel like I am the person going on dates, having loads of fun." Jenny, a fourteen year-old black middle-class student at Jefferson, describes the impact that one novel, *Princess Amy* (3:1982) has on her: "My favorite part is when the girl and the guy first kiss. That gives me a squishy feeling in my stomach, sorta like I'm actually there, being the girl that's gettin' kissed." The girls' endorsement of the worthiness of these relations between the sexes affirms traditional gender relations. The girls never disputed the desirability of heterosexual romance, but rather tried to capture it over and over in their reading of other romance fiction and wished for this specialness in their own lives. This was even the case when the girls' relationships with boys were fraught with conflicts to such a degree that the only satisfying romance they could imagine was one occuring in a novel.

How does this view fit with the strong assertive heroines the girls preferred to read about? The girls' version of feminine assertiveness was in many ways one bounded by traditional views. Girls could certainly "best" boys in everyday life and in the world of romance fiction, but the bottom line was that one could not be "too pushy" because this could result in alienating boys and destroying any romantic prospects. The latter was clearly something the girls would not do, even when boys did not treat them well in the case of Marge and Pam, or in the "get even" fantasy of Annie. Hence, the girls' conception of the proper relationship between the sexes featured some assertiveness along with staying in the good graces of boys.

The girls' romance reading was characterized by this tug of war between conventional femininity and more assertive modes. This central tension was considerably sharpened when the girls conveyed their thoughts on their future in the world of work and at home.

Material girls

These girls' visions of the present and future were shaped through their romance-reading in contradictory ways. Working for pay while in school was important for most of these girls since it was the ticket to consumption which, in turn, fed into romance. Along with jobs, marriage and children were also on the distant horizon. The girls' reading tapped into their desires for material objects and centered the gender, class, and racial aspects of their identities around consumption.

Beautification with an eye to romance motivated the girls' wage work and consumption. The girls saw a direct relation between appearance, popularity and romance. All the girls believed in the notion that "pretty girls get nice boyfriends." Although having a nice personality was equally important, attractiveness was something that a girl could not do without. These beliefs were validated through everyday life in which the prettiest, most popular girls at their schools also had their pick of the boys. These descriptions of the most popular girls and ideal romance-fiction heroines mirrored one another. The linking of beauty with romance not only fueled the girls' consumption, but also provided the reason for working for pay.

All the girls were involved in various kinds of casual work, like babysitting and performing odd jobs, to augment allowances or earn all spending money. The girls' earnings were spent on clothes, beauty products, movies, fast food, records, and videos—with the majority going for clothes and beauty products. With larger allowances, the white, black, and Chinese middle-class girls babysat to buy "little extras" or "something extravagant" that allowances would not cover. For the white, black, and Hispanic working-class girls, consumption was on a more limited scale. Little or no spending money from parents required amazing entrepreneurship to earn pocket money. This involved not only the usual odd jobs, but also doing paid domestic work in homes where they babysat. The girls had plans to continue working in high school in retail sales, clerical work, or the fast-food industry in order to have more spending money. They saw having a job as making the difference between doing without and having money to spend. This reality bumped up against the universe of the romance novel.

Affluence and even luxury generally characterizes the world of romance fiction. as I have previously indicated. Although most of the heroines do casual work, they enjoy a kind of familial economic stability. This is a world different from that of the twenty-nine girls. The working-class girls glimpsed this world as bystanders. The designer clothes, elaborate homes, and glamorous vacations were not for them. Several middle-class girls saw this world slipping away. During the recent recession in Lakeview, many of the girls' relatives had lost good paying jobs and were still unemployed, or were working for drastically reduced wages. There was austerity in the middle-class as massive white collar layoffs continued. These glimpses of an economy still in trouble did not prevent the girls from dreaming of a secure and confortable future. Romance novels with their economically secure world, allowed the girls to "realize" their dreams.

The girls' future plans included marriage, children, some further schooling and work for pay.[12] Over half of the twenty-nine girls expected to marry before the age of twenty and work for a few years before having children. However, they rejected the dominant vision in romance novels of married women as full-time housewives and child-minders. The working- and middle-class girls coming from two-paycheck families acknowledged that they would have to work for a while after marriage in order to help out. Along with the girls' rejections of this model, however, was a strong longing for a more conventional feminine role. This tension was an outcome of their dawning knowledge of the difficulty of juggling housework, children, and paid work. The girls' own considerable domestic responsibilities at home and their mothers' dawn-to-dusk work routine gave them sobering glimpses of what might be in store for them.

Summary

Romance fiction does not merely supply readers with "mass produced fantasies" as Modleski (1984) suggests. Rather, these books influence young women's self-conceptions through complex and often contradictory processes. For the twenty-nine girls, the pleasure of the text involved reflecting on aspects of their social identities. Romance-fiction reading became a way to ponder femininity within the context of heterosexuality. The fantasy life the girls lived in reading cut across race and class by engaging with many of their already-existing wishes and desires.[13] For many of the girls, these novels satisfied their longing for romance, a sense of importance, and the feeling of being cared for in the absence of nurturing romantic relationships and warm school and home environments. Their reading confirmed yet another important aspect of girls' gender identity: their desire to be seen as competent young women. Hence, their vision of femininity was not characterized by passivity and docility in contrast to Snitow's (1983) suggestion that romance novels categorically promote these characteristics. However, the girls' femininity more often featured testing boundaries rather than transcending them.

The very act of buying and reading romance novels put the girls in the position of consumer. In one sense the novels can be viewed as a series of commercials for beauty products and clothes. This supports Gitlin's observation (1982) that symbolic relations are becoming more and more linked to econòmic relations, especially within popular culture. Romance novels reinforce the worthiness of consumption and tap into the girls' yearnings for material goods and a comfortable life. They also lay the groundwork for their future of marriage and work. The girls' recognition of a life divided between home and work did not erase their longing for someone to take care of them. That this view of femininity might be possible only for women of the privileged class, did not occur to the girls.

Both the structure of romance novels and the kinds of oppositions of the twenty-nine girls engaged in point to the tensions surrounding romance reading in school. The girls' identities as reluctant readers, and their desire to transcend what this meant, fueled their reading. However, there is a dark side here as girls substituted the romance novel for other instructional texts, and as teachers condoned this practice, all contributing to the girls' opposition to the more strictly academic aspects of school. The teachers' practice was ultimately not defensible as this reading was done without meaningful communication between students and teachers regarding student's reflections on what they read. This practice militated against what is perhaps the most important aspect of learning from reading, that of making sense of books through discussion with others.[14] Although the championing of romance-novel reading momentarily empowered girls to assert claims for a schooling related to their interests, this empowerment turned back upon them. Their resistances perpetuated and reinforced these girls' identities as students that would not finish school or would graduate with skills that would qualify them only for low-skill exploitative jobs. The latter was a strong probability in view of changes in the larger Lakeview economy. Keeran (1985) claims that by 1990, service-sector industries will employ almost three-quarters of the workforce, with most of these workers women. Romance-reading prepared Lakeview girls for entering this future society as middle- and working-class women.

Through this chapter I have placed the phenomenon of teen romance novels in the context of readers and their schools. I now take romance fiction one step further by connecting novels and readers with the important historical events in the United States from 1942–82, exploring the relationship between literature and society.

8
The World of Romance and Beyond

Any analysis of literary texts must take into account the fact that literature is produced and read within an historical context. This does not imply that literature is a mere reflection of history. Rather, the point is to examine the intersection of society, art, and politics at the time that the texts were written. Kaplan argues that this step is necessary in understanding the claims to truth that fiction presents (Kaplan, 1985, p. 161). Far from reflecting history, literature constructs meaning. It often articulates the tensions and contradictions within a society. According to Moi (1985), popular literature is especially involved in producing consent to gender, class, and race meanings.[1] These tensions are quite apparent in teen romance fiction which presents a striking example of the impact of history and politics on literature.

To exemplify these and other points, I discuss the important events that have shaped women's lives in the United States before and during the time the novels were written. Because space does not permit a full and detailed account of these events, I will mainly focus on the home, work, and political climate from 1942 to 1982. I will then look at the ways in which these aspects of women's lives made their way into novels and the forms that their representations took. Finally, I will turn to the social functions of literature, tying together the analysis of teen romance fiction and its readers with the possible social impact of this reading.

Women's lives, women's work

From the colonial era, the lives of many women in the United States were shaped by both domesticity and wage labor (Wertherheimer, 1977). This was a fact of life for most working-class women, regardless of color, and was an emerging trend for white middle-class women as well. Yet society considered domesticity to be "true womanhood" and downplayed women's contributions in the workplace and on the political scene.[2] The period of 1942 to 1982 is especially important because it is the point of convergence of over one hundred years of women's struggles on various fronts for political power, better pay, and reproductive and marital rights. This period also displays the tremendous tensions within American society over women's desire to determine their place in the world.

The beginning of World War II witnessed thousands of women responding to the call to wartime employment. Although opposition to married women in the workforce was decreasing, a fundamental ambivalence towards this aspect of women's lives remained.[3] This was apparent in the practice of first hiring unemployed men and those outside of military duty. Not until 1942 did business fill jobs with women, partly under pressure from the the Women's Bureau.[4] More than three million married women became wage workers from 1940–1944. Job stratification was common as employers imported rural white women to fill the well-paid factory jobs. Black women responded with demonstrations in Detroit and elsewhere, and thus gained some higher-paying factory work. The lucrative jobs in steel mills and shipfitting, however, were closed to many of them.

Despite the fact that many mothers worked outside the home as well, women still had total responsibility for home and children. Although there was a concerted effort to secure childcare and help with housework, the federal government did little to relieve women of their double burden. The childcare provided was often available only to women working in heavy industry and on a temporary basis. Working twelve to fourteen hours meant that most women had to depend on relatives and older children for care of younger children. In this way, the bonds between women and the home were kept intact for the day when they would once again become full-time homemakers.

During World War II, many women received their union cards for the first time. This was due in part to union concerns of preserving the wage level of jobs for male workers (Kessler-Harris, 1982). The steady influx of women into smokestack industries brought a fourfold increase in the number of women trade unionists. However, the unions walked a tightrope where women were concerned. On the one hand, they sought ways to involve women in union activity and labor issues; on the other hand, they worked to prepare women for postwar layoffs. Sensing what

The world of romance and beyond

was to come, the Women's Bureau of the Department of Labor called a national conference in December, 1944 and a series of resolutions on working conditions was passed. However, women relented on the issue of layoffs out of a sense of the union's conflicting interests when it came to giving jobs to women rather than to returning veterans.[5] As the war drew to a close, women experienced pressure from all sides to trade in their soldering irons for ironing boards gracefully. By the end of the war, over three million women had resigned or been fired from their jobs, especially in heavy industry (Rosen, 1973, p. 216). As in World War I, women did not willingly give up their jobs. For example, they picketed over unfair practices at the Ford Highland Park Motor Plant. However, the inflationary tendencies at work during 1945–47 forced many women to come to grips with the necessity of working for pay despite low wages.

Although the 1950s is known as the heyday of domesticity, it also contained many countercurrents. There was an overwhelming consensus that women belonged at home. Yet women's wages meant some stability for families in the face of a roller-coaster economy. Women's work would also be a factor in maintaining a level of spending necessary to keep corporate coffers full. Increased support for women workers came from the federal government in the form of a 1955 White House Conference on Effective Uses of Woman-power (Kessler-Harris, 1982). Although the conference affirmed women's traditional roles as wives and mothers, it also encouraged them to participate more fully in the world of work. Where waged work had been an interlude in many women's lives, more and more women were staying in the work force. Many women opted for full-time instead of part-time work and increasing numbers of women over forty-five became wage workers for the first time in their lives. These trends combined to make women twenty-nine percent of all workers in 1950.

The dominant idea that women worked for "pin money" and to "help out" in the family was called into question as women sought recognition and more pay for the work they performed. The outbreak of the cold war with the gearing up of the military industries produced some labor shortages that were filled by women workers. This was used as an opportunity to push for training, maternity leave, and equal pay by the Women's Bureau and women's groups. Women's growing discontent with the mismatch between their supposed social contributions and the reality of less than desirable pay and working conditions was translated into floods of complaints to unions and to the Women's Bureau. Women were barred from job security in the civil service system. Women Ford Motor workers charged the United Auto Workers and Ford Motor with collusion in bypassing senority lists. The drive to break down barriers based on sex rekindled interests in an Equal Rights Amendment, this time with some support from the Women's Bureau.[6] Black women's struggles became increasingly centered on the developing civil rights movement which identified the eradication of racism as the key to a better life.

These cracks in the ideology of femininity coexisted uneasily with the strong "feminine mystique" of the 1950s. Women's questioning of their social positions bumped up against larger social definitions of femininity, ones that stressed passivity, nurturance, and dependence. Working mothers were blamed for juvenile delinquency and for the growing tension within families (Baxandall, Gordon, & Reverby, 1976). Women were forced to speak out of both sides of their mouths when it came to their futures. To prefer the workplace to the kitchen meant being classified as abnormal. However, more and more women had to work or simply wanted to do so. The feminine mystique combined with guilt, provided the ideological mechanism for keeping women in their place. This double bind produced in some women an anger that would boil over in the next decade with the second women's movement.

For many women, the 1960s turned the "marriage-baby carriage" ideology upside down; for others, few aspects of their lives changed. Women continued to enter the work force in increasing numbers for financial and personal reasons. The two-paycheck family was on the rise as married women constituted 30.5 percent of all workers in 1960 (Kessler-Harris, 1982, p. 302). However, labor market segmentation kept eighty percent of these women in stereotypically feminine occupations.[7] After decades of struggle, the Equal Pay Act became law in 1963. In theory it prohibited pay differentials between women and men who worked equivalent jobs. It covered few jobs, however, and specifically excluded domestic and farmworkers. In the next year, the Civil Rights Act, which had been designed to prohibit employment discrimination by race, color, and religion, was modified to include sex in an attempt to make the bill look "ridiculous." However, women in the House and Senate took the matter very seriously and lobbyied to ensure the bill's passage. Although this Act and the resulting Equal Employment Opportunity Commission had the potential to help women fight job-related sexual discrimination, the reality was that mainly class-action suits were handled, and most women were left to individual struggles in the work place (Freeman, 1975).

What had begun in the nineteenth century as a bid for women's right to vote now developed into a large national movement to end sex discrimination at home and on the job.[8] Spurred by the growing Black Power movement, women demanded expanded employment opportunities, education, reproductive rights, childcare centers, and legislation that would formally recognize women's legal rights. Women's confinement to the home and their status as sex objects were identified as key elements of their oppression. The women's movement often presented itself as speaking for all women's concerns. However, it would be erroneous to assume that this was indeed the case. Although many middle-class women spent meaningless days confined to their homes in the dreary suburbs, working-class women were clocking 9 to 9 between their jobs and housework. Still other women seized new educational opportunities for careers, filling the ranks of the feminine professions such as teaching and nursing. Others continued the decades of struggle for entrance into traditionally male jobs. Many women of color found themselves still battling the racism, sexism, and classism that confined them to low-paying deadend work. Differences in class and race cut through the women's movement as working-class and black women remained at its margins or worked within the civil rights movement (Freeman, 1975).[9]

It is equally wrong to assume that all women embraced what the women's movement represented. The many tensions within organizations concerned with women's rights reflected the conflicting attitudes of women themselves regarding their social positions. Although women's groups were successful in forcing the repeal of many anti-abortion laws and freeing biological reproduction from sexuality, women were not of one opinion as to the meaning of these events. As the decade drew to a close, several counter movements would challenge this new femininism. Under the names of HOW (Happiness of Womanhood) and Fascinating Womanhood, such groups would celebrate the intrinsic differences between women and men and promote a traditional femininity (Kessler-Harris, 1982).

In the 1970s women continued to balance both home and work; at the beginning of the decade, forty percent of married women worked for pay. The number of women in skilled, traditionally male work increased to half a million, an eighty percent increase over 1960. Although by the

The world of romance and beyond

late 1970s seven out of ten women were employed full time, their wages still hovered around sixty percent of men's pay. The situation was even more dismal for black women who earned only ninety percent of white women's wages according to Kessler-Harris (1981, pp. 146–147). As in the past, bringing home a paycheck did not change women's responsibility for housework and childcare. Under pressure from women's groups, the federal government would make feeble attempts at childcare, but women would find themselves once again depending on their own ingenuity and on traditional support networks.

As women were making inroads into almost every segment of society, conservative political forces began to erode slowly these hard-won changes. "Profamily" and anti-femininist groups took strong stands against the relaxing of laws on divorce and cohabitation. The campaign for the passage of the ERA by the states was accompanied by a strong countermovement that coalesced around Phyllis Schlafly's "Stop ERA" organization. Reproductive rights, upheld by the 1973 Roe vs. Wade decision, were challenged by emerging anti-abortion groups. By the late 1970s, funding for hot-lunch programs, childcare, and increased social service payments were being cut. These changes would occur in tandem with the onset of the worst economic crisis since the 1930s.

The early 1980s were characterized by persistent inflation and waning economic growth. Women found themselves fighting battles identical to those of earlier decades. The struggle for better pay, better jobs, education would assume a new urgency. Although there were more women than ever in the workforce, their wages continued to lag behind male workers; women were making fifty-nine cents to every dollar men earned (Blinkhorn, 1982, p. 2). Unemployment continued to rise in 1980–82, women's position became more precarious. In 1981, the President's National Advisory Council on Economic Opportunity acknowledged that women and children were the new poor. At the root of this phenomenon was the increase in single female heads of families and the Reagan administration's cuts in all social services. Women were under fire in other areas as well.

Women became the special targets of fierce campaigns to reassert traditional views on femininity. Conservative political groups that had gone underground somewhat during the 1960s emerged with full force in the 1980s in the form of the New Right and the "Reagan Revolution." The New Right, a coalition of various conservative organizations, combining "pro-life," religious fundamentalist, anti-unionist, and anti-gay-rights interests, was particularily concerned with the defense of patriar-

The world of romance and beyond

chy and defined women through their roles as wives and mothers.[10] This was evident through its strong campaign to prevent passage of the ERA in 1982 and in its position on abortion. The New Right also used the continuing recession to argue that women should not be in the work place and that their bids for increased political power should not be met. As in the past, women's paid work was linked to old themes of the disintegration of the family and the naturalness of traditional social hierarchies.

The Reagan administration not only fully rejected the goals of the women's movement, but also held it openly in contempt. Where the Carter administration had given some approval to certain women's issues like the ERA, Reagan embraced the rightwing and the Moral Majority. The congressional campaign by Orrin Hatch and Jesse Helms to secure support for a constitutional ban on abortion, combined with the firebombings of abortion clinics, emerged as signs of tensions within the area of reproductive control. The Family Protection Act[11] and other legislation were introduced to reassert traditional notions of the nuclear family. In 1981, federal programs providing money to the states for childcare were reduced to twenty-one percent, as were AFDC funds for job training. As the 1980s progressed, many other measures benefiting women would be similarly challenged by the New Right. For many women, these measures represented an onslaught against the fruits of decades of struggle. As in the past, women's resistance manifested itself in demonstrations by reproductive rights groups, welfare mothers, and women workers. As the decade continued, the tensions among the New Right, feminists, and progressive women would escalate.

Historical context and the femininity in romance fiction

This historical survey underscores the continuing uneasiness of American society with women's changing positions and displays the political forces involved the contest for women's hearts and minds. Popular fiction plays on the tensions emanating from women's attempts to redefine femininity. Teen romance fiction plays a key role here because it rearranges and recodes certain larger social themes regarding women, romance, sexuality, work, and power.

What one finds in the books published in period 1 is a version of gender relations that stresses the harmony between girls and boys, with

The world of romance and beyond

romance as the natural form of these relations. Period 1 books like *Going on Sixteen* (1:1946), *Wait for Marcy* (1:1950), *The Boy Next Door* (1:1956), *Sorority Girl* (1:1952), and *Blueberry Summer* (1:1956) demonstrate an interest in the aspects of feminine experience that pertain to heart and hearth to the exclusion of anything else. *Seventeenth Summer* (1:1942) and *Junior Miss* (1:1942) abound with references to women and girls continually cleaning, cooking, and caring for children. There is no doubt in heroines' minds that their futures will be structured around marriage and children just like the lives of their mothers before them.

The domestic themes from this romance fiction converge in the 1940s and 1950s with the promotion of consumerism, childcare, and homemaking as women's chief occupations—despite the presence of women working for pay. The wartime employment of women of all social classes is not mentioned in the three novels from the period 1942–43 nor is there any mention of women's involvement in postwar clerical work and manufacturing. However, the expansion of consumer-goods industries requiring the development of firm markets to maintain profitability resonates throughout the novels. The fictional emphasis on domesticity provides testimony to the worthiness of consumption. It can also be interpreted as fiction's mediation of the unresolved ambiguities concerning women's wage work. However, these gender themes are anchored in specific class and race relations that are an expression of white middle-class femininity. The novels provide an almost seamless version of race and gender relations within this class, giving readers the impression of an unchanging universe. This belies the historical context previously discussed, which shows that gender tensions exist across class and racial lines. This confidence over social relations in the novels of period 1 would be undermined by the events of the 1960s and 1970s.

Many period 2 novels have heroines that question and challenge gender relations: *My Darling, My Hamburger* (2:1971), *Hey, Dollface* (2:1978), *Very Far Away From Anywhere Else* (2:1976), *Ruby* (2:1976) and *Up in Seth's Room* (2:1979). The controversies with parents and boyfriends regarding sexuality challenge aspects of heterosexuality. These themes reflect the questioning of traditional relationships between women and men in American society at this time. Sexuality becomes the focus of struggle in the novels as it is the only area where adolescent girls can legitimately protest in view of their age, which precludes other struggles around jobs, childcare, and education. However, the novels' focus on sexuality does go to the heart of women's struggles during the 1960s and 1970s.

At that time, many women and girls abandoned models of romantic love and experimented with different forms of sexual expression and orientation. Reproductive rights and the question of whether to have children at all were paramount for many women. Novels like *Ruby* and *Hey, Dollface* reflect struggles over sexual orientation. *My Darling, My Hamburger* and *Mr. and Mrs. Bo Jo Jones* directly deal with reproductive rights, although in a conservative fashion. Although the women's movement per se does not appear in the novels, its momentum and energy are apparent in these heroines' struggles with boyfriends over romance and in the increased numbers of adult women working for pay. *Ruby* contains a fine portrait of black women's involvement in the Black Power movement through the characters of Daphne and Phyllisia. However, this is the only novel to specifically represent any women who are politically active. The novels in their own ways include these changes in women's lives although domestic concerns still outweigh wage work. Heroines' more active role in romance and questioning of heterosexuality are related to women's general dissatisfaction with traditional gender relations in the larger society. Although these struggles do not decenter the dominant version of femininity in the novels, they do represent a recognition of the crisis in white middle class femininity at the time.

The novels of period 3 represent a harkening back to a femininity from the 1940s and 1950s which is now overlaid with life in the 1980s. Conspicuously absent are the gender issues posed in period 2 novels. In their place is a gender harmony most evident in *P.S. I Love You* (3:1981), *Princess Amy* (3:1981), *California Girl* (3:1981), and *Seven Days to a Brand-New Me* (3:1982). These novels, like those of period 1, make domestic and romantic concerns the center of heroines' lives. Heroines think only of being popular and of getting a boyfriend. Career plans are such a low priority that Jennie Webster of *California Girl* can think of throwing away years of athletic training rather than being separated from her boyfriend. Heroines' lack of concern with work and careers is paralleled in how few adult women are represented as being in the workforce. Although teenage sexuality is much discussed in period 2 novels, it appears in only one period 3 novel, *I'll Always Remember You . . . Maybe* (3:1981). Here, intercourse poses no difficulty for the heroine as each novel presents a relationship that is unique and unlike other romances. Otherwise, sexuality in period 3 fiction is reminiscent of the hugging and chaste kissing of period 1 novels.

A comparison of the historical context of the early 1980s with the

The world of romance and beyond

novels of this period reveals many contradictions. The few working mothers in period 3 belie the growing number of two-paycheck families. A similar mismatch occurs with teenage girls' career-work aspirations. The domestic future that period 3 heroines envision is not one that many young women in the 1980s could hope to achieve as adults, given an economy in crisis and the necessity of women's wage work. The silence in the novels regarding teenage sexuality is striking in light of society's continuing concern with this topic (Goodman, 1983). These novels may be mediating several perspectives on sexuality: sexuality is reserved for adults, and teenage sexuality is unproblematic. The former links period 3 novels with traditional gender sentiments; the latter ignores emerging feminist rethinking of the consequences of the sexual revolution (Vance, 1984).

Two threads within period 3 novels merit more discussion. First, there seems to be a large discrepancy between the gender relations in the novels and those in society at large. The early 1980s saw a concern with more equitable relationships between women and men along with strong tendencies to reassert traditional patterns. In the novels, however, traditional gender interactions dominate. Secondly, period 1 and 3 novels have much in common. The 1940s and 1950s contained countercurrents to domestic femininity in the form of women's growing discontent. Similarly, the years 1980–82 also contained gender struggles stemming from the legacy of the 1960s and 1970s. Conservative gender perspectives associated with New Right femininity appear in period 3 novels as the old domesticity and silence on sexuality and wage work in young women's lives. These domestic themes are part of the strong reemergence of traditional views on femininity that underly all the books.

The very consistent representation of femininity in teen romance fiction illustrates some important observations about the relationship of popular fiction to historical context. The text does not represent reality, but in fact constructs meaning. For romance fiction, this involves offering readers particular gender, class, race, and sexual identities that maintain the social order, instead of challenging it. Although it is true that gender sentiments from everyday life can make their way into fiction, they are recoded through the literary convention that operates within a selective tradition (Christian-Smith, in press). Taxel (1984) suggests that this tradition is especially strong in children's fiction, determining what versions of lived experience are represented in books. The absence of any discussion of women's resistance to New Right gender ideologies and the continuing struggles over home and job is illustrative of this phenomenon.

Humm, Stignant, and Widdowson (1986) observe that literature, like any other cultural form, has a dynamic of its own, with a history and set of relations between authors, publishers, and audiences. Children's publishing has long been characterized by conflicting perspectives regarding what constitutes appropriate content for young readers (Rose, 1984) to such a degree that books dealing with teen sexuality, such as *Mr. and Mrs. Bo Jo Jones* and *My Darling, My Hamburger*, have been the object of controversy.[12] However, literature can be influenced by sociohistorical context. A case in point is the traditional femininity of period 3 novels, which is a transformed version of New Right fears and resentment of today's more independent women. Swingewood (1975) proposes that the relationship between literature and society may be that of contraction and mediation. That same version of gender relations in period 3 fiction contradicts the present reality of women's double shift and mediates conservative gender perspectives with the ways women's lives have changed since the 1940s. All of these set limits on any simple correspondence between life and art. However, one of the roles of literature, especially fiction, involves rendering the fictional world so believable that it can be taken for the real thing.

Adolescent romance fiction and society

Cultural products such as romance fiction provide both an escape from and reconciliation to modern life. Romance novels present imaginative resolutions to gender relations, allaying fears, and creating hope and desire, along with reconciling readers to dominant social relations of gender, class, race, age and sexuality. Lovell contends that a contradiction lies at the center of postindustrial society as to its construction of women's and men's identities (Lovell, 1987, pp. 15–16). On the one hand, reliable and stable individuals are required, people who attend to their social responsibilities. On the other hand, these individuals must be receptive to the "enticements of the marketplace" associated with pleasure and leisure. The novel plays a role in maintaining both aspects of identity along with expressing this "fracture" within capitalism. To

The world of romance and beyond

understand these conflicting aspects of novels, it is necessary to return to romance-fiction readers and the texts themselves.

An important aspect of girls' romance-reading is the escape from pressures of home, school, and an uncertain future. The buffer zone created during reading gave many of the girls hope for a better future. Do teen readers really escape when reading romances? The girls' hopes and desires for a domestic future show that the novels actually prepare them for marriage and motherhood, not for an escape from them. This aspect of romance fiction involves reconciling readers to their social positions. The affluent world of romance fiction is a lodestone that exerted considerable influence on the readers I studied. They felt that they could realize their dreams of a comfortable life through a "good" marriage and their own efforts. However, this quest for a better life turned upon accepting traditional gender and class positions. Although some girls saw the mismatch between their own world and that of the romance novel, they were not willing to abandon hope. The well-appointed homes and abundance of consumer goods in the novels appeared out of thin air, thereby mystifying the fundamental economic and social reasons behind such affluence. Through this magic, the girls gained hope that as individuals they might be able to "grab the brass ring." The girls created an "Horatia Alger" myth of feminine endeavor, one that somewhat softened the rough exterior of modern life. Yet, in dreaming the "impossible dream," the girls assumed their positions as reliable and stable future wives and workers.

The consumption-driven universe of romance fiction helps to make individuals receptive to the marketplace. This individual bears a striking resemblance to the "possessive" individual who as Apple and MacPherson (1962) claim, characterizes modern society (Apple, 1979, p. 10). According to Apple, the abstract individual is severed from larger social connections and movements and is "ideally suited to both maintain a rather manipulative ethic of consumerism and further the withering of political and economic sensitivity" (Apple, 1979, p. 10). Romance novels situate women readers as primarily consumers and not producers. Yet the life conditions of the twenty-nine readers point to the necessity of women's wage work. The novels mediate this contradiction by making the domestic and romantic aspects of life women's reality. For many of the twenty-nine girls, the romance text gave them, in the face of isolation and loneliness, a sense of belonging. Davis (1987) notes that readers make friends with characters, endow them with personalities, and create a kind of fictional community. This practice was very common among the twenty-nine readers. On the surface, this practice seems to be innocuous. However, concern arises when one examines the kind of community romance fiction constructs. It is a community of individuals experiencing their unique romances and problems. Here self-understanding, *not* collective action is the key to change. This view of community is yet another face of the "possessive individualism" permeating the novels.

Summary

Coward and Ellis (1977) suggest that the function of ideology is to establish social positions and secure people's consent to existing power arrangements. Ideology accomplishes these tasks by fixing certain meanings while eliminating or containing alternatives. Although teen romance fiction plays a key role in this process of winning consent, it is also implicated in major fractures within gender ideology and capitalism over the past forty years. The frequent mismatch between the historical context and the content of romance fiction expresses the tensions within femininity. Light argues that "the acquisition of gendered subjectivity is a process, a movement towards a social 'self' fraught with conflicts and never fully achieved" (Light: 1984, p. 9). Romance fiction's purpose is the exact opposite: it fixes the self into patterns that reaffirm dominant social arrangements. This does not discount readers' important questioning of gender relations through their interpretations of the novels. The subject positions readers assumed represent an assessment of what is possible in a complex and fragmented world.

Romance fiction has the power to engage young women readers on the level of their most intimate hopes and dreams. It is on this level that the socially reproductive aspects of romance novels achieve their effect. In Chapter 9, I return to various issues in previous chapters and discuss constructive ways of using romance fiction to explore versions of femininity.

9
A Place in the World

This study of romance fiction and its readers demonstrates that popular culture is Janus-faced in that it articulates what Williams (1977) calls residual and emergent sentiments. Traditional and emerging cultural meanings coexist in an uneasy fashion within any cultural form, especially within popular literature. Popular fiction does not so much impose meanings on its readers, but rather constructs readers' gender, class, race, age, and sexual identities in complex ways. Textual analysis indicates that the social and political currents within romance fiction are often very traditional as to women's place in society. The novels written from 1970 to 1980 chronicle the rise of the conservative right wing and the restoration of traditional gender perspectives. They articulate the many tensions within dominant gender ideologies. Hovering about the margins of romance fiction is a discourse of feminine hope for the future where young women's own desires and aspirations count even when those lives are centered around romance. My study of the twenty-nine young women readers demonstrates that popular fiction often involves oppositional readings that enunciate the desires of readers, as well as their fears, and also a resentment of the power of men and the subordination of women. Romance fiction allows readers to escape, momentarily, into a world where the emotional side of their lives is fulfilled, and their feelings of competence as young women are validated. Popular culture, especially popular romance fiction, exploits the many ideological strains that exist within society and represents the continuing struggle over women's place in the world. In this final chapter I return to several of the issues outlined in the previous chapters, provide recommendations for educators and parents, and discuss the implications of popular romance for a feminist politics of popular culture.

Popular romance and schooling

Chapter 7 demonstrates that there is considerable tension surrounding the practices at Kominsky, Jefferson, and Sherwood Park that eventually endow romances with the authority to speak to students. The larger institutional context, where teachers were under mandates of state testing and pressured into demonstrating student growth in reading, was a factor in allowing popular materials into classrooms. The five teachers also acknowledged that the intensification of their work load, the increase in the number of students, and the immense paper work for Chapter I teachers made it difficult to select materials carefully. Consequently, they strongly relied on the reputation of publishers. The selective rendering of experience in tradebooks and textbooks, along with recent charges of censorship in school editions discussed in Chapter 8, make this reliance politically problematic. The "higher production quotas," increase in accountability, and intensification of teachers' work are aspects of the continuing expansion of capitalist practices and values within the schools (Apple, 1979). Romance fiction itself represents the continuing expansion of the capitalist marketplace in the schools. As Chapters 1 and 7 indicate, this practice has consequences for the content of school texts given the ownership of publishing by multinational corporations whose interests are often politically conservative. While Chapters 2 through 6 and 8 demonstrate that teen romances are elements in the ongoing conservative political restoration, they are also the space where resistances to conservative gender perspectives manifests itself.

Although popular romances are key elements in the process of rule by consent, the act of reading also involves political actions around gender meanings and authority relations. As Tina, Tomeika, Jan, and Carol wrested some control over their reading from Mrs. B. they called into question a teacher's authority to determine choice of reading materials. Their actions contested the power of teachers to decide what is best for students. In many ways, their actions here were an exemplification of the assertive femininity the girls constructed during their reading. They were able to substitute this mode of femininity in place of the compliant femininity expected in the classroom. The struggles between these girls and their teacher were ultimately over whose gender meanings had legitimacy. However, as Chapter 7 demonstrates their actions were contradictory in that they hardened the girls' opposition to "legitimate" texts and the official knowledge they contain. Although the romances generated a high engagement with reading, and provided the readers with "really useful" gender knowledge, this knowledge did not count towards achieving academic success. The twenty-nine girls remained marked as reluctant readers despite their rich and complex interpretations of romance fiction. Although their ability to make sense of the books validated in their own minds their personal and academic competence, because of the contradictory status of romance fiction, teachers did not interpret their reading as competence. Romance novels were not legitimate texts in teachers' eyes, despite student efforts to confer authority on these texts. The political dynamic underlying teachers' work, in combination with the absence of communication with students regarding the substance of romance reading, continued to reinforce the view of romance readers as less capable. This study shows that textual authority is a political process that is enacted in the power struggle between students and teachers. Although teachers and students compromised, the power to define a legitimate text ultimately rested with teachers. Teachers dispense the rewards on which academic success rests. There are few such rewards for teen romance readers.

Radway (1984) indicates that the isolation of reading at home facilitates the privatization of the reading experience. It cements the individual interpretations of adult women readers, and prevents readers from acting politically on their insights regarding gender relations. The girls' romance reading in schools involved a somewhat similar dynamic. Their private mode of reading allowed many of the traditional gender meanings derived from the romances to go relatively unchallenged. The model of individualized reading promoted at Kominsky, Sherwood Park, and Jefferson played a role in shaping an individualistic ethic in the girls, an ethic with larger political consequences. The reading practices not only reinforced the ideology of individualism contained in romance fiction, but also helped to shape the girls' political identities as individual subjects. The ideology of individualism is at the core of traditional American politics. These practices also support Luke's (in press) contention that literacy instruction is a form of ideological practice through the social values and "sensibility" it promotes regarding ways of approaching texts. Texts are to be read individually, and their meanings are to be related to the life of the individual. Although I cannot claim that the political actions of some of the girls in the classroom emanated from their insights into the workings of patriarchy, it is the case that the pleasure of romance reading inspired the collective action of the five readers in Mrs. B.'s class. Although this action challenged important aspects of teachers' authority, it did not extend to the mode of reading itself. Once the romances were secured, the girls read individually. I will return to the significance of this reading mode at a later point.

Form, content and readers

McRobbie (1978b) argues that the young women in her study endorsed conventional femininity because it seemed to them as an "unalterable aspect of life." The twenty-nine readers also accepted dominant gender, class, race, age, and sexual relations, although their responses contained oppositional elements. Key factors in the girls' reconciliation to domestic futures are the textual features of romance fiction that are discussed in Chapters 2 through 6 and 8. Although readers interpret texts in various ways, the text acts as a constraint on reader's activity, as Iser (1980) and Rosenblatt (1978) have stated, through its very form and content. Romances are examples of Eco's notion of "closed texts" which through their very structure attempt to shape readers' responses by virtue of "a range of rigidly pre-established and ordained interpretive solutions" (Eco, 1979, p. 51).[1]

According to Hodge and Kress features like sequence and causation not only characterize events, but also signify "coherence, order, and closure" (Hodge and Kress, 1988, p. 230). I have suggested that the codes of *romance, sexuality,* and *beautification* order the fictional universe and reinforce each other regarding their form and content to such an extent that readers are presented with a coherent set of messages. Romance and heterosexuality, as the controlling discourses in the novels, attempt to funnel readers toward accepting the inevitability of romance and the dominance of men in women's lives. In romance fiction, women exist to please men by looking beautiful, they must relegate their wishes and desires to second place. The twenty-nine girls accepted this image of femininity, although they saw their own wishes as important. The happy endings and individual solutions that are characteristic of romance novels engage with readers' desires to experience a happier, more problem-free version of existence. The happy ending gives order and coherence to the world of romance, thus drawing readers towards a simplified version of social interaction where individual and not collective solutions

A place in the world

count. As readers escape into this less complicated universe, they are taught political lessons about the negative nature of conflict and change.

Eco notes that another feature of closed texts is redundancy of narrative structure within a genre (Eco, 1979, p. 33). Teen romances feature a consistent narrative form historically and across texts. Without exception, the novels hinge on the counterpoint between the "good girl" and "other girl" and all feature an ingenue who accepts romance and becomes strong through the love of the boy of her dreams. This redundancy is built into teen romances through their status as series novels and because they are the product of marketing. Many of the thirty-four novels analyzed, and especially those favored by the twenty-nine readers, are written using "tip sheets," formulas that specify audience, character traits, writing style, length, and appropriate themes.[2] Eco (1979) describes the effect of redundancy and the pleasure of repetition as blocking the possibility of using the text for imagining change. Although each of the twenty-nine readers established various meanings for the romance novels they read, they mostly accepted the novels' versions of social relations. They never disputed the desirability of becoming a girlfriend and recapture that moment of heterosexual specialness through their continual reading of romances.

Although there are many signposts in the text to shape readers' interpretations, the novels offer occasions for speculating on outcomes and pondering femininity, as discussed in Chapter 8. The textual analysis and the study of readers are in agreement on several points. The textual analysis shows that romance-fiction heroines are not always as stereotypically passive and pliable as an Angie Morrow. Readers' preference for strong heroines and impatience with passive ones represents their desire to transcend gender stereotypes and imagine a more assertive femininity. However, closer examination of the meaning of assertiveness reveals a bottom line of caution that stops short of confronting boys. Like Radway's adult-romance readers (1984), teenage readers read as an antidote to loneliness and experience feelings of specialness during reading. Reading romances and the fantasies of love they set in motion represent ways of counteracting the increasing anomie and coldness of life today. Through romance reading, readers transform gender relations so that men cherish and nurture women rather the other way around. The readers' collective rejection of a macho masculinity represents their partial overturning of one aspect of patriarchy. However, their final acceptance of romantic love and its power structure undercuts the political potential of these insights. Romance reading does not alter the girls' present and future circumstances, but rather is deeply implicated in reconciling them to their place in the world.

Anyon (1981) and Taxel (1984) argue that tradebooks and textbooks often offer students models of social action that help young readers make sense and meaning in their lives. In romance fiction these models not only have elements of gender and sexuality, but class and race as well. The discussion of the textual features of romance fiction in Chapter 5 indicates that these models of action are based in the white middle class, although they are not textually identified as such. Readers are addressed from this perspective despite their own class or racial identities. In Chapter 7 I discussed how readers did not unilaterally accept the novels' definitions of married women's lives as primarily domestic with paid work only undertaken out of economic necessity. The narrative organization at times allowed readers to question romance fiction's rendering of women's home and work experiences. Readers' Horatia Alger fantasy represents the point where readers transform gender and class relations by substituting breadwinning women for the June Cleavers of romance fiction. Along with this fantasy, there was a longing for a domestic life, one that emanates from the girls' dawning realization of the burdens represented by home and work. Romance fiction's universe of conspicuous consumption meshes with the girls' longing for a life of comfort and affluence. The school identities of these twenty-nine girls as reluctant readers, and the work undertaken to buy commodities, help to consolidate their class identites around low-paying service-sector work.

Instructional recommendations

Romance-novel reading occurs at a crucial time in adolescent girls' lives when many are looking for their place in the world. As Chapter 1 indicates, many educators and parents are concerned about the versions of reality romance fiction offers young women readers. Clearly, the answer is not to ban romance novels from classrooms. As the reading study shows, girls devoted to this genre will find creative ways to continue their reading despite teacher disapproval. Romance novels per se should not be viewed as unilaterally oppressive and sexist. Romances do offer readers the space to reflect on the dilemmas surrounding female-male relations. I believe that the lack of communication between teachers and students regarding their reflections is implicated in these readers' final endorsement of conventional femininity. The individual mode of reading plays a role here as well. I also believe that the reflective aspect of romance reading may provide a meeting ground between readers, teachers and parents for constructively approaching these novels. Any recommendations involving romance fiction must address readers themselves and larger questions of political practice around popular culture. Although I treat these separately for the purposes of clarity, I do not imply that they are separate in practice. I begin with a number of strategies that I recommended to Lakeview teachers to help readers examine and extend their responses to romance fiction. I follow this by a discussion of book selection. Most of the strategies are designed to develop "reader communities" where readers collectively read and respond. Many of these strategies can also be used by individual readers when reading at home.

Corcoran suggests four cognitive processes underlying aesthetic reading which I believe are also common to critical reading; picturing and imaging; anticipating and retrospecting; engagement and construction; and valuing and evaluating (Corcoran, 1987, pp. 44–51). Picturing and imaging involves the "mental pictures" that readers get when they read. Anticipating and retrospecting occur when readers' minds race ahead or lag behind what their eyes are perceiving. Engagement and construction involve readers' emotional reactions to the text, especially to its characters, and the potential of reading to change readers somehow. Valuing has to do with the judgments readers make concerning whether a book is worth reading. Evaluation concerns readers' appraisal of structural elements of texts. Corcoran's perspective is useful for shedding light on the role readers play in determining literary meaning. This perspective can provide a point of departure for the designing of critical reading strategies that both tap into the experiences that young women readers bring to their reading and also help readers clarify their emotional responses to fiction.

There are several ways to foster picturing and imaging when reading romance novels. "Literary journals" (Farris, 1989) can be used to record reactions and reflect in writing about stories. "Free writing," where students write using self-generated topics, represents readers' authentic responses. Readers can share their journals with classmates. This lays the groundwork for reader communities where students can be challenged and enriched through comparing their responses to those of others. Journals can also be used as the basis of small group discussions

A place in the world

of books when readers share their writing with one another and discuss the implications of their writing. A variation involves teachers asking students to read the first few pages of a new book and then brainstorm regarding what they think of as they read a new book. Writing or mapping in a reading journal are also effective ways of preserving important psychological and cognitive first impressions of books. This is especially important for romance novels, as these novels so strongly engage readers on the level of emotion and fantasy. Teachers and students can then read the logs or maps, commenting on the important gender themes that this first account of reading may reveal.

Anticipating and retrospecting can be facilitated by teaching readers how to use various parts of books before and during reading to speculate on the actions of characters. For example, teachers can prepare a modified version of an Anticipation Guide (Vacca & Vacca, 1986, p. 128) in which students are asked to do the following before reading either individually or in groups:

1. Look at the cover artwork and title.
2. Think about each and write down what the book might be about.
3. Read the back cover.
4. What additional information does this give you regarding what the book might be about?
5. Add this new information to what you have already written.
6. Read with your predictions in mind.
7. As a prediction comes true, put a check mark over it.
8. As things are different, mentally note this or write it down.

While reading a particular chapter, teachers can guide readers towards identifying the gender problems that characters have to solve. Readers then predict the outcome of these problems and read to determine the actual outcome. Readers can record this process in their journals, determining whether they are satisfied with the outcome and how they might want to change it. Again, individual and collective group reading models can be used. Corcoran recommends interrupted reading, where teachers ask readers to stop reading at a particular point and ask themselves questions such as:

A place in the world

1. Why is this event important?
2. What might happen next?
3. How does this event change my understanding of what has come before?
4. What might the ending be?
5. How do I feel about what has happened to the characters?
6. Do I accept what the author might be saying about romance?
7. How do I feel about romance? (Corcoran, 1987, p. 67)

Responses can be verbal or in writing. This strategy requires readers' to connect previous events in stories with future events, thus strengthening both anticipating and retrospecting.

Romance-novel readers often identify positively with the heroine, maintaining a high degree of engagement with the story line and characters. Teachers can tap into this pleasurable aspect of reading to help readers critically reflect on the meaning of identification with characters who are textually defined as "the girlfriend." Once again, response journals are excellent vehicles for readers to reflect on characters and actions in novels. In their journals readers can use "speed mapping" (Corcoran, 1987, p. 67), making diagrams or visual representations of their impressions of characters and events. They can imagine a dream that characters could have and speculate on the meaning of the dream (Adams, 1987), or imagine themselves to be a certain character and retell an episode from the vantage point of how they would handle it. Young and Robinson recommend a "reading shoe box" as a way of helping students to recreate, in the imagination, a particular character's story (Young & Robinson, 1987, p. 170). Teachers can ask students to bring in items that might belong to a character. Students examine the contents of a shoe box and retell the story through a collection of things that might be connected with romance. A shoe box that a group of seventh-grade Sherwood Park girls made contained prom photographs, ads from a teen fashion magazine, a "used" kleenex, a button saying "love," and an anonymous love note where a dissolved romance is described. These students discussed the contents of the shoe box and settled on collectively writing pages from a girl's diary reporting the ups and downs of her romance. In this activity girls critically reflected, as a group, on the meaning of the items, romance itself, and their feelings about boys.

Evaluating and valuing are crucial aspects of reading and response. Romance readers often have very strong reactions to individual books and characters. Visual representations of the story, in the form of bar graphs, can be used to help readers plot the events of a story and how they would evaluate them on a scale from "interesting" to "boring" (Corcoran, 1987, p. 65). In small group settings, students could "wonder aloud" by raising personal questions and issues about the story. One prevalent "wonder" question is why authors write romances. Much spirited discussion can result from this thinking aloud. Wigtuoff and staff from the Council on Interracial Books for Children (1981) recommend that teachers copy particularly telling episodes from romance novels, provide questions that tap reasons for characters' thoughts and actions, and ask readers what they would do in a similar situation. This activity enables readers to see that romance has many possibilities other than the stock ending of "they lived happily ever after."

These strategies can help readers to examine critically the gender issues surrounding romance novels. It is also vital that teachers be familiar with books to help students in the selection process. Professional journals such as *School Library Journal, Journal of Reading, English Journal,* the *Alan Review,* and *The New Advocate* all regularly review new young adult books. These sources are helpful for guiding readers towards books that incorporate gender themes but do not make romance the only important experience in a heroine's development. Readers should also be exposed to what Taxel (in press) calls "oppositional texts." These are texts that go against the grain of conventional gender, class, and racial sentiments in literature for young readers. For instance, Bill and Vera Cleaver's *Trial Valley* deals with sixteen-year-old Mary Call who has been mother to her younger brothers and sisters since their parents' death. Mary is a self-reliant young woman. Although a romantic motif is present in the novels—two young men propose marriage to Mary—she prefers to work out her problems on her own terms. Another example of a strong young woman may be found in Viglucci's *Cassandra Robbins, Esq.*[3] In this novel, Cassie must discover who she is. The theme of identity takes on a special edge because Cassie is the only girl and the only brown person in a white family. Cassie's questioning of where she belongs becomes crucial after she meets Josh Lindsay, her brother's handsome black roommate from college, who spends the summer with Cassie's family. The subsequent romance between Cassie and Josh fills Cassie with concerns about sexual attraction, the meaning of love, and how romance fits into her plans for a future career. The novel ends with uncertainty regarding their relationship as Cassie decides that she must find herself before she can consider what role Josh may play in her life. Lukas's *Center Stage Summer* invites readers to consider the political as an aspect of femininity through the character of budding actor Johanna Culp. This heroine seriously questions the power relations of romance and becomes committed to social change through her involvement in the local "No Nukes" movement. Johanna's ability to stand up to men ranging from her boyfriend Neil to the chairman of the board of a war munitions industry signals her new identity. This novel sends clear messages that possessiveness is not love; and girls, not boys, must create their own realities and take responsibility for it. By placing political activity at the center of the story, *Center Stage Summer* promotes the importance of collective action in effecting social change.[4]

One aspect of gender that is rarely examined in books are the ways that male characters are portrayed. A book that goes a long way toward exploring the stereotypes that surround masculinity is Sach's *A Summer's Lease*. Here, fifteen-year-old Gloria competes with Jerry for the editorship of the school newspaper and must come to terms with her dislike of Jerry's patient and gentle manner. Both Gloria and Jerry represent nontraditional ways of viewing femininity and masculinity. This novel can help female readers examine how limiting gender stereotypes can be for both girls and boys.

Romance-novel reading can be balanced with the reading of other books that provide glimpses of the wide range of activities and interests that comprise women's life experience both today and yesterday. These books help to instill in readers the knowledge of women's immense social contributions. As friendship is an important aspect of an individual's social and emotional development, novels about the joys of friendship can help girls understand that it is important to have friends of both sexes. Fiction dealing effectively with this theme is represented by Garrigue's *Between Friends*, Paterson's *Bridge to Terabithia*, and Levoy's *Alan and Naomi*. Nonfiction reading is especially important because narrative still involves ideological closure by virtue of its characteristics discussed in Chapter 6 even in books where authors deliberately set out to overturn gender stereotypes. Sobol's *Woman Chief*, Kingston's *Woman Warrior*, and Smucker's *Runaway to Freedom* are grounded in the lives of actual women of the past.

As Volosinov (1973) has observed, language itself involves a "struggle over meaning," one which I have shown to be at the center of young women's romance reading. The activities I have outlined can help sharpen these struggles and give readers the critical tools to make deconstructive readings that unearth the political interests shaping romance fiction's form and content. Although it is important to facilitate critical reflection and make available books with more progressive content, that is only part of the picture. Popular-culture forms can be used to shape a feminist cultural politics.

Feminist politics of popular culture

Bennett (1986) characterizes popular culture as the "area of negotiation" between dominant and opposing cultural elements. In many ways the struggles of young women readers within classrooms and in the realm of meaning represent the kind of cultural politics that has long concerned feminists. These struggles are part and parcel of a traditional feminist cultural politics one centering on "the politics of the personal" in which consciousess and everyday life have taken on a political character (Barrett, 1980, p. 37). However, the latter have become "public" political issues as they are the sites where individuals' consent and resistance to dominant patterns of power and control are negotiated. There are many political issues in popular culture that can form the basis of a feminist politics of popular culture.

Popular culture is one of the more important forces in the school and leisure lives of youth, especially young women. A visit to almost any school attests to the omnipresence of popular culture from styles of dress to the books young women read. Their leisure is dominated by the beat of popular music, MTV, soap opera, and videos, most of which are made for young women largely without their participation. Given the double-edged quality of popular culture, its oppositional components can contain political challenges to existing gender, class, race, age, and sexual divisions. For this potential to be realized, it will be important to continue helping students to locate the contradictions between popular culture's version of social relations and their own lives. Central to this goal is establishing a political practice around the consumption of popular culture. In the case of popular romance fiction, this involves redefining reading from an apolitical, internal, and individual activity to a socially and historically situated political practice.[5] The theory and practice of feminist pedagogy (Schniedewind, 1987; Shrewsbury, 1987) and that of Freire's political literacy approach (Freire, 1987) represent points of departure for a "politics of reading."[6] Many of the reading strategies I outlined above are steps in this direction.

A place in the world

Politicizing reading is vital because much of the hegemonic power of ruling elites in the United States is consolidated through written forms, especially textbooks and tradebooks as Anyon (1981), Taxel (1984), and I have shown.

As the control of popular culture in its commodity form is in the hands of large corporate interests representing the New Right, it is vital that cultural struggles continue to be directed towards the corporate sector. Cultural forms like film, television, and literature were targeted early on by feminists as crucial areas for analysis and political struggle (Millett, 1977; Stacy, Bereaud, & Daniel, 1974). It is important to continue struggling against such interests along with seeking new spaces for competing cultural practices. When Bantam issued to "Sweet Dreams" book-club subscribers a "Slumber Party Kit" that featured "The Boy of My Dreams" crossword puzzles, and when Scholastic developed "Wildfire" magazine, parents and educators mobilized popular support for large protests against the sexist content of these materials. Both of these marketing devices were quickly eliminated. That teen romances today contain slightly less traditional themes than the original series romances is also the outcome of the collective struggle of many groups for more varied gender representations. The political struggle over representation extends to supporting alternative presses such as the Feminist Press, Square One Publishers, and Women's History Collective as key components in political strategies against gender, class, race, age, and sexual hegemony.

There is yet another area of popular culture that is vital to a feminist politics of popular culture. I have previously argued that capitalism is especially adept at manipulating pleasure through popular culture forms in ways that heighten the tensions within the social subject who "takes care of business" and is receptive to the pleasure that such cultural forms bring. As Barrett (1980) notes, pleasure has been problematic for feminists as those happy endings in romance fiction and restoration of order at the end of popular films and television programs are often pleasurable. There are also the "pleasures of identifying" with characters and situations and "remaking" the text in fantasy. These elements are important for feminist struggles because they can represent the point of ideological closure and the utopian potential of popular culture.

Although the politics of popular culture that I have outlined poses tremendous challenges, it is precisely the challenge that makes these struggles so important. Barrett clearly states what is at stake: "Cultural politics, and feminist art, are important precisely because we are not the helpless victims of oppressive ideology. We take some responsibility for the cultural meaning of gender and it is up to us all to change it" (Barrett, 1980, p. 58). Gender, class, race, age, and sexuality are not immutable categories in teen romance or anywhere else, but cultural constructs that are produced and can be transformed.

Appendix A
Methodology

Any study is based in certain methodological practices and assumptions that guide inquiry. I conclude this study with a description of the two sets of methodologies underlying the analysis of adolescent romance fiction and its readers. This appendix describes sampling procedures, techniques for analyzing teen romance fiction, and the methods employed in the study of readers.

Textual analysis

The sample of thirty-four adolescent romance novels

The period of 1942–82 was chosen since it represents the very beginnings of teen romance fiction (Burton, 1965; Edwards, 1952) and includes the development of the new series romances. In stories written for girls prior to the 1940s, romance was an interlude in girls' lives. Gradually, it became the focus of novels so that a new kind of book was available to readers by 1942. This date marks the publication of Daly's *Seventeenth Summer*, the first novel to feature romance as its proper subject matter (Patterson, 1956). The novels also span four decades which have significance for women in terms of home, work, politics and education indicated in Chapter 8. The sample of thirty-four books is a fraction of the 150 books on the original list. It represents those books having strong romantic components that were highly recommended by a number of selection tools (see Appendices B and C).

Appendix A

Sampling involved a two-tier procedure. The original list of 150 novels was developed through the use of various bibliographies of recommended adolescent literature and critical works providing a discussion of individual novels. Among the first set of sources consulted during the compliation of titles were *Young Adult Literature* (Lenz & Mahood, 1980), *Literature Study in the High Schools* (Burton, 1965), *Literature for Today's Young Adult's* (Donelson & Nilsen, 1980), and *Paperbooks in the Schools* (Butman, Reis, & Sohn, 1963). Annotated and topical bibliographies contained in *Books and the Teenage Reader* (Carlsen, 1967) and *Your Reading* (Frogner, 1954; Neville, 1946; Walker, 1975; Willard, 1966) were also used. An individual title had to be positively recommended by two different selection tools in order to remain on the first list of novels. The intention was to locate books that would be representative of adolescent romance fiction and provide a somewhat even distribution of titles over the forty year period. The first list was then narrowed to those books meeting the above criteria, producing a second list. *The Junior High School Library Catalog, Senior High School Library Catalog, Kliatt Young Adult Paperback Book Guide, Booklist, Hornbook,* and *School Library Journal* are prominent selection tools used by educators and school and public librarians when selecting books for young readers. All available editions and issues of these books and journals were consulted beginning with the 1942 edition/issue whenever available. The books in the second list were evaluated against this second set of selection guides to determine which books would possibly be included in school, classroom and public libraries. To remain on the second list, a book had to be positively reviewed in at least one selection guide. The new romances presented a problem because of their recent appearance and the lag between publication and book reviews. Subsequently, it was very difficult to locate reviews in the major selection guides. As these new romances represent an important development in teen romance fiction, as many titles as possible were included given these constraints.

The present sample of thirty-four novels represents those books positively reviewed in at least three selection guides and are books available through libraries and book stores as indicated by my search of several school, metropolitan and suburban libraries. In reality, most books were recommended by a number of sources and some had won awards from the American Library Association like the ALA Best Book and YASD Notable Book.

Appendix A

Analysis of Literature

The approach to literature used in this study regards texts as meaning producing systems. Shifting the analysis away from the traditional identification of meanings to how texts make meanings necessitates a methodology that can account for this process. Semiotics provides such a method through its focus on understanding both the meaning of social practices and how these meanings are constructed. Semiotics studies culture as a message system structured like language. Central to semiotics are the categories of "sign" and "codes." The following discussion will focus on semiotics as applied to literary analysis.

Semiotics is concerned with the relationship between a sign or word and its meaning along with the way signs are combined into codes (Belsey, 1980). Language is a system of signs where any sign has a dual nature: the "signifier," or sound, and the "signified," the concept or meaning. For example, the relationship between the concept of a house (the signified) and the sound made by the word "house" (the signifier) constitutes the linguistic sign. According to Barthes (1964), each part of the sign exists in an arbitrary relationship, one established socially through convention and custom.[1] Language is a system of difference in which a relationship of opposition exists between items with the meaning of one item understood in relation to another (Barthes, 1964, 1967). The opposition between the sounds /t/ and /d/ form the basis of meaning at the phonetic level while the meaning of each word resides in the difference between its own sounds and those of other sounds such as in "pin" and "bin." Words such as "mother," "sister," and "woman" derive their meanings in contrast with other words. Hence, language operates on the basis of a complex pattern of paired differences or binary oppositions which form the basic structure of meaning.

Differentiation and meaning occur through the relationship between two planes—the paradigmatic and the syntagmatic. According to Fiske and Hartley (1978, p. 50), a paradigm is "a 'vertical' *set* of units [each unit being a sign or word], from which the required one is selected." On the other hand, a syntagm is "the 'horizontal' *chain* into which it [a word or sign] is linked with others, according to agreed rules and conventions." Each word will have a syntagmatic relationship with words that precede or succeed it. This relationship provides the "grammar" for linking signs into a meaningful whole. The paradigmatic rela-

Appendix A

tionship determines the rules governing word choice or "vocabulary." The concept of difference becomes important as words not chosen to be part of an utterance also define the meaning of the chosen word. Semiotic structures are formed through processes of joining and separating.

Signs themselves can be organized into meaningful systems called *codes*. A code is a "vertical" set of signs (paradigm) that can be combined according to certain "horizontal" rules or grammar (syntagm). Codes are inherently social since their very existence is dependent upon the agreement of users. Monaco (1977) explains that the code is the medium through which cultural products transmit their messages. Codes are dynamic structures which contain tensions between traditional and innovative aspects. Traditional aspects enable a code to communicate and convey meanings by conventions formed in the past that exert influence in the present. The innovative character of codes involves new practices and developments that coexist with traditional ones. Codes are critical constructions derived from the analysis of signs which permit the interpretation of literature. Interpretation then involves identifying the codes, analyzing their meaning and making connections between the codes in individual texts or among texts.

The social dimensions of semiotics have been recently developed by Hodge and Kress (1988) who argue that semiotic systems cannot be studied in isolation from the social context. The meaning of a particular semiotic system like the novel is shaped by the social, economic and political conditions surrounding its writing along with the larger configuration of power and control within the society. Semiotic processes themselves are the site of struggles over meanings as various opposing images contend for control. Codes are shaped through the differential positions individuals and groups occupy by gender, class and race. Social semiotics joins the close analysis of the text to the political uses of language. Interpretation then entails bringing the unifying as well as the oppositional elements of codes to the surface while accounting for the ways texts deal with these tensions.

A semiotically grounded methodology for analyzing narrative structure was adapted from A. J. Greimas's work on the structure of the folktale. Both folktales and teen romances are examples of Barthes's notion of the "readable" text, a coherently organized and unadorned text designed for wide readership. Greimas's (1966) study of the folktale revealed a system of binary opposites such as Subject vs. Object, Sender vs. Receiver and Helper vs. Opponent which was responsible for generat-

Appendix A

ing characters in the stories. Greimas then theorized that three sets of binary oppositions in various combinations would produce the characters in almost any story. For example, the category of Subject vs. Object generated stories of quest which is the pattern for simple romances. Here, Subject vs. Object and Sender vs. Receiver would combine to produce patterns for male and female characters as Sender/Subject and Receiver/Object respectively. Character is only one dimension of narrative structure. To understand how the characters act, one must look to action as a kind of performance by characters. Greimas uses the concept of "function" in the form of pairs of oppositions to describe action. In the folktale, Greimas noted twenty pairs of oppostions such as prohibition/violation and command/acceptance that generate the actions of the characters. For example, if command/acceptance is synonymous with establishing contracts then its opposite prohibition/violation would involve breaking contracts. The combination of these functions would generate a distinctive narrative structure concerned with establishing or breaking contracts, alienation and reintegration (1966, pp. 195–196) in the manner of the tale "Rapunzel." Hence, the meaning of a folktale or any other story is the result of form and content—characters and actions working in tandem.

Semiotics lends itself to the analysis of teen romances. The thirty-four novels were read to determine not only what meanings they might have, but how they constructed meaning. To understand this, two dimensions of the novels would have to be analyzed: actions and characters. The novels were first read in order to gain as many impressions as possible. Later, a close textual analysis revealed that certain actions entailing *romance, beauty,* and *sexuality* dominated regardless of when the novels were written. Nearly every action in the thirty-four novels was an expression of these three ideas. Their pervasiveness convinced me that they constituted the recurring patterns of actions or codes of the novels. McRobbie (1978a) also identified these ideas which she called the codes of *romance, sexuality,* and *beautification* as structuring the teen magazine *Jackie* thus providing verification for the existence of these codes in popular culture forms. Through further analysis I was able to reduce the various aspects of each code into a number of sentences that represented the "logic" operating in each code. By comparing and contrasting the elements of each of the codes, the meanings of these actions within individual novels and across the sample emerged. The intention was not to seek unified meanings, but to be sensitive to what-

Appendix A

ever twists and turns the novels might provide. Nevertheless, patterns emerged that appeared to be historical in origin, that is, novels written during specific years had similar code characteristics. By separating the novels into groups according to the content of the codes of *romance, sexuality,* and *beautification* the three periods emerged. The periodization provided the analytical tool for detecting any tensions or changes in the codes over time and allowed for the analysis of the relationship of the novels to the historical context.

Greimas's methodology is useful for analyzing the narrative form of teen romance fiction. The idea that characters perform actions and resolve conflicts provided the key to locating and understanding the narrative structure of the novels. I first analyzed the elements of the three codes to determine the kind of characters performing the various actions involving romance, sexuality and beautification. I determined that two pairs of oppositions, the Good/Bad and Strong/Weak, generated virtually all female characters in the novels. I then analyzed the meaning of these oppositions, drawing profiles of the major characters. Through analysis of the oppositional structure, the tensions within these characters clearly emerged. Further research into fiction focusing on women's lives revealed that the Good/Bad and Strong/Weak oppositions have a long history from the Brontës to today's romances as the major character structuring mechanisms (Brownstein, 1984; Modleski, 1984).

The actions in romance novels were not reducible to a set of functions as was the case in Greimas's study. However, there was one action dominating all the novels. This concerned the central role of romance in heroines' becoming women. This leitmotif, or overriding theme encapsulated the dominant traits of the heroine and provided the link between the binary opposites and the codes of *romance, beautification,* and *sexuality*. The leitmotif provided the mechanism for exploring how form and content might work together or against each other regarding meaning production. It allowed me to continue to be atuned to the diversity of romance fiction's meanings.

Semiotics describes the systems of conventions that shape meaning in the form of codes and binary oppostions. This textual analysis accounts for one aspect of romance fiction. The other part involves the actual readers and their interpretations of the novels. This study continues the semiotic focus on meaning production through ethnography which can provide insights into readers in schools and the knowledge they construct through their reading.

Appendix A

The Study of Readers

Defining the Issues

My interest in romance fiction began some years before this study, and is a reflection of my continuing concern with understanding popular literature and readers. The initial focus of the research was influenced by the existing research on the role of popular literature in the formation of subjectivity along the lines of gender, class, race, sexual orientation, and age (Rose, 1984; Walkerdine, 1984). Critical feminist accounts of schooling also shaped the theoretical orientation (Griffin, 1985; McRobbie, 1978b; Weiner & Arnot, 1987) However, the school as a context for romance reading has not been explored to date. The grounding in these pertinent issues generated what Malinoski (1922, pp. 8–9) calls "foreshadowed problems," a set of research-based issues and problems.

The issues relating to romance fiction and readers in my study were influenced by this literature and Radway's (1984, p. 8) *Reading the Romance*. She was concerned not only with "how the women understand the novels themselves but also how they comprehend the very act of picking up a book in the first place." Radway has especially analyzed the strong fantasy and gender component of romance fiction reading among adult women reading at home, although she has not made class and race integral to her study. However, her focus on the significance of the act of reading itself paralleled my interest in the meaning of reading within the school, a setting where reading not only occurs, but is taught.

In light of this research, I formulated the initial issues into a series of questions: Who reads romances? Why are romances read? What meanings do readers make when they read? What significance can be attached to reading in school? While these questions guided the initial phases of research, during the fieldwork they became more narrrowed while unexpected categories developed. An example of the latter concerned my initial assumption that age might play a significant role in young women readers' rationale for romance reading, that is, their reading might significantly differ from that of adults. This presumption was quickly dispelled. I also found that many issues swirled around the school and classroom as site for reading, especially who had the authority to define "proper" reading material. Readers' academic status and their

Appendix A

present and future aspirations also became increasingly important as was the very status of romance novels in the classroom.

Access and sample

My choice of middle school and junior high school as sites was the outcome of widespread reports in the literature (Lanes, 1981; Harvey, 1982; Madsen, 1981) of romance reading in schools among girls ages 9–15. As a former teacher, reading specialist and supervisor at those levels, I had also witnessed this reading, particularly in reading and language arts classes. Because I wanted to seek as much diversity in readers as possible, I decided to seek a class and racially mixed school district. I first decided to secure access to a school district where I had no professional acquaintants since a preexisting identity perhaps might limit the nature and quality of interactions with participants.

Access to a school district proved difficult since the very idea of studying teen romance novels in schools was not viewed favorably. This is in part due to the stigma attached to this kind of reading and lack of seriousness on the part of the public regarding romance fiction despite widespread readership and the presence of a body of distinguished scholarship on the subject. After failing to secure access to several districts, I was faced with the decision of whether to discontinue the research or draw on my status as a reading specialist with a wide range of acquaintances among other reading professionals. Using such measures for entree is not without precedent in the literature (Gouldner, 1954). As a reading specialist researcher, I was readily accepted by the urban Lakeview School District for field work at Kominsky Junior High School, Jefferson and Sherwood Park Middle Schools.

Although elated at the prospect of beginning the field work, I was concerned that my professional identity might limit aspects of the study. Furthermore, my contact person in each site was the school reading specialist. I decided to exert a concerted effort not to appear too closely associated with any particular groups or individuals. I now saw downplaying my reading specialist background as crucial. Reading specialists often occupy the tenuous position of curriculum developer, teacher and quasi-administrator which require a constant juggling act to balance (Burg et al., 1978; Wylie, 1969). This tripartite role subsumes evaluation of programs and teachers as well as advocacy for students. At times

Appendix A

these three roles produce much tension when programs designed for particular students may collide with teachers' and administrators' visions of proper reading instruction. Despite these realities and my concerns, I felt I had success in maintaining a wide range of acquaintances, although requiring constant work on my part.

Roberts (1981) notes that gender is a significant factor in field research. Being a woman allowed me access to the girls in a variety of school settings, and was instrumental in helping me to gain their trust and that of their women teachers. Hammersley and Atkinson (1983) note that ethnicity can set limits on a field study as well. As a white woman, I more easily secured the trust of other white women. I had to constantly "win" the trust of the black, Hispanic and Chinese girls. There were areas about the girls' lives and reading which they would not divulge or only answered in generalities even towards the end of the study. The reasons for this stem from the complex and troubled racial relations in Lakeview and its surrounding communities. Lakeview schools were the site of racial tensions among students, parents and teachers in the period before and during the field work. These circumstances set limits on the field work with girls of color. I do not feel that the data on the racial dimensions of reading represent the depth I would have liked to attain.

Along with the field work in schools, I had initially intended to interview informants and parents in their homes. I was interested in how home background might condition the act of reading and the meanings of romance novels. Like McRobbie (1978a, 1978b) I experienced difficulty in gaining access to young women's homes mainly because I had no ready introduction. Hence, I was confined to reporting statements made by young women about their home lives and was not able to actually observe and interview them at that site.

Once I had secured my sites, locating the romance fiction readers in the schools became an important concern. Glaser and Strauss (1967) discuss "theoretical sampling," a strategy in which the selection of informants emerges as the research progresses and according to the researcher's knowledge background. Since librarians usually possess much knowledge regarding reading patterns with a school, I spent the first several weeks becoming acquainted with librarians in the three schools. Eventually I secured their permission to examine the book checkout cards. To identify books as romances I used the card catalog topic designations as well as librarians and my own knowledge of prominent series and titles. The three librarians were generous in their assistance and showed their keen interest in the study by supplying names of individual girls who they knew to be frequent romance readers. Through the librarians, I was in turn introduced to reading and language arts teachers who also might be able to supply names. Several teachers shared book club order forms as well. I was interested in girls who read at least three romances a month.[2] Through these sources the initial sample of seventy-five girls from the three schools was compiled. Since this number was a bit large in terms of time available and resources, the sample was narrowed by choosing girls who read at least five romances a month. This resulted in a group of twenty-nine girls in the three schools. Checking the class schedules of these girls revealed that they shared five women teachers for language instruction. Initially I had few preconceptions regarding teen romance readers other than age and gender. It came as quite a surprise that the girls as a whole received Chapter I reading support service and/or were tracked into low ability language classes.

Data collection

From October, 1985 to May, 1986 I spent approximately two to three days a week in the schools. This schedule was dictated by my teaching responsibilities and writing schedule. Although I was not present in each school every week, over the eight months I was able to balance the time available among the three sites. To find out about readers and romances, I employed a variety of techniques from ethnography and existing studies of readers. This is in keeping with ethnography's practice of combining interview and observation with data from other sources. In the initial stages, I informally interviewed several of the seventy-five girls about their reading to establish the basis for a "reading survey" which I planned to administer to all seventy-five girls. I also drew categories for items from Radway (1984) and Thurston (1987). The reading survey is recognized in studies of romance readers (Jensen, 1984; Radway, 1984; Thurston, 1987) as a valuable technique for gathering a wide range of rich data that would require a staggering number of interviews to secure. The survey was administered in November to the seventy-five girls (see Appendix D).

I was also a participant and observer in the five classrooms and any others where I had access. A typical day would consist of observing in language arts or Chapter I classrooms, having lunch with students or

Appendix A

teachers, attending extra-curricular activities and teachers' meetings. Realizing that a researcher cannot do everything in-depth, I interacted with teachers and students to the fullest extent possible and what would make sense in the various contexts. Since I am a middle aged woman with graying hair, there were places students ordinarily inhabit such as lockerooms and lavatories that were clearly out of bounds. My presence there would have made the girls uncomfortable and perhaps jeopardized the trust I had established. However, I was accepted in the cafeteria since many adults ate lunch with students. Several teachers did so as well as retirees acting as volunteers. I was present at extra-curricular activities, although most of the twenty-nine girls were not involved in these activities. However, I felt it was important for insights into the culture of the schools. I attended as many faculty meetings both formal and informal as possible. I informally talked with students and teachers as well as formally interviewing them individually and in groups. I asked many questions and did a great deal of listening. I examined school documents such as curriculum guides, reading folders and other pertinent information to have as wide a range of sources as possible.

As the basis of some of my formal interviews with students and teachers I drew on Hargreaves, Hester and Mellor's (1975) "non-directive" questioning. This involved observing a lesson and extracting what I felt were significant statements or occurrences. During the interview I would describe the event or quote what the individual had said and then pose a "why" question or ask for an explanation. At other times I would center student interviews around the issues of romance reading, school, home, and future and present work plans. I found these issues to trigger interviewees into talking about not only those issues, but others as well. However, interviews were open-ended and interviewees' responses significantly shaped their content. I also used some of the Reading Survey questions when appropriate. The teacher interviews followed a similar format and were focused on romance reading in their classroom, teaching, language arts curriculum and student interactions.

Recording data

The methods of recording data depended upon context and purposes. I took notes during classroom observation and meetings whenever possible. I used a system of speed note taking that I had developed over a course of years. I always began my notes by indicating the the time, location, participants and circumstances. There were times when note taking would be unfeasible such as during casual encounters. I would then depend on my memory and reconstruct the event in writing as soon as possible. I tried to be as concrete and detailed as possible in my accounts. Whenever possible, I used a tape recorder for the individual and group interviews. For the most part, interviewees were comfortable with the tape recorder. Although the taped interview provided rich detail, a drawback was the amount of transcription required. I often took notes from the tape first and then had it fully transcribed later on. This allowed me to use the tape data as soon as possible to guide further inquiry. I also made use of "analytic memos" (Hammersely & Atkinson, 1983). Following an interview or observation, I would review my notes and bracket statements or ideas that represented important avenues to explore or might be useful for data analysis. I also periodically reviewed my notes and wrote small narratives in which I "took stock" of my progress, developed emerging ideas and synthesized events.

I organized my notes into the three primary categories of observation, interview and documents along with keeping the student and teacher notes separate. The use of different color paper and folders helped to maintain this framework. I made several copies of each set of notes to facilitate data analysis. Although I used a basic chronological system, I maintained a topical subsystem which emanated from my constant sifting through the data.

Analysis and Reporting

By placing the process of data analysis at this point, I do not imply that it was separate from collection. Rather, I continuously analyzed notes, formulated categories and reviewed the background literature as the study proceeded. Data was coded, categorized according to overriding ideas or themes. I used Glaser and Strauss's (1967) "constant comparison" method in which categorized data would be compared to other categorized sources. I checked the inferences I had drawn from the data against different periods in the field work and different respondents. I coded data on the typed and hand written records and made comments in the ample left hand margins. I reviewed all the data on four separate occassions. Initially, I felt that gender and class would be the overriding

Appendix A

categories. Gender became a slightly more dominant category. I continued to consider how reading might relate to respondents lives as women and as members of a social class. Work and the notion of the "reluctant" reader also emerged as significant themes. In terms of the relation of the school to romance reading, the idea of authority relations was dominant. A dynamic of resistance and accommodation on the part of both teachers and students emerged within the latter category. The various reasons for reading romances and the characteristics of a good romance novel seemed to hinge on the idea of fantasy. Although I initially thought that fantasy would be important, I was not prepared for the way it closely related to gender and class. With these categories in mind, I wrote several working papers using both the field data and the relevant literature. These papers clarified the categories and helped me refine the framework.

I envision writing as a major mode of making sense of romance fiction reading. The field notes, analytic memos and the working papers all represent points where analysis and writing merged. In the various drafts I have written , I have attempted to maintain a tension between the actual events or words of participants and my interpretations. Generalizations have been almost always supported by observations or quotations from interviews. The names of the school district, schools and participants have been fictionalized in accordance with confidentiality. Some of the girls chose their own pseudonyms. In writing the account appearing in this book, I have organized it according to topics since this seemed an appropriate way to give a thorough account of an idea or event. It also follows the general pattern of the book. I have focused the account on the readers and their teachers, and have reserved this appendix as the means for reflections on my role as researcher. The various written accounts of this field work have been shared with the participants. They have commented upon them and their criticisms are reflected in the present account.

Limitations

Any study has limitations, especially when it attempts to link girls' romance fiction reading with schooling and other significant aspects of their lives. One limitation involves my inability to gain access to homes to include this important dimension in the study. Although the five teachers were most generous in their cooperation, there were sensitive topics involving reading curriculum for "reluctant" readers and teaching. I had to proceed so cautiously that at times I simply abandoned the area altogether for fear of jeopardizing my status. I also felt that my identity as a reading specialist and former supervisor at times resulted in guarded responses on the part of teachers. Because I was not granted permission to observe the twenty-nine girls in their other classes, I was unable to use these observations as points of comparison. Another limitation involves the absence of male readers from the study. Do boys read romance novels? There are few novels that deal with the male perspective on romance and it is not known if boys read them. While this dimension was not included in the present study, a future study might shed considerable light on the role of intimacy and literature in shaping femininity and masculinity. Kominsky, Sherwood Park and Jefferson and its seventy-five teen romance readers represent a small fraction of Lakeview Schools and the larger teen romance reading population. Readers must decide for themselves regarding the conclusions drawn and the importance of this study. If readers are moved to probe more deeply into the relationship of instructional materials and the construction of students' hopes and dreams as women, then this study has achieved its goal.

Appendix B
Novels Used In This Study

Author	Title	Publisher	Date	Recommended by
PERIOD I (1942–1959)				
Benson, S.	*Junior Miss*	Pocket Books (Originally 1942)	1969	*Senior High School Library Catalogue*, 1947, 1952, 1957, 1962; Schechter & Bogart, 1965, 1970; *Booklist*, 1941; Burton; Carlsen; Donelson & Nilsen; Lenz & Mahood; Neville
Daly, M.	*Seventeenth Summer*	Simon & Schuster (Originally 1942)	1968	*Senior High School Library Catalogue*, 1947, 1952, 1957, 1962; Schechter & Bogart, 1965, 1970, 1975, 1980; *Booklist*, 1942, 1943; *Hornbook*, 1942; Frogner; Neville; Walker; Willard
DuJardin, R.	*Practically Seventeen*	Scholastic	1943	*Senior High School Library Catalogue*, 1948, 1950, 1952, 1957, 1962; Schechter & Bogart, 1965; *Booklist*, 1950; Burton; Frogner
Cavanna, B.	*Going on Sixteen*	Scholastic	1946	*Senior High School Library Catalogue*, 1947, 1952, 1957, 1962; Schechter & Bogart, 1965; *Booklist*, 1946, 1954; Burton; Carlsen; Donelson & Nilsen; Frogner; Lenz & Mahood

Appendix B

Author	Title	Publisher	Date	Recommended by
Freedman, B. Freedman, N.	*Mrs. Mike*	Berkley	1947	*Senior High School Library Catalogue*, 1952, 1957, 1962, 1967; Schechter & Bogart, 1965, 1970, 1975, 1980; *Booklist*, *Hornbook*, 1948; Carlsen; Frogner; Walker
Cavanna, B.	*Paintbox Summer*	Westminster	1949	*Senior High School Library Catalogue*, 1951, 1952, 1957, 1962; Schechter & Bogart, 1966; *Booklist*, 1951; Donelson; Lenz & Mahood
Du Jardin, R.	*Wait for Marcy*	Scholastic	1950	*Senior High School Library Catalogue*, 1951, 1952, 1957, 1962; Schechter & Bogart, 1966; *Booklist*, 1951; Donelson & Nilsen; Lenz & Mahood
Emery, A.	*Sorority Girl*	Westminster	1952	*Senior High School Library Catalogue*, 1951, 1952, 1957, 1962; Schechter & Bogart, 1966; *Booklist*, 1951; Donelson & Nilsen; Lenz & Mahood
Cavanna, B.	*The Boy Next Door*	William Morrow	1956	*Senior High School Library Catalogue*, 1957, 1962; Schechter & Bogart, 1965; *Booklist*, 1956; Burton
Ogilvie, E.	*Blueberry Summer*	Scholastic	1956	*Senior High School Library Catalogue*, 1957, 1968; *Booklist*, 1956; *Hornbook*, 1956

Appendix B

Novels Used In This Study (continued)

Author	Title	Publisher	Date	Recommended by
Stolz, M.	*The Day and the Way We Met*	Harper & Row	1956	*Senior High School Library Catalogue*, 1957, 1968; *Booklist*, 1956; *Hornbook*, 1956; Burton; Donelson & Nilsen
Cleary, B.	*Jean and Johnny*	Dell	1959	*Senior High School Library Catalogue*, 1965; Schechter & Bogart, 1965; *Booklist*, 1959; *Hornbook*, 1959; YASD Notable Book
PERIOD II (1963–1979)				
Cleary, B.	*Sister of the Bride*	Dell	1963	*Senior High School Library Catalogue*, 1964; Schechter & Bogart, 1965, 1970, 1975; *Booklist*, 1963; *Hornbook*, 1963; Kliatt, 1981; *School Library Journal*, 1963
Eyerly, J.	*Drop-Out*	Berkley	1963	*Senior High School Library Catalogue*, 1965; Schechter & Bogart, 1965, 1970, 1975; *Booklist*, 1964; *School Library Journal*, 1963; Carlsen; Walker; Willard
L'Engle, M.	*Camilla*	Delacorte	1965	Schechter & Bogart, 1970, 1975, 1982; *Hornbook*, 1965, 1983; *School Library Journal*, 1982; Carlsen, Walker

Appendix B

Author	Title	Publisher	Date	Recommended by
Hunt, I.	*Up a Road Slowly*	Grosset	1966	*Senior High School Library Catalogue,* 1968; Schechter & Bogart, 1967, 1970, 1975, 1980, *Booklist,* 1967; *Hornbook,* 1967; Donelson & Nilsen; Walker; Newbery Award Winner
Head, A.	*Mr. and Mrs. Bo Jo Jones*	New American Library	1967	*Senior High School Library Catalogue,* 1972; *Booklist,* 1967; Donelson & Nilsen; Lenz & Mahood; Walker
Zindel, P.	*My Darling, My Hamburger*	Bantam	1971	Schecter & Bogart, 1972, 1975, 1980; Donelson & Nilsen; Lenz and Mahood; *Hornbook,* 1969; Walker
Guy, R.	*The Friends*	Holt	1973	Schechter & Bogart, 1975, 1980; *Booklist,* 1974; *Hornbook,* 1974; *Kliatt,* 1974; *School Library Journal,* 1973; Donelson & Nilsen; Walker; YASD Notable Book
Lyle, K. L.	*I Will Go Barefoot All Summer For You*	Dell	1973	Schechter & Bogart, 1974, 1975, 1980; *Kliatt,* 1975; *Booklist,* 1973; Donelson & Nilsen; Walker
Guy, R.	*Ruby*	Viking	1976	*Kliatt,* 1979; *Hornbook,* 1976; Donelson & Nilsen; Lenz and Mahood; ALA Best Book

Appendix B

Novels Used In This Study (continued)

Author	Title	Publisher	Date	Recommended by
Le Guin, U.	*Very Far Away From Anywhere Else*	Bantam	1976	*Senior High School Library Catalogue*, 1978; Schechter & Bogart, 1977; *Booklist*, 1976; *Hornbook*, 1976; Donelson & Nilsen; Lenz and Mahood; YASD Notable Book
Wilkinson, B.	*Ludell and Willie*	Bantam (Originally 1977)	1981	Schechter & Bogart, 1978, 1980; *Kliatt*, 1981; *Booklist*, 1977; *Hornbook*, 1977; *School Library Journal*, 1977; Donelson & Nilsen
Hautzig, D.	*Hey, Dollface*	William Morrow	1978	Schechter & Bogart, 1980; *Kliatt*, 1980; *Booklist*, 1978; *Hornbook*, 1978; *School Library Journal*, 1978; Donelson & Nilsen
Gauch, P.	*Fridays*	Pocket Books	1979	Schechter & Bogart, 1981; *Kliatt*, 1981; *Booklist*, 1979; *School Library Journal*, 1980
Mazer, N. F.	*Up in Seth's Room*	Dell	1979	*Senior High School Library Catalogue*, 1981; Schechter & Bogart, 1981; *Kliatt*, 1981; *Booklist*, 1979; *School Library Journal*, 1980; Donelson & Nilsen; ALA Best Book

Appendix B

Author	Title	Publisher	Date	Recommended by
Pascal, F.	My First Love and Other Disasters	Viking	1979	Schechter & Bogart, 1980; *Kliatt*, *Booklist*, 1977; *School Library Journal*, 1979; YASD Best Book
PERIOD III (1980–1982)				
Pevsner, S.	Cute is a Four-Letter Word	Archway	1980	Schechter & Bogart, 1981; *Hornbook*, 1981; *School Library Journal*, 1980
Conklin, B.	P.S. I Love You	Bantam	1981	*Kliatt*, 1982; *School Library Journal*, 1982; *Booklist*, 1982
Pevsner, S.	I'll Always Remember You . . . Maybe	Houghton	1981	Schechter & Bogart, 1982; *Booklist*, 1981; *Hornbook*, 1981; *School Library Journal*, 1981
Pollowitz, M.	Princess Amy	Bantam	1981	*School Library Journal*, 1981; *Hornbook*, 1981; *Booklist*, 1981
Quin-Harkin, J.	California Girl	Bantam	1981	*School Library Journal*, 1981; *Hornbook*, 1981; *Booklist*, 1981
Vernon, R.	The Popularity Plan	Bantam	1981	*School Library Journal*, 1981; Donelson & Nilsen
Conford, E.	Seven Days to a Brand-New Me	Atlantic, Little, Brown	1982	Schechter & Bogart, 1982; *Booklist*, 1981; *Hornbook*, 1981, 1983

Appendix C

Books and Journals Used in the Selection of the Sample of Thirty-Four Books

Booklist. Chicago: American Library Association, all issues from 1942–1983.
Burton, D. (1965). *Literature study in the high schools*. New York: Holt, Rinehart and Winston.
Butman, A., Reis, D., & Sohn, D. (1963). *Paperbacks in the schools*. New York: Bantam.
Carlesen, G. R. (1967). *Books and the teenage reader*. New York: Bantam.
Donelson, K. L., & Nilsen, A. P. (1980, 1985). *Literature for today's young adults*. Glenview: Scott, Foresman and Company.
Frogner, E. (1954). *Your Reading*. Champaign: National Council of Teachers of English.
Hornbook. Boston: Hornbook, Inc., all available issues from 1942–1983.
Kliatt Young Adult Paperback Book Guide. Newton: Kliatt Paperback Book Guide, all available issues from the first issue in 1972 through 1983.
Lenz, M., & Mahood, R. M. (1980). *Young adult literature*. Chicago: American Library Association.
Meigs, C., Eaton, A., Nesbitt, E., & Viguers, R. (1969). *A critical history of children's literature*. New York: MacMillan.
Neville, M. (1946). *Your reading*. Chicago: National Council of Teachers of English.
Schecter & Bogart. *Junior high school library catalogue*. New York: M. H. Wilson, various editions.
School Library Journal. New York: R. R. Bowker, all issues from the first issue in 1973 to 1983.
Senior high school library catalogue. New York: H. W. Wilson, various editions.
Smith, L. (1967). *The unreluctant years: A critical approach to children's literature*. New York: Viking Press.

Walker, E. (1979). *Book bait*. Chicago: American Library Association.
Walker, J. L. (1975). *Your Reading*. Urbana: National Council of Teachers of English.
Willard, C. B. (1966). *Your Reading*. Urbana: National Council of Teachers of English.

Appendix D
Reading Survey*

I would appreciate your taking time to answer these questions about your reading. I am conducting this survey to find out your reading preferences and opinions about romance novels for teens. You should not place your name on this survey as it is confidential. Mark items with a check in the space provided. Mark all that apply.

1. What kind of teen romances do you read?

   ____ Wildfire   ____ Heavenly Romances

   ____ Sweet Dreams   ____ Signet/Vista Romances

   ____ Silhouette's First Love   ____ Wishing Star

   ____ Caprice   ____ Windswept

   ____ Young Love   ____ Sweet Valley High

2. What kinds of *other* books do you read?

   ____ Adventure   ____ School Stories

   ____ Biography   ____ Mysteries

   ____ "How To" Books   ____ Science Fiction

   ____ Sport Stories   ____ Nature

---

*Some questions adapted from Radway (1984) and Thurston (1987)

Appendix D

____ Humor   ____ Collections—
                                              Poetry, Short Story

____ Western   ____ Other

3. How many romances for teens do you usually read in a month? ____

4. Where do you usually obtain the books you read?

    ____ Bookstore   ____ School Library

    ____ School Book Club   ____ Public Library

    ____ Supermarket   ____ Friend or Relative

    ____ Other _____

5. What influences you the most when you choose a romance?

    ____ Author   ____ Back Cover Summary

    ____ Cover Illustration   ____ Publisher or Series Name

    ____ Price   ____ Title

    ____ Someone Recommended It To Me

    ____ Other _____

6. At what age did you first begin reading romances?

    ____ 5–8   ____ 12–15

    ____ 9–12   ____ 16 or older

7. Does your mother or female guardian read romances?

    ____ Yes   ____ Sometimes

    ____ No

Appendix D

8. Do you read every day?

   _____ Yes

   _____ No

9. Which best describes when you mostly read?

   _____ I read in _____ class (subject)

   _____ I read at home

   _____ I read during lunch hour

   _____ I read while babysitting

   _____ I read during study hall

10. What do you usually do with the books you buy after you finish reading them?

    _____ Keep

    _____ Trade

    _____ Give Away

11. Have you read a book by any of the authors listed below?

_____ Stella Pevsner	_____ Betty Cavanna
_____ Maureen Daly	_____ Anne Emery
_____ Mary Stolz	_____ Patricia Gauch
_____ Deborah Hautzig	_____ Norma Fox Mazer
_____ Francine Pascal	_____ Ellen Conford
_____ Elaine Harper	_____ Your Favorite Author(s)

Appendix D

12. Do you think romances generally are

    _____ Well Written

    _____ So-So

    _____ Not Well Written

13. How often do you discuss your romance reading with others?

    _____ Often

    _____ Sometimes

    _____ Seldom

    _____ Never

14. Who do you discuss romances with *most* often?

    _____ My Mother/Female Guardian

    _____ My Sister

    _____ My Teacher(s)

    _____ My Friend(s)

    _____ Other _____

15. What are the most important ingredients in romance stories?

    _____ Happy Ending

    _____ Easy to Read

    _____ Fast Moving Story

    _____ Lots of Love Scenes

    _____ Exciting, Interesting Story

    _____ Other _____

Appendix D

16. What qualities do you like to see in the heroine?

    _____ Intelligence

    _____ Strength

    _____ Honesty

    _____ Caring

    _____ Wealthy

    _____ Independence

    _____ Sense of Humor

    _____ Friendliness

    _____ Assertiveness

    _____ Beauty

    _____ Aggressiveness

    _____ Other _____

17. What qualities do you like to see in the hero?

    _____ Intelligence

    _____ Caring

    _____ Protectiveness

    _____ Strength

    _____ Honesty

    _____ Sense of Humor

    _____ Friendliness

    _____ Good Looking

    _____ Independence

Appendix D

_____ Wealthy

_____ Other (please specify) _____

18. How closely do you think the characters in romances are like people you meet everyday?

    _____ Identical

    _____ Very Similar

    _____ Kind of Similar

    _____ Not at All Similar

19. Do you think the things happening in romances do happen in real life?

    _____ Always

    _____ Very Often

    _____ Sometimes

    _____ Seldom

    _____ Never

20. Are the boys in the romances like boys you know?

    _____ Yes

    _____ No

    _____ Somewhat

21. Why do you read romances?

    _____ To Relax

    _____ to Escape My Problems

    _____ To Learn About New Things

Appendix D

_____ Because I Like to Read About Strong Heroes

_____ Because Romances Are Rarely Sad

_____ Other _____

22. What is your source of spending money?

_____ Allowance

_____ Gifts

_____ Babysitting

_____ Housework

_____ Other _____

23. What do you spend your money on?

_____ Clothes

_____ Records, CD's, and Tapes

_____ Videos

_____ Movies

_____ Cosmetics

_____ Stereo, Radio Equipment

_____ Food

_____ Concert Tickets

_____ Hair Products

_____ Other _____

Please complete the questions on the back of this page

Appendix D

1. Sex

    _____ Female _____ Male

2. Age

    _____

3. Year in School

    _____

4. Which best describes your school?

    _____ Middle School _____ Junior High

5. Residence

    _____ City _____ Suburbs

    _____ Own Home/Condo _____ Rented House or Apartment

6. Race or Ethnic Identity

    _____ White _____ American Indian

    _____ Black _____ Hispanic

    _____ Oriental _____ Other _____

7. Family Income

    _____ Under $10,000 _____ $40,000–$49,000

    _____ $10,000–$19,000 _____ $50,000–$75,000

    _____ $20,000–$29,000 _____ $76,000–$100,000

    _____ $30,000–$39,000 _____ Over $100,000

Appendix E
Ten Most Popular Teen Romance Novels Among Readers

1. *Perfect Summer*, Francine Pascal (Bantam's Sweet Valley High)
2. *Love at First Sight*, Elaine Harper (Silhouette's Blossom Valley)
3. *Turkey Trot*, Elaine Harper (Silhouette's Blossom Valley)
4. *P.S. I Love You*, Barbara Conklin (Bantam's Sweet Dreams)
5. *My First Love and Other Disasters*, Francine Pascal (Viking)
6. *A Passing Game*, Tobey Tyler (Silhouette's First Love)
7. *California Girl*, Janet Quin Harkin (Bantam's Sweet Dreams)
8. *Against the Odds*, Andrea Marshall (Silhouette's First Love)
9. *Seven Days to a Brand-New Me*, Ellen Conford (Atlantic)
10. *Cute is a Four-Letter Word*, Stella Pevsner (Archway)

Notes

Series Editor's Introduction

1. Michael W. Apple, "Redefining Equality," *Teachers College Record* 90 (Winter 1988), pp. 162–84.
2. Allen Hunter, *Children in the Service of Conservatism* (Madison: University of Wisconsin Institute for Legal Studies, 1988), p. 16.
3. Quoted in Rebecca E. Klatch, *Women of the New Right* (Philadelphia: Temple University Press, 1987), p. 128.
4. Linda Christian-Smith, "Romancing the Girl: Adolescent Romance Novels and the Construction of Femininity," in Leslie Roman and Linda Christian-Smith with Elizabeth Ellsworth, eds., *Becoming Feminine: The Politics of Popular Culture* (Philadelphia: Falmer Press, 1988), p. 78.
5. Lewis Coser, Charles Kadushin, and Walter Powell, *Books: The Culture and Commerce of Publishing* (New York: Basic Books, 1982). See also Michael W. Apple, *Teachers and Texts: A Political Economy of Class and Gender Relations in Education* (New York: Routledge, 1986).
6. Compare this to the degradation of other forms of intellectual labor in Michael W. Apple, *Education and Power* (New York: Routledge, ARK Edition, 1985).
7. Christian-Smith, "Romancing the Girl," p. 76.
8. Ibid., p. 78.
9. See Elizabeth Ellsworth, "Illicit Pleasure: Feminist Spectators and *Personal Best*," in Roman and Christian-Smith with Ellsworth, eds., *Becoming Feminine*, pp. 102–19, and Paul Willis, Simon Jones, Joyce Canaan, and Geoff Hurd, *Common Culture: Symbolic Work at Play in the Everyday Culture of the Young* (New York: Routledge, in press).
10. Dorothy Hobson, *Crossroads: The Diary of a Soap Opera* (London: Methuen, 1982).
11. Leslie Roman and Linda Christian-Smith, "Introduction," in Roman and Christian-Smith with Ellsworth, eds., *Becoming Feminine*, pp. 3–4.
12. Ibid., p. 4.

Notes

1 Introduction

1. See Modleski (1982), Radway (1984), Thurston (1987), and Snitow (1983).
2. All names are fictitious.
3. For a more thorough discussion of the theory and practice of cultural studies see Hall, Hobson, Lowe, and Willis (1980).
4. Refer to McRobbie (1980) and Acker (1981) for a critique of cultural studies research.
5. See Appendix A for a discussion of semiotics.
6. Other studies supporting the socially reproductive qualities of comics and books are Light (1984), Radford, (1986) and Walkerdine (1984).
7. According to Whiteside (1981), the first publishing merger was between Random House and Knopf in 1961, to preserve the companies after the death of its owners. Other publishing mergers were spurred on by electronics companies, who were interested in tapping into the enormous amounts of federal funds available to schools for equipment and materials. The publishing houses, with their long-standing relationship to the schools, were a key factor in electronic firms' plans to sell computerized teaching machines to the schools.
8. For a listing of ownership of these corporations see Dun & Bradstreet (1984).
9. It is important to note that romance fiction is not all of one piece. The series romances of Harlequin Enterprises are more conservative in content. The paperback original romances such as Woodiwiss's *The Flame and the Flower* are more varied in content with stronger character development. The new "erotic historical" romances evolved from the bodice-rippers. Thurston (1987) claims that these romances are dramatically different than the previous types because they have a specific erotic content and feature more independent and older heroines.
10. According to Thurston (1987), Harlequin's lagging sales in the early 1970s promoted a change in management. Harlequin brought in Lawrence Heisey of Proctor and Gambel, who used mass-production marketing techniques to put Harlequin at the top of the mass-market publishing industry.
11. For a discussion of the controversy over teen romances, see Harvey (1982), Lanes (1981), Madsen (1981), and Pollack (1981)
12. Madsen (1981) notes that Xerox's *Read* and Scholastic's *TAB* book clubs had sales of over ninety thousand per copy per year.
13. The growing implementation of literature-based curriculum for reading instruction featuring many trade books lends an added urgency to the critical examination of romance fiction and its use in schools.

Notes

14. The American Library Association has accused Scholastic of expurgation and censorship in its preparation of "special school" editions of previously published books (Keresy, 1984).

2 Love Makes the World Go 'Round: The Code of Romance

1. Throughout the text "girls" refers to young women.
2. See McRobbie (1978b), Sarsby (1983), Sharpe (1977), and Thompson (1984).
3. The parenthetical citations stand for the following: 1—period 1, 2—period 2 and 3—period 3.
4. The major male character in almost all of the novels is very popular. Other popular boys from period 1 are Ken Sanderson (*The Boy Next Door*, 1956), Steve Judson (*Wait for Marcy*, 1950), Adam Ross (*Blueberry Summer*, 1956) and Johnny Chessler (*Jean and Johnny*, 1959). In period 2 boys such as Bo Jo Jones (*Mr. & Mrs. Bo Jo Jones*, 1967), Sean Collins (*My Darling, My Hamburger*, 1971), Willie Johnson (*Ludell and Willie*, 1977,1981), Seth Warnecke (*Up in Seth's Room*, 1979), and Jim Freeman (*My First Love and Other Disasters*, 1979) are popular. Period 3 also has its share of popular boys represented by Skip Svoboda (*Cute is a Four-Letter Word*, 1980), Paul Slade (*P. S. I Love You*, 1981), and Paul Leonard (*I'll Always Remember You . . . Maybe*, 1981).
5. The "vamp" has a long history in women's literature. The defining features of this character concern her ability to transcend the conventions governing the actions of the heroine. Other vamps in teen romance fiction include Kentucky Jackson (*Practically Seventeen*, 1943), Luanne Chapman (*California Girl*, 1981), and Betsey Talbert (*Princess Amy*, 1981).
6. Romance as a solution to unhappiness is a prevalent motif in period 2 novels particularly in *Drop-Out* (1963), *I Will Go Barefoot All Summer For You* (1973), and *My Darling, My Hamburger* (1971).
7. Boys endow girls' lives with meaning even in novels where girls have status in their own right. An excellent case is the period 3 novel *California Girl* (1981), where Junior National swimming champion Jennie Webster has little confidence until she becomes Mark Waverly's girlfriend.
8. The novels in which the dynamic of specialness is evident are: 1—*Going on Sixteen* (1946), *Mrs. Mike* (1947), *Paintbox Summer* (1949), *Wait for Marcy* (1950), and *Blueberry Summer* (1956); 2—*Drop-Out* (1963), *Camilla* (1965), *I Will Go Barefoot All Summer For You* (1973), *Up in Seth's Room* (1979), and *My First Love and Other Disasters* (1979); and 3—*Cute is a Four-Letter Word* (1980), *P.S. I Love You* (1981), *Princess*

Notes

      Amy (1981), *California Girl* (1981), and *Seven Days to a Brand-New Me* (1982).
9. Boys also have a system of surveillance. In *Seventeenth Summer* (1942) it is the "checker" system in which younger boys occupy street corners to determine the company girls keep when they are not with boyfriends.
10. See Elshtain (1981) for further discussion of the public versus private.

3 Sealed with a Kiss: The Code of Sexuality

1. See Chapter 4 for additional treatment of the connection between the body and sexuality.
2. Other criticism of Foucault is contained in Haug (1987), Sawicki (1986), Seidler (1987), and Smart (1983).
3. These novels include a "punishment" motif, where boys leave when heroines become pregnant.
4. The novels in which intercourse occurs are: 2—*Mr. & Mrs. Bo Jo Jones* (1967), *My Darling, My Hamburger* (1971), *Up in Seth's Room* (1966); and 3—*I'll Always Remember You . . . Maybe* (1981).
5. Similar warnings occur in *Up in Seth's Room* (1966), *My Darling, My Hamburger* (1971), and *Ludell and Willie* (1977, 1981).
6. Angie Morrow also voices this reticence concerning being assertive with boys: "You can't ask a boy, 'When will I see you again?'" (1942, p. 21). Similar feelings are also expressed in *Wait for Marcy* (1950), *Practically Seventeen* (1943), *Going on Sixteen* (1946), and *The Boy Next Door* (1956), *Sister of the Bride* (1963), *My Darling, My Hamburger* (1971), *Ludell and Willie* (1977, 1981); *Cute is a Four-Letter Word* (1980), *P.S. I Love You* (1981), and *Princess Amy* (1981).
7. Thorne and Yalom (1982) contend that the idea of common interests in families facilitates the invisibility of patterns of dominance and subordination while minimalizing conflict, violence, and the unequal division of labor. For further treatment of this topic, see Barrett and McIntosh (1982) and Hartmann (1981).
8. For example, Jack Duluth and his friend Swede (*Seventeeth Summer*, 1942) are not compelled to report to parents. Ken Sanderson also (*The Boy Next Door*, 1956) has a great deal of freedom. Parents never check on Ken Rhodes's whereabouts in *Wait for Marcy* (1950).
9. This view of women's sexuality has its origins in the nineteenth century. Women were seen as asexual, virtuous, moral, and the providers of a certain "cleanliness" that could remove the taint of men's association with the "uncleanliness" of commerce and public life. According to Bland, men's sexuality was seen as rampant, and it was women's responsibility

Notes

to keep themselves pure to serve as examples of moral virtue (Bland, 1981, pp. 56–58).

4 Mirror, Mirror on the Wall: The Code of Beautification

1. As discussed in Chapter 5, beautification lays the groundwork for heroines' position in the division of labor as consumers and homemakers.
2. I do not imply that these patterns arose with capitalism. Rather, capitalism has both sharpened old aspects and created new aspects of sexism.
3. The relationship between beautification and romance is also found in period 1 romances such as *Junior Miss* (1942, 1969), *Going on Sixteen* (1946), *Paintbox Summer* (1949), and *Jean and Johnny* (1959). This is also evident in period 2 in *I Will Go Barefoot All Summer For You* (1973) and in period 3 books *Seven Days to a Brand-New Me* (1982) and *Cute is a Four-Letter Word* (1980).
4. See also period 1 novels *Junior Miss* (1942, 1969), *Practically Seventeen* (1943), *Going on Sixteen* (1946), *Sorority Girl* (1952), period 3 *Cute is a Four-Letter Word* (1980), *California Girl* (1981), *Seven Days to a Brand-New Me* (1982), and *The Popularity Plan* (1981).
5. Similarly, in *Junior Miss* (1942, 1969) Judy Graves astounds her family with her new grace when she sweeps into the living room in party dress, makeup, and curled hair.
6. This also occurs in other period 2 novels such as *My Darling, My Hamburger* (1971), *Ludell and Willie* (1977, 1981) and, *Fridays* (1979).
7. The absence of any work underlying beautification is found in *Up in Seth's Room* (1979), *Mr. & Mrs. Bo Jo Jones* (1967), *Ruby* (1976), and *Hey, Dollface* (1978).
8. In period 2 parents are very concerned that girls' dress and makeup may convey "the wrong impression." In *My Darling, My Hamburger* Liz Carsten's stepfather appraises her party dress as "too low-cut and too tight" (2:1969, p. 49).
9. The sexualizing of the heroine's body occurs in *Drop-Out* (1963), *Mr. & Mrs. Bo Jo Jones* (1967), and *Fridays* (1979).
10. Other novels in which heroines complain about their plainness are period 1—*Seventeenth Summer* (1942), *Going on Sixteen* (1946), and *Jean and Johnny* (1959); period 2—*Sister of the Bride* (1963), *The Friends* (1973), and *Hey, Dollface* (1978); and (period 3) *P.S. I Love You* (1981), *California Girl* (1981), and *The Popularity Plan* (1981).
11. The term "seamless" derives from film theory: in Hollywood-style films all vestiges of production techniques are erased and the fact that film itself is composed of separate frames and gaps is not readily apparent to viewers.

Notes

5 Keepers of Heart and Hearth: Gender, Class and Race in Romance Fiction

1. There are a number of interpretations regarding the precise way in which gender, class, and race relate to one another. See Anthias and Yuval-Davis (1983), Barrett and McIntosh (1985), Hooks (1984), and Swerdlow and Lessinger (1983).
2. For the purpose of analysis, I will discuss class and race separately. In reality, it is difficult to separate them.
3. For further discussion see Davis (1982) and Hooks (1984).
4. Wright uses the classical criteria of economic ownership (control over investments), possession (control over physical aspects of production and labor), legal ownership (control of property or being an employer of labor power), and wage labor (sale of labor power) (Wright, 1978, pp. 76–78). In a later study, Wright (1982) added domination (patterns of authority) and authority (individuals controlling the authority hierarchy).
5. Wright claims fifty-four percent of women are working-class from the view of wage labor as compared to forty percent for men (Wright, 1982, pp. 722, 724). Sixty-five percent of black women are working-class.
6. Wright's (1978) answer to the question of how to theorize the class position of homemakers is the idea of "class interest." By viewing the housewife as part of her family and the family itself as a unit, one can determine the housewife's class position by the larger position of the family. This position, however, hinges on the wage-earning spouse and implies that the sexual division of labor does not create a clash of class interests between women and men. Wright's position is limited because it encases women in their families and does not address these factors: paid work and the hidden economic contributions of housework and consumption.
7. See Armstrong and Armstrong (1983) for a critique of the domestic labor debates.
8. The history of slavery in the United States conditions the relationship of black women to their homes in view of slaveowners' deliberate attempts to eradicate any vestiges of domestic life.
9. Amott (1985), Scott (1985), and J. Smith (1984) provide detailed accounts of how the combination of gender, class, and race are pulling women into poverty.
10. Davis (1982) notes that even as late as the 1980s thirteen percent of black women were maids and domestic workers.
11. I focus on women in families as this is the dominant representation in adolescent romance fiction. Few single adult women are found, and young women are always depicted within the family context.
12. That men's wages do contribute to family wealth is seen in the growing poverty of single women heads of households (Scott, 1984). J. Smith

Notes

13. Other period 2 novels where white women tote briefcases and shopping bags are *Drop-Out* (1963), *Hey, Dollface* (1978), and *Up in Seth's Room* (1979).
14. This portrayal of single women is also found in *Up a Road Slowly* (1966) and *Going on Sixteen* (1946).
15. Although heavy-handed, Calvin Cathy's words show that education has a special significance when viewed from the vantage point of race: "Whatever in your head, get it out now. Is one thing to think about—getting into college. You're going [to college] if I got to beat your tail in . . . You ain't come all the way to this country to end up no washerwoman nor clerk in a stinking office" (*Ruby* ,1976, p. 40).

6 Becoming a Woman: Narrative and Femininity

1. For a more detailed treatment, see the essays in Mitchell (1981).
2. I also discuss this aspect of romances in Chapter 7.
3. See Appendix A for a discussion of the theory behind and origins of the oppositional structure.
4. Although the representation of femininity through form is consistent, I do not wish to downplay the importance of the two narrative variations.
5. Robinson (1978) notes that these oppositions have long characterized the structure of the women characters in novels featuring women's experiences.
6. This pattern of defining the heroine's goodness through her ability to follow the rules regarding male initiative is also evident in *Mrs. Mike* (1976) and *Going on Sixteen* (1946).
7. Like Angie Morrow (*Seventeenth Summer*, 1942), Maddy Kemper (*Seven Days to a Brand-New Me*) is also speechless where Adam is concerned: "I realized he actually spoke to me; and I stood there, panting and sweating, and didn't say a word" (3:1982, p. 9).
8. Other "good girl"/"other girl" pairs are:

Novel	*Period*	*Good Girl*	*Other Girl*
Practically Seventeen	(1)	Tobey Heydon	Kentucky Jackson
Wait for Marcy	(1)	Marcy Rhodes	Devon Merriott
The Boy Next Door	(1)	Jane Howard	Linda Howard
Paintbox Summer	(1)	Kate Vale	Misty Seaton
Seven Days to a Brand-New Me	(3)	Maddie Kemper	Mary Louise Dryden

Notes

9. Fathers are essentially good individuals in period 1 novels as Jane Howard's father in *The Boy Next Door* (1956).
10. In period 1 there are only two male characters who are not favorably viewed. Tom Kitchell (*Sorority Girl*, 1942) begins to take girlfriend Jane Burnaby for granted; Tony Becker (*Seventeenth Summer*, 1942) has a reputation of being a "fast boy."
11. Additionally, Lou is called a "murderess" by Nick and "no good" by Bo Jo.
12. This is indicated by Angie's observations that "even [her] thoughts had changed" (Daly, 1942, p. 85). Jack continues to dominate her thoughts while she does her daily activities.
13. The following period 2 novels also contain the contestation variant: *Drop-Out* (1963), *Up in Seth's Room* (1979), *Very Far Away From Anywhere Else* (1976), and *My First Love and Other Disasters* (1979).
14. At the beginning of the novel, Maggie's naivete is shown when she accepts the advice of Miss Fanuzzi, the sex education teacher, on what to do "when things get out of control" on a date. Miss Fanuzzi suggests "going to get a hamburger" (3:1969, p. 6).
15. The novel closes with the possibility of a renewal of Maggie's romance with Dennis.
16. The reluctance variant is also found in *Fridays* (1979) and *The Boy Next Door* (1956).
17. In *Fridays* (1979) Corey Martin and her friends decide that they do not need boys and plan Friday night all-girl parties. However, several of the girls subvert the original plan by revealing the location of the parties to potential boyfriends so they can crash the parties. This is another way of attracting the attention of romantically uncommitted boys.
18. Judy and Fluffy are very nonchalant about the presence of boys. During a card game, they proceed as if the boys were not in the room.

7 Romancing Girls: Romance Fiction and Its Readers

1. I focus mainly on students, with some reference to teachers.
2. Readability, or the level of difficulty of reading and writing, is most often estimated through counting sentence length and word length. A number of the Hi-Low's that I have analyzed using readability measures are written at the fourth to fifth grade level. Publisher's routinely estimate readability and print it in terms of grade level on the copyright page.
3. The outlying schools tracked students in math, science, and language arts as well. Most of the girls in my sample were tracked together so they interacted with one another across a range of subject areas.

4. In 1965 Congress passed the Elementary and Secondary Education Act known as Title I (now Chapter I) as a part of its "War on Poverty." Chapter I focused on improving the reading and mathematics knowledge of the poor and educationally disadvantaged. Although Chapter I funding has been severely curtailed of late, it still remains the major form of compensatory education within many urban school districts.
5. I focus exclusively on the school because access to homes was difficult.
6. There are very few romance novels in which characters are not white. West's *Promises* (1986) features black main characters. However, the novel has no specifically black cultural dimensions.
7. All pauses and hesitations have been omitted.
8. The major adolescent book awards in the United States are the American Library Association's Notable Books, the Laura Ingalls Wilder Award, the Newbery Award, and The National Book Award.
9. Mrs. B. characterized "quality literature" as a superbly told story, rich characters, and a concise "literary" style. She did not view book quality as connected to the way women were represented.
10. The findings of the 1983 Consumer Research Study on Reading and Book Purchasing by the Book Study Group found that the average reader read 24.9 books for leisure or work over a six-month period.
11. The young women of color were resigned to the lack of models of black femininity in teen romance fiction. In their estimation, the books merely reflected the way blacks are treated in the media in general.
12. Their plans beyond high school were technical college, beauty school, and training in computers.
13. The girls looked to an ideal femininity that was not seen as essentially white middle-class. This model in teen romance fiction was presented as the one to which all should aspire.
14. Unlike Radway's (1984) readers, the twenty-nine girls did not exchange books or share their reading. They read mostly as isolated individuals.

8 The World of Romance and Beyond

1. See Gramsci (1980) and Bennett, Mercer, and Woollacott (1986) on the role of popular culture in the struggle for hearts and minds.
2. See Welter (1966) for a more detailed discussion of the concept of "true womanhood."
3. A *Time* magazine article for September 14, 1942, encapsulates dominant attitudes toward women working during World War II. The article argued that women's presence at Douglas Aircraft was causing an intrusion into

Notes

work discipline. A Santa Monica branch bombshelter had to be closed during the lunch hour because of "hanky panky" (Rosen, 1973, p. 215).

4. Established in the 1920s, The Women's Bureau of the Department of Labor monitored compliance with protective labor legislation and women's opportunities to secure paid work. Protective legislation had a double-edged quality as much of it was directed at women alone and prevented them from engaging in certain types of work such as printing. However, both women and men benefited somewhat from the health and safety regulations. The Bureau continued its work with women well into World War II (Kessler-Harris, 1981, pp. 93–94).

5. See Kessler-Harris (1982) for a more detailed discussion.

6. In August 1920 the Nineteenth Amendment extended voting to women. But by 1923 the National Women's party felt that women could only be truly free if they had equal rights as individuals. This thinking culminated in the introduction of an Equal Rights Amendment to the Constitution. The campaign for passage of this amendment would occupy the next five decades. However, by the 1950s major women's groups like the League of Women Voters, the National Consumers League, and the major trade unions still opposed the amendment on the grounds that it would eradicate protective legislation.

7. According to Kessler-Harris, women's wages had fallen to sixty percent of the rate for men by 1960 (Kessler-Harris, 1982, p. 305).

8. See Freeman (1975) for a complete history and analysis of the second women's movement.

9. Hooks (1981) contains a thorough discussion of black women and the women's liberation movement.

10. The following is a partial listing of right-wing activists and the groups with which they are affiliated.

Paul Weyrich	Heritage Foundation
Richard Viguerie	Conservative Caucus
Pat Robertson	National Conservative Political Action Committee
Jerry Falwell	Gun Owners of America
Jimmy Swaggert	Committee for the Right to Keep and Bear Arms
Sen. Jesse Helms	Life Amendment PAC
Sen. Malcom Wallop	Liberty Federation
Rep. Jack Kemp	Concerned Women of America

Notes

11. In 1981, Senators Roger Jepsen, Paul Laxalt, and Congressperson George Hansen introduced the Family Protection Act (FPA), which received strong backing from the right. Several of the FPA's sections relate to women. These included forbidding the federal government to preempt local laws pertaining to child and spouse abuse. The FPA would also limit federal funding of abortion, contraception, or treatment of sexually transmitted diseases when patients are minors, unless parents were notified ("Family Protection Cloaks Reaction," 1981, p. 3).
12. Judy Blume's books continue to attract controversy as have Maurice Sendak's *In the Night Kitchen* and *Outside Over There*.

9 A Place in the World

1. See Luke (1987) for an extended discussion of open and closed texts.
2. The tip sheet from Silhouette's "First Love" prescribes standard English and the sparing use of "slang or dialect." "The tone of a First Love is upbeat, the ending optimistic. Values stressed are implicit and humanistic." Our aim is to give teenagers a good, light read that indicates young characters, contemporary situations, and universal themes."
3. *Cassandra Robbins, Esq.* and *Center Stage Summer* are offered by Square One Publishers, a small independent press. Square One proclaims its intent on book covers as publishing stories of young people from various races and classes who "speak out on contemporary political and social issues and who challenge traditional sex role stereotypes."
4. Other oppositional texts are Miller-Lachmann's *Hiding Places* and Hawks's *Twenty-Six Minutes*.
5. On a critical model of reading see Luke and Baker (1989).
6. In calling for a combining of the two approaches, I acknowledge the different traditions represented by feminist pedagogy and Freire's political literacy.

Appendix A

1. Hodge and Kress (1988) provide a critique of the arbitrariness of the sign.
2. According to a 1983 study by the Book Industry Study Group (Market Facts, 1984), readers can be classified as light (one to three books), moderate (four to twenty-five) and heavy (twenty-six or more) in a six-month period.

Bibliography

Acker, S. (1981). No-woman's-land: British sociology of education 1960–79. *Sociological Review, 29,* 77–97.

Adams, P. (1987). Writing from reading—'Dependent authorship' as a response. In B. Corcoran & E. Evans (Eds.), *Readers, texts, teachers* (pp. 119–152). Milton Keynes, England: The Open University Press.

Altbach, E. (1974). *Women in America.* Lexington, MA: D.C. Heath.

Amos, V., & Parmar, P. (1984). Challenging imperial feminism. *Feminist Review, 17,* 3–19.

Amott, T. (1985). Race, class and the feminization of poverty. *Socialist Politics, 3,* 5–12.

Anyon, J. (1981). Ideology and United States history textbooks. In R. Dale, G. Esland, R. Fergusson, & M. MacDonald (Eds.). *Politics, patriarchy & practice* (pp. 21–40). Sussex: The Falmer Press.

Apple, M. W. (1985). The culture and commerce of the textbook. *Journal of Curriculum Studies, 17,* 147–162.

Apple, M.W. (1979). *Ideology and curriculum.* Boston: Routledge & Kegan Paul.

Apple, M. W. (1982). *Education and power.* Boston: Routledge & Kegan Paul.

Apple, M. W. (1988). *Teachers and texts.* New York: Routledge.

Apple, M. W. (1989). The politics of common-sense: Schooling, populism, and the New Right. In H. Giroux & P. McLaren (Eds.), *Critical pedagogy, the state, and cultural struggle* (pp. 32–49). Albany: State University of New York Press.

Anthias, F., & Yuval-Davis, N. (1983). Contextualizing feminism—gender, ethnic and class divisions. *Feminist Review, 15,* 62–75.

Armstrong, P., & Armstrong, H. (1983). Beyond sexless class. *Studies in Political Economy, 10,* 7–43.

Baker, N. C. (1984). *The beauty trap*. New York: Franklin Watts.

Baker, C., & Freebody, P. (1989). Talk around text: Constructions of textual and teacher authority in classroom discourse. In S. de Castell, A. Luke & C. Luke (Eds.), *Language, Authority and Criticism* (pp. 263–283). London: The Falmer Press.

Barrett, M. (1980). *Women's oppression today*. London: Verso.

Barrett, M., & McIntosh, M. (1982). *The anti-social family*.London: Verso.

Barrett, M., & McIntosh, M. (1985). Ethnocentrism and socialist-feminist theory. *Feminist Review,20*,35–48.

Barthes, R. (1967). *Elements of semiology*.London: Jonathan Cape.

Barthes, R. (1977). *Image, music, text*.New York: Hill and Wang.

Bartky, S. (1982). Narcissism, femininity and alienation. *Social theory and practice,8*,127–141.

Bartky, S. (1979). On psychological oppression. In S. Bishop & M. Weinzweig (Eds.), *Philosophy and Women*(pp. 33–41). Belmont, CA: Wadsworth.

Baxandall, R., Gordon, L., & Reverby, S. (1976). *America's working women*.New York: Vintage Books.

Belsey, C. (1980). *Critical practice*.London: Methuen.

Bennett, T. (1986). The politics of 'the popular' and popular culture. In T. Bennett, C. Mercer, & J. Wollacott (Eds.), *Popular culture and social relations* (pp. 6–21). Milton Keynes, England: The Open University Press.

Bennett, T., Mercer, C., & Wollacott, J. (1986). *Popular culture and social relations*. Milton Keynes, England: Open University Press.

Bhavnani, K.-K., & Coulson, M. (1986). Transforming socialist-feminism. *Feminist Review, 23*, 81–92.

Bland, L. (1981). The domain of the sexual: A response. *Screen Education, 39*, 56–67.

Blinkhorn, L. (1982, September 12). The feminization of poverty. *The Milwaukee Journal, 297*, pp. 1–3.

Bridgman, A. (1984, March 7). A.L.A. study of book-club alterations prompts shifts in policy. *Education Week*, pp. 6–7.

Brownstein, R. (1984). *Becoming a heroine*. New York: Penguin Books.

Burg, L. A., et al. (1978). *The compleat reading supervisor*. Columbus: Merrill.

Buroway, M. (1979). *Manufacturing consent: Changes in the labor process under monopoly capital*. Chicago: The University of Chicago Press.

Bibliography

Caplan, P. (1987). *The cultural construction of sexuality.* London: Tavistock.

Carter, E. (1984). Alice in the consumer wonderland. In A. McRobbie & M. Nava (Eds.), *Gender and Generation* (pp. 185-214). London: Macmillan.

Castells, M. (1980). *The economic crisis and American society.* Princeton: Princeton University Press, 1980.

Chapkis, W. (1986). *Beauty secrets.* Boston: South End Press.

Christian-Smith, L. K. (1986). The English curriculum and current trends in publishing. *English Journal, 75,* 55-57.

Christian-Smith, L. K. (1987). Gender, popular culture and curriculum: Adolescent romance novels as gender text. *Curriculum Inquiry, 17,* 365-406.

Christian-Smith, L. K. (1989). Power, Knowledge and Curriculum: Constructing femininity in adolescent romance novels. In S. de Castell, A. Luke & C. Luke (Eds.), *Language, Authority and Criticism* (pp. 17-31). London: The Falmer Press.

Christian-Smith, L. K. (in press). In different voices: Morality and femininity in literature. *Curriculum Inquiry.*

Cleaver, B., & Cleaver, E. (1977). *Trial Valley.* Philadelphia: Lippincott.

Corcoran, B. (1987). Teachers creating readers. In B. Corcoran & E. Evans (Eds.), *Readers, texts, teachers* (pp. 41-74). Milton Keynes, England: The Open University Press.

Coser, L.A,, Kadushin, C., & Powell, W. W. *Books.* New York: Basic Books, 1982.

Cott, N. F. (1978). Passionlessness: An interpretation of Victorian sexual ideology, 1770-1850. *Signs, 4,* 219-236.

Coulson, M., Magas, B., & Wainwright, H. (1975). The housewife and her labor under capitalism—a critique. *New Left Review, 89,* 59-71.

Coward, R. (1984). *Female desire.* London: Palladin Books.

Coward, R., & Ellis, J. (1977). *Language and materialism.* London: Routledge & Kegan Paul.

Crossen, C. (1988, February 11). Book publisher finds lucrative niche in soap-opera series for teen-age girls. *The Wall Street Journal,* p. 25.

Dalla Costa, M. (1972). Women and the subversion of the community.In M. Dalla Costa & S. James (Eds.), *The power of women and the subversion of community.* Bristol: Falling Wall Press.

Davin, A. (1987). 'Mind that you do as you are told': Reading books for Board School. In G. Weiner & M. Arnot, *Gender under scrutiny* (pp. 143-149). London: Hutchinson.

Davis, A. (1982). *Women, race & class*. London: The Women's Press.

Davis, L. (1987). *Resisting novels*. New York: Methuen.

De Castell, S., Luke, A., & Luke, C. (1989). *Language, authority and criticism*. London: The Falmer Press.

Delphy, C. (1976). *The main enemy*. London: Women's Research and Resource Center.

Douglas, M. & Isherwood, B. (1979). *The world of goods: Towards an anthropology of consumption*. London: Allen Lane.

Douglas, A. (1980). Soft-porn culture. *New Republic, 30,* 25–29.

Dun & Bradstreet. (1984). *Who owns whom, North America?* London: Dun & Bradstreet.

Dyer, R. (1979). *Stars*. London: British Film Institute.

Eagleton, T. (1979). Ideology, fiction, narrative. *Social Text, 2,* 62–80.

Eco, U. (1976). *A theory of semiotics*. Bloomington, IN: Indiana University Press.

Eco. U. (1979). *The role of the reader*. Bloomington:IN Indiana University Press.

Edwards, M. (1952). How do I love thee? *English Journal, 41,* 335–340.

Ehrenreich, B., & Ehrenreich, J. (1977, March/April). The new left: A case study in professional-managerial class radicalism. *Radical America, 11,* 7–23.

Eidman-Aadahl, E. (1988). The solitary reader. *The New Advocate, 1,* 165–176.

Elshtain, J. B. (1981). *Public man, private woman*. Princeton: Princeton University Press.

Employment in perspective: Minority workers. (1988). Report 755. Washington: U.S. Bureau Labor Statistics.

Employment in perspective: Women in the labor force. (1987). Report 749. Washington: U. S. Bureau of Labor Statistics.

Estes, T., & Vaughn, J. (1973). Reading interests and comprehension: Implications. *The Reading Teacher, 27,* 149–153.

Fader, D., & McNeil, D. (1968). *Hooked on books: Program and proof*. New York: Berkeley Books.

Family Protection Act cloaks reaction. (1981). *The People, 9,* p. 3.

Farris, P. J. (1989). Story time and story journals. *The New Advocate, 2,* 179–184.

Bibliography

Fetterly, J. (1978). *The resisting reader*. Bloomington, IN: Indiana University Press.

Fiske, J., & Hartley, J. (1978). *Reading television*. London: Methuen.

Foucault, M. (1980). *The history of sexuality*. London: Allen Lane.

Freeman, J. (1975). *The politics of women's liberation*. New York: Longman.

Freire, P. (1987). *Reading the word & the world*. Granby, MA: Bergin & Garvey.

Gardiner, J. (1977). Women in the labor process and class structure. In A. Hunt (Ed.). *Class and class structure* (155–163). London: Lawrence and Wishart, 1977.

Garrigue, S. (1978). *Between friends*. Scarsdale, NY: Bradbury.

Gaskell, J. (1983). The reproduction of family life: Perspectives of male and female adolescents. *British Journal of Sociology of Education, 4,* 19–37.

Gitlin, T. (1982). Television's screens: Hegemony in transition. In M. W. Apple (Ed.), *Cultural and economic reproduction in education* (pp. 202–246). Boston: Routledge & Kegan Paul.

Glaser, B., & Strauss, A. (1967). *The discovery of grounded theory*. Chicago: Aldine.

Gordon, A., & Hunter, A. (1977/78). Sex, family & the New Right. *Radical America, 12,* 9–25.

Gouldner, A. W. (1954). *Patterns of industrial bureaucracy*. New York: Free Press.

Gramsci, A. (1980). *Selections from the prison notebooks*. New York: International Publishers.

Greimas, A.J. (1966). *Semantique Structurale*. Paris: Larousse.

Greimas, A.J. (1970). *Du sens*. Paris: Seuil.

Griffin, C. (1985). *Typical girls?*. London: Routledge & Kegan Paul.

Hall, S. (1985). Authoritarian populism: A reply. *New Left Review, 151,* 115–124.

Hall, S., Hobson, D., Lowe, A., & Willis, P. (1980). *Culture, media and language*. London: Hutchinson.

Hall, S., & Jefferson, T. (1976). *Resistance through rituals*. London: Hutchinson.

Hammersley, M., & Atkinson, P. (1983). *Ethnography principles in practice*. London: Tavistock.

Hargreaves, D. H., Hestor, S., & Mellor, F. (1975). *Deviance in classrooms*. London: Routledge & Kegan Paul.

Harlequin: A romance publisher adds men's novels and a touch of mystery. (1981, July 6). *Business Week*, pp. 93–94.

Hartmann, H. L. (1981). The family as a locus of gender, class, and political struggle. *Signs, 16*, 366–393.

Harty, S. (1979). *Hucksters in the classroom*. New York: Center for Responsive Law.

Harvey, B. (1982, February 10–16). How far can you go in a teen romance? *Village Voice, 27*, 48–49.

Haug, F. (1987). *Female sexualization*. London: Verso.

Hawks, R. (1988). *The twenty-six minutes*. Madison, WI: Square One Publishers.

Hebdige, D. (1979). *Subculture: The meaning of style*. London: Methuen.

Herrick, H. (1952, January). Compliments collector—you! *Screen Stories, 1*, 49–50.

Hodge, R. & Kress, G. (1988). *Social Semiotics*. Ithaca, NY: Cornell University Press.

Hooks, B. (1981). *Ain't I a woman*. Boston: South End Press.

Hooks, B. (1984). *Feminist theory from margin to center*. Boston: South End Press.

Howe, F. K. (1978). *Pink collar workers*. New York: Avon.

Humm, P., Stigant, P., & Widdowson, P. (1986). *Popular fictions*. London: Methuen.

Hunt, I., & Starrs, C. (1983). Dynamics of class and the new middle class. *Social Theory and Practice, 9*, 85–114.

Hunter, A. (1984). *Virtue with a vengeance: The pro-family politics of the New Right*. Unpublished doctoral dissertation, Department of Sociology, Brandeis University, Waltham, MA.

Hunter, A. (1985). Why did Reagan win? Ideology or economics? *Socialist Review, 79*, 29–41.

Iser, W. (1974). *The implied readers: Patterns of communication in prose fiction from Bunyan to Beckett*. Baltimore, MD: The Johns Hopkins University Press.

Iser, W. (1980). Interaction between text and reader. In S. R. Suleiman and I. Crosman (Eds.). *The reader in the text* (pp. 106–119). Princeton, NJ: Princeton University Press.

Jensen, M. (1984). *Love's sweet return*. Bowling Green, OH: Bowling Green State University.

Johnson, R. (1983). *What is cultural studies, anyway?* Stencilled Occasional Paper. Centre for Contemporary Cultural Studies, Birmingham, England.

Kaplan, C. (1985). Pandora's box. In G. Greene & C. Kahn (Eds.). *Making a difference* (pp. 146–176). London: Methuen.

Kaplan, C. (1986). *Sea Changes*. London: Verso.

Kaplan, C. (1986). *The thorn birds*: Fiction, fantasy, femininity. In V. Burgin, J. Donald & C. Kaplan (Eds.). *Formations of fantasy* (pp. 142–165). London: Methuen.

Keeran, R. (1985, October). AFL-CIO report: Service sector. *Economic Notes, 53*, p. 4.

Kelly, J. (1983). The doubled vision of feminist theory. In J. L. Newton, M. P. Ryan, & J. R. Walkowitz (Eds.), *Sex and class in women's history* (pp. 259–270). London: Routledge and Kegan Paul.

Keresy, G. (1984). School bookclub expurgation practices. *Top of the News, 40*, 131–138.

Kessler-Harris, A. (1982). *Out to work*. Oxford: Oxford University Press.

Kessler-Harris, A. (1981). *Women have always worked*. Old Westbury, CT: The Feminist Press.

Kingston, M. (1977). *Woman warrior*. New York: Random House.

Kuhn, A. (1982). *Women's pictures*. London: Routledge & Kegan Paul.

Kryk, H. (1923). *A theory of consumption*. Boston: Houghton Mifflin.

Kuhn, A., & Wolpe, A. M. (1978). *Feminism and materialism*. London: Routledge and Kegan Paul.

Lakoff, R. T., & Scherr, R. L. (1984). *Face Value*. Boston: Routledge & Kegan Paul.

Lanes, S. (1981). Here comes the blockbusters—teen books go big time. *Interracial Books for Children Bulletin, 12*, 5–7.

Lefevre, L., & Martin, H.-J. (1976). *The coming of the book*. London: New Left Books.

Levoy, M. (1977). *Alan and Naomi*. New York: Harper.

Light, A. (1984). 'Returning to Manderley—romance fiction, female sexuality and class. *Feminist Review, 16*, 7–25.

Lovell, T. (1987). *Consuming fiction*. London: Verso.

Lukas, C. K. (1988). *Center stage summer*. Madison: Square One Publishers.

Luke, A. (1987). Open and closed texts: A theoretical model for the critical analysis of curricular narratives. Manuscript submitted for publication.

Bibliography

Luke, A. (in press). The secular word: Catholic transformations of Dick and Jane. In M. W. Apple and L. K. Christian-Smith (Eds.), *The Politics of the Textbook*. New York: Routledge, Chapman, and Hall.

Luke, A., & Baker, C. D. (1989). *Towards a critical sociology of reading pedagogy*. Amsterdam: John Benjamins.

Luke, C., De Castell, S., & Luke, A. (1989). Beyond criticism: The authority of the school textbook. In S. de Castell, A. Luke and C. Luke (Eds.), *Language, authority and criticism* (pp. 245–260). London: The Falmer Press.

MacPherson, B. (1978). *The political theory of possessive individualism*. London: Oxford University Press.

McRobbie, A. (1978a). *Jackie: An ideology of adolescent femininity*. Stencilled Occasional Paper. Birmingham, England: The Centre for Contemporary Cultural Studies.

McRobbie, A. (1978b). Working class girls and the culture of femininity. In Women's Studies Group (Eds.), *Women take issue* (pp. 97–108). London: Hutchinson.

McRobbie, A. (1980). Settling accounts with subcultures. *Screen Education*, *34*, 37–50.

Madsen, C. T. (1981). Teen novels: What kind of values do they promote? *The Christian Science Monitor*, *18*, B14–17.

Malinowski, B. (1922). *Argonauts of the Western Pacific*. London: Routledge & Kegan Paul.

Market Facts. (1984). *1983 consumer research study on reading and book purchasing: Focus on juveniles*. New York: Book Industry Study Group.

Millett, K. (1977). *Sexual politics*. London: Virago Press.

Miller-Lachmann, L. (1987). *Hiding Places*. Madison, WI: Square One Publishers.

Millman, V. (1985). Breadwinning & babies: A redefinition of careers education. In G. Weiner (Ed.), *Just a bunch of girls*. Milton Keynes, England: Open University Press.

Mitchell, W. J. T. (1981). *On narrative*. Chicago: The University of Chicago Press.

Modleski, T. (1984). *Loving with a vengeance*. London: Methuen.

Moi, T. (1985). *Sexual/textual politics*. London, New York: Methuen.

Morely, D. (1980). Texts, readers, subjects. In S. Hall, D. Hobson, A. Lowe, & P. Willis (Eds.), *Culture, media and language* (pp. 163–173). London: Hutchinson.

Motion Picture Magazine. (1953, April), pp. 10–11.

Mulvey, L. (1975). Visual pleasure and narrative cinema. *Screen, 3,* 6–18.

Mussell, K. (1975). Beautiful and damned: The sexual woman in gothic fiction. *Journal of Popular Culture, 9,* 84–89.

Oakley, A. (1972). *Sex, gender and society.* London: Temple Smith.

Oakley, A. (1976). *Woman's work.* New York: Random House

Oakley, A. (1981). *Subject women.* New York: Pantheon Books.

Olson, D. (1980). On the language and authority of textbooks. *Journal of Communications, 30,* 146–186.

Omi, M., & Winant, H. (1986). *Racial formation in the United States.* New York: Routledge & Kegan Paul.

O'Toole, P. (1979).Paperback virgins. *Human Behavior, 8,* 62–67.

Otto, W., Peters, C. W., & Peters, N. (1977). *Reading problems.* Reading: Addison-Wesley.

Paterson, K. (1978). *Bridge to Terabithia.* New York: Avon.

Patterson, E. L. (1956). The junior novels and how they grew. *English Journal, 45,* 381–387.

Plotke, D. (1986). Reaganism and neoliberalism. *Socialist Review, 86,* 7–23.

Pollock, P. (1981). The business of popularity. *School Library Journal, 28,* 25–28.

Poulantzas, N. (1975). *Classes in contemporary capitalism.* London: New Left Books.

Radford, J. (1986). *The progress of romance.* London: Routledge & Kegan Paul.

Radway, J. (1984). *Reading the romance.* Chapel Hill, NC: The University of North Carolina Press.

Rich, A. (1976). *Of woman born.* New York: Norton.

Roberts, H. (1981). *Doing feminist research.* London: Routledge & Kegan Paul.

Robinson, L. S. (1978). *Sex, class and culture.* Bloomington, IN: Indiana University Press, 1978.

Romantic Times. (1987, April/May). Romance video news. p. 74.

Rose, J. (1984). *The case of Peter Pan.* London: MacMillan.

Rosen, M. (1973). *Popcorn Venus.* London: Avon.

Rosenblatt, L. (1978). *The reader, the text, the poem.* Carbondale, IL: Southern Illinois University Press.

Sacks, K., & Remy, D. (1984). *My troubles are going to have trouble with me.* New Brunswick, NJ: Rutgers University Press.

Sarsby, J. (1983). *Romantic love and society.* Harmondsworth, England: Penguin books.

Sawicki, J. (1986). Foucault and feminism. *Hypatia, 1,* 23–26.

Schneider, K. (1983). Monroe doctrine. *The Progressive.* 6. p. 38.

Schick, F. L. (1958). *The paperbound book in America.* New York: R. R. Bowker Company.

Schniedewind, N. (1987). Teaching feminist process. *Women's Studies Quarterly, 15,* 15–31.

Scholastic Inc. *Scholastic Inc.—An overview.* (1985). New York: Scholastic Inc.

Scott, H. (1984). *Working your way to the bottom.* London: Pandora Press.

Seidler, V. (1987). Reason, desire and male sexuality. In P. Caplan (Ed.). *The cultural construction of sexuality* (pp. 82–112). New York: Tavistock.

Sharpe, S. (1978). *Just like a girl.* Hammondsworth: Penguin Books.

Shatzkin, L. (1982). *In cold type.* Boston: Houghton Mifflin Company.

Shrewsbury, C. M. (1987).What is feminist pedagogy? *Women's Studies Quarterly, 15,* 6–14.

Smart, B. (1983). *Foucault, Marxism and critique.* London: Routledge & Kegan Paul.

Smith, J. (1984). The paradox of women's poverty: wage earning women and economic transformation. *Signs, 10,* 291–310.

Smith, W. (1981, November 13). An earlier start on romance. *Publishers' Weekly, 220,* 56–61.

Smucker, B. (1979). *Runaway to freedom.* New York: Dell.

Snitow, A. B. (1983). Mass market romance: Pornography for women is different. In A. Snitow, C. Stansell & S. Thompson (Eds.). *Desire: The politics of sexuality* (pp. 258–275). London: Virago Press.

Snitow, A., & Stansell, C., & Thompson, S. (1983). *Desire: The politics of sexuality.* London: Virago Press.

Sobol, R. (1976). *Woman chief.* New York: Dell.

Spelman, E. V. (1982). Woman as body: Ancient and contemporary views. *Feminist Studies, 8,* 109–131.

Stacy, J., Bereaud, S., & Daniel, J. (1974). *And Jill came tumbling after.* New York: Dell.

Bibliography

Swerdlow, A., & Lessinger, H. (1983). *Class, race and sex.* Boston: G. K. Hall and Co.

Swingewood, A. (1975). *The novel and revolution.* New York: Harper & Row.

Taxel, J. (1984). The American Revolution in children's fiction: An analysis of historical meaning and narrative structure. *Curriculum Inquiry, 14,* 7–55.

Taxel, J. (in press). Reclaiming the voice of resistance: The fiction of Mildred Taylor. In M. W. Apple & L. K. Christian-Smith (Eds.). *The Politics of the Textbook.* New York: Routledge & Chapman Hall.

Thompson, S. (1984). Search for tomorrow: On feminism and the reconstruction of teen romance. In C. S. Vance (Ed.). *Pleasure and danger* (pp. 350–384).

Thorne, B., & Yalom, M. (1982). *Rethinking the family.* New York: Longman.

Thurston, C. (1987). *The romance revolution.* Urbana and Chicago: The University of Illinois Press.

Turow, J. (1978). *Getting books to children.* Chicago: American Library Association.

Vacca, R. T., & Vacca, J. L. (1986). *Content area reading.* Boston: Little, Brown and Company.

Vance, C. (1984). *Pleasure and danger.* Boston: Routledge & Kegan Paul.

Viglucci, P. C. (1987). *Cassandra Robbins, Esq.* Madison: Square One Publishers.

Volosinov, V. N. (1973). *Marxism and the philosophy of language.* New York: Seminar Press.

Walkerdine, V. (1984). Some day my prince will come: Young girls and the preparation for adolescent sexuality. In A. McRobbie & M. Nava (Eds.). *Gender and generation* (pp. 162–184). London: Macmillan Publishers.

Weinbaum, B., & Bridges, A. (1979). The other side of the paycheck: Monopoly capital and the structure of consumption. In Z. Eisenstein (Ed.). *Capitalist patriarchy and the case for socialist feminism* (pp. 190–203). New York: Monthly Review Press.

Weiner, G., & Arnot, M. (1987). *Gender under scrutiny.* London: Hutchinson, The Open University.

Welter, B. (1966). The cult of true womanhood, 1820–1860. *American Quarterly, 18,* 151–174.

Wertheheimer, B. (1977). *We were there.* New York: Pantheon.

West, T. (1986). *Promises.* New York: Silhouette.

Wexler, P. (1983). *Critical social psychology.* Boston: Routledge & Kegan Paul.

White, H. (1981). The value of narrativity in the representation of reality. In W. J. T. Mitchell (Ed.). *On narrative* (pp.1–23). Chicago: The University of Chicago Press.

Whiteside, T. (1981). *The blockbuster complex*. Middletown, CT: Wesleyan University Press.

Wigutoff, S. (1981). Examining the issues: What teachers can do. *Interracial Books for Children Bulletin, 12,* 23–24.

Williams, R. (1977). *Marxism and literature*. Oxford: Oxford University Press.

Willis, P. (1977). *Learning to labour*. Westmead, England: Saxon House.

Winship, J. (1978) Woman's world: Woman—an ideology of femininity. In Women's Studies Group (Eds.). *Women take issue* (pp. 135–167). London: Hutchinson.

Winship, J. (1987). *Inside women's magazines*. London: Pandora Press.

Wolff, J. (1981). *The social production of art*. London: The MacMillan Press.

Women's Studies Group.(1978). *Women take issue*. London: Hutchinson.

Wright, E. O. (1978). *Class, crisis and the state*. London: Verso.

Wright, E. O. (1982b). The status of the political in the concept of class structure. *Politics and Society, 11,* 321–341.

Wright, E. O., Costello, C., Hachen, D., & Sprague, J. (1982a). The American class structure. *American Sociological Review, 47,* 709–726.

Wylie, R. E. (1969). Diversified concepts of the role of the reading consultant. *The Reading Teacher, 22,* 511–522.

Young, C. , & Robinson, E. (1987). Reading/writing in the culture of the classroom. In B. Corcoran & E. Evans (Eds.). *Readers, texts, and teachers* (pp. 153–175). Milton Keynes, England: The Open University Press.

Index

Accomodation, 42, 156
Acker, S., 176
Action, 99–100
Active/passive coding, 85–89
Adams, P., 138
Adult romance novels, 12–13, 115; erotic, 3, 176
Adventure books, 100–101
Age, 8, 67, 101, 127, 133, 141–143, 153
Against the odds, 110–111, 174
Alan and Naomi, 140
Alan Review, 139
American Library Association's (ALA) Best Books, 145, 161–162
Amott, T., 59, 180
Analytic memos, 155–156
Anthias, F., 180
Anti-abortion groups, 121–122
Anticipating and retrospecting, 136–137
Anticipation Guide, 137
Anyon, J., 135, 142
Apple, M., 3, 10, 60, 128, 131, 175
Armstrong, H., 180
Armstrong, P., 180
Arnot, M., 150
Atkinson, P., 152, 155
Austen, J., 3
Authority, 70, 180; and power, 52; relations, 131

Baker, C., 185
Bantam, 13, 142, 161–163, 174
Barthes, R., 146–147
Bartky, S., 44
Barrett, M., 42, 141–143, 178, 180
Baxandall, R., 120

Beautification, 114, 149, 179; and class, 45, 53; code of, 4–6, 16, 43–55, 79, 81, 97, 133, 149; and femininity, 51–53; and gender, 52; and identity, 52; politics of, 43–46; and power, 52, 44; and race, 45, 53; and romance, 47, 114, 179
Beauty/fashion complex, 44–46
Belsey, C., 146
Bennett, T., 141, 183
Benson, S., 20, 26, 160
Bereaud, S., 142
Bertraux, D., 62
Between friends, 140
Binary oppositions, 146–147, 181
Black Power Movement, 93, 125
Bland, L., 178–179
Blanks, 109–111
Blinkhorn, L., 122
Blossom Valley, 104, 108, 124
Blueberry summer, 47, 63–64, 124, 159, 177
Blume, J., 185
Body, 31, 38, 43–45, 47, 178; and consciousness, 38; fragmentation of, 43, 45; objectification of, 45, 51; sexualization of 50, 179
Bogart, 158–163
Book Industry Study Group, 101, 183, 185
Booklist, 158–164
Books and the teenage reader, 145
Book selection, 139–140
Boyfriend, 17–18, 29, 43, 48, 86, 106, 125, 178, 182
The boy next door, 34, 51, 63, 81,

Index

84, 122, 124, 159, 177–178, 181–182
Bridges, A., 60
Bridge to Terabithia, 140
Brontës, 3, 149
Brownstein, R., 149
Buehl, R., 2, 14
Burawoy, M., 57
Burg, L., 151
Butman, A., 145, 164
Burton, D., 144–145

California girl, 25–27, 34, 64, 72, 77, 85–86, 91, 125, 163, 174, 177–179
Camilla, 69–70, 73, 81, 160, 177
Canaan, J., 175
Capitalism, 9, 43, 57–58, 127, 129, 142, 179
Capitalist marketplace, 131
Caplan, C., 42
Carlsen, G., 158–159, 160, 164
Carter, E., 9, 61
Cassandra Robbins, Esq., 139, 185
Castells, M., 59–60
Cavanna, B., 14, 18, 22, 158–159
Censorship, 131, 177
Center stage summer, 140, 185
Chapkis, W., 44
Chapter I Program, 100–103, 153, 183
Christian-Smith, L., 4, 146, 175
Civil Rights Act, 120
Civil rights movement, 120; black women's involvement in, 120
Class, 4, 8–9, 45, 53, 55–62, 67, 73, 78, 116, 124, 127, 133, 135, 139, 141–143, 150, 156; and gender, 56–62, 180; identity, 8; interest, 180; and race, 56, 62, 180; theory, 56–62, 180; trajectories, 62
Class position, 57–58; of families, 56, 58, 180; girls, 62; housewives, 58–58, 180; women, 56–62; 71
Classroom libraries, 99
Cleary, B., 20, 26, 160
Cleaver, B., 139
Cleaver, V., 139
Co-ed, 8
The Cold War, 119
Commodities, 61, 68

Competence, 112
Concerned Women of America, 3
Code, 147–149; and gender, class and race, 147
Conford, E., 26, 104, 163, 174
Conklin, B., 163, 174
Consciousness, 3–5, 7, 42
Conservative Caucus, 3
Constant comparison method, 155
Consumerism, see consumption
Consumption, 6, 56–57, 60–62, 68–71, 74, 114, 116, 124, 131, 135; class aspects; 60–62, 68–70, 135; cultural dimensions, 61, 180; economic dimensions, 60; gender aspects, 60–62, 68–71; and race, 60–62, 68–71
Contestation Variant, 92–95, 182
Contradiction, 6, 9, 37, 95,102, 113
Contradictory class location, 57–59, 61
Control, 16; of the body, 38–39, 41
Corcoran, B., 135–139
Corporate merging, see publishing, mergers
Coser, L., 2, 10–11, 175
Cott, N., 42
Coulson, M., 58
Council on Interracial Books for Children, 14, 139
Coward, R., 31, 45, 129
Critical reading, 136–139, 185
Culture, 9
Cultural capital, 25–26
Cultural politics, 141
Cultural studies, 5, 7–10, 176
Cute is a four-letter word, 26, 48, 72, 74, 82, 163, 174, 177–178

Dalla Costa, M., 58
Daly, M., 14, 18, 28, 144, 158, 182
Daniel, J., 142
Data analysis, 154–156
Davis, A., 56, 60, 80, 128, 180
The day and the way we met, 48, 51, 63–64, 67, 74, 160
De Castell, S., 98–99
Dell, 13
Delphy, C., 58
Desire, 21, 37, 41, 112, 115, 128; object of, 36
Difference, 146–147
Discourse, 130, 133; sexual, 23

Index

Division of labor, 67, 73, 75, 178–179
Domesticity, 57, 62–63, 65–67, 73, 76, 78–79, 117, 119, 124, 126, 128
Domestic labor, see housework
Domestic labor theory, see housework, theory
Domestic themes, see domesticity
Domination, 29, 178
Donelson, K., 145, 158–162, 164
Double Action, 99
Double standard, 35–36, 53
Douglas, A., 12
Drop-out, 18, 32–33, 37, 66, 72, 88, 160, 177, 179, 181–182
DuJardin, R., 13, 26, 158–159
Dun & Bradstreet, 76
Dyer, R., 46

Eagle Forum, 3
Eagleton, T., 80
Eaton, A., 164
Eco, U., 133–134
Economic crisis, 2, 114
Economic ownership, 180
Economic relations, 116
Economy, 61, 114–116, 119
Edwards, M., 144
Ehrenreich, B., 57
Ehrenreich, J., 57
Eliot, G., 3
Ellis, J., 129
Ellsworth, E., 175
Elshtain, J., 178
Emergent cultural forms, 130
Emery, A., 13, 22, 159
"Employment in perspective: Minority workers," 59
"Employment in perspective: Women in the labor force," 59
Engagement and construction, 136, 138
English Journal, 139
Equal Pay Act, 120
Equal Rights Amendment (ERA), 3, 120–123, 184
Equality Employment Opportunity Commission, 120
Escape, 105, 112, 128, 130
Estes, T., 99
Ethnography, 149, 153

Exchange relations, 18–20, 29
Eyerly, J., 19, 160

Fader, D., 99
Family, 2, 14, 20, 56, 64, 75, 120, 122, 178, 180; and consumption, 61, 68; and romance, 37; and sexuality, 29, 35–37, 141; and women, 56, 119–120
Family Protection Act, 123, 185
"Family protection cloaks reaction," 185
Fantasy, 9, 38, 105, 108, 115, 135, 137, 142, 150, 156
Farris, P., 136
Fascinating Womanhood, 121
Fashion, see beauty/fashion complex
Fathers, 21, 35–36, 62, 66, 87–88, 182
Female-male relations, see gender relations
Feminine initiative, 29
Feminine mystique, 120
Femininity, 4, 6, 8, 15–19, 33, 44, 48, 51, 66, 74, 76, 78–79, 81, 84–85, 89, 92, 96, 98, 104, 109, 111, 113, 116, 120, 121, 131, 133, 140, 181; assertive, 17, 113, 131, 134; creating, 109–113; culture of, 8; components of, 56; discourse on, 54–55; domestic, 78; and historical context, 123–127; ideology of, 3, 5, 78, 51; passive, 134; pondering, 109–113, 115; and race and class, 56, 62, 78–79, 116, 124–125, 183
Feminism, 2
Feminist movement, 121, 123, 125, 184; and black women, 184
Feminist pedagogy, 141, 185
Feminist politics of popular culture, 136, 144–143
Feminist Press, 142
Fetterly, J., 99
First Love, 13–14, 104, 185
Fiske, J., 146
Foreshadowed problems, 150
Formula approach, 13
Foucault, M., 30–31, 178
Freedman, B., 159
Freedman, N., 159
Freeman, J., 121, 184

Index

Freire, P., 141, 185
Fridays, 72, 162, 179, 182
The friends, 53, 64, 67, 70, 74–75, 161, 179
Frogner, E., 145, 158–159, 164

Gardiner, J., 59
Garrigue, S., 140
Gaskell, J., 16
Gauch, P., 162
Gaze, 49–50, 54
Gender, 2, 4, 8, 15, 63–64, 67, 77, 124, 127, 137, 139, 141–143, 150, 153, 156; and careers, 76–78, 125–126; and class, 56, 124, 128, 180; and education, 76–78; ideology, 79, 98, 129–130; identity, 8, 79; issues, 130; meanings, 43, 131–132; and race, 56, 124, 180; relations, 38, 45, 54, 74, 96–98, 113, 123–124, 126–127, 129, 132–135; subjectivity, 9, 109; and work, 112
Girlfriend, 18, 23–24, 26, 86, 89–91, 94, 134, 177
Gitlin, T., 116
Glamour, 46
Glaser, B., 152, 155
Going on sixteen, 64, 68, 71, 76, 124, 158, 177–179, 181
Good/Bad opposition, 4, 80–89, 85, 149
Good girl, 4, 20, 81–83, 86, 134, 181
Goodman, E., 126
Gordon, L., 2, 120
Gramsci, A., 7, 183
Grandmothers, 36–37, 65, 67, 70
Greimas, A. J., 147–149
Griffin, C., 16, 150
Guy, R., 21, 161

Hall, S., 2, 8, 176
Hammersley, M., 152, 155
Happiness of Womanhood (HOW), 121
Hargreaves, D., 154
Harlequin, 3, 12–13, 176
Harper, E., 174
Hartley, J., 146
Hartmann, H., 56, 178
Harty, S., 15
Hatch, O., 123

Haug, F., 178
Hautzig, D., 21, 162
Hawks, R., 185
Head, A., 23, 161
Hebdige, D., 8
Hegemony, 7, 142
Helms, J., 123
Hestor, S., 154
Hey, dollface, 21–22, 72, 124–125, 162, 179, 181
Hiding-places, 185
High-Low texts, 99–100
History of sexuality, 30
Hobson, D., 175–176
Hodge, R., 80, 133, 147, 185
Home, 3, 16, 58, 63, 65, 68, 70–74, 76, 78–79, 113, 115–116, 118–119, 121, 144, 150, 152, 156, 183
Homemaker, see housewife
Homemaking, see domesticity
Hooks, B., 56, 56, 180, 184
Horatia Alger myth, 128, 135
Hornbook, 158–164
Household, see home
Housekeeping, see housework
Housewife, 58–59, 61, 180
Housework, 9, 57–60, 62–68, 115, 118, 124, 180; and class, 62–190; and gender, 63–64, 67–68; and race, 63–64, 67–68; theory, 58–59, 180
Howe, F., 60
Humm, P., 127
Hunt, I., 58–59
Hunt, I., 18, 161
Hunter, A., 2, 175
Hurd, G., 175

Identification, 113, 138
Ideological closure, 140
Ideological struggle, 2
Ideology, 16, 96, 120–129, 143; of individualism, 132
I'll always remember you . . . maybe, 33–34, 41, 72, 77, 124, 163, 177–178
Instructional strategies for romance novels, 135–141
In the night kitchen, 185
Iser, W., 109, 133
I will go barefoot all summer for you, 66, 94, 161, 177, 179

Jackie, 8–9, 148
Jefferson Middle School, 100–101, 106–108, 131–132, 151, 157
Jefferson, T., 8
Jensen, M., 153
Jobs, see work
Johnson, R., 7
Jones, S., 175
Journal of Reading, 139
The junior high school library catalog, see Schecter & Bogart
Junior miss, 20, 57, 94–95, 124, 158, 179

Kadushin, C., 2, 10–11, 175
Kaplan, C., 9, 117
Keeran, R., 59, 116
Keresy, G., 115, 177
Kessler-Harris, A., 56, 118–119, 121–122, 184
King, S., 11
Kingston, M., 140
Kiss, see sexuality
Klatch, R., 175
Kliatt Young Adult Paperback Book Guide, 161–164
Kominsky Junior High School, 100–102, 105, 131–132, 151, 157
Knowledge, 31, 105; really useful, 82; of romance, 27, 82; of sexuality, 30, 39, 41, 149, 152; valid knowledge, 98, 130, 132
Krantz, J., 11
Kress, G., 80, 133, 147, 185
Kuhn, A., 78
Kyrk, H., 61

Lakeview School District, 5, 100, 112, 114, 116, 136, 151–152, 157
Lakoff, R., 43–44, 46
Lanes, S., 13–15, 151
Laura Ingalls Wilder Award, 183
League of Women Voters, 184
Lefevre, L., 10
Le Guin, U., 38, 162
Leitmotif, 149
L'Engle, M., 160
Lenz, M., 145, 158–159, 161–162, 164
Lessinger, H., 180
Levoy, M., 140
Librarians, 14, 145, 152–153
Life Amendment PAC, 3

Light, A., 129, 176
Literature for today's young adults, 145
Literature study in the high schools, 145
Looking, see gaze
Love at first sight, 174
Lovell, T., 10, 127
Low ability reading classes, see reading courses, reluctant readers
Lowe, A., 176
Ludell and Willie, 26, 36–37, 53, 64, 67, 70, 73, 75–76, 162, 177–179
Lukas, C., 140
Luke, A., 98–99, 132, 185
Luke, C., 98–99,
Lyle, K., 161

MacPherson, B., 128
McIntosh, M., 178. 180
McNeil, D., 99
McRobbie, A., 8, 16, 112, 133, 148, 150, 152, 176–177
Madsen, C., 151, 176
Magas, B., 58
Mahood, M., 145, 158–159, 161–162, 164
Malinowski, B., 150
Market Facts, 13, 101, 185
Marriage, 3, 5, 13, 71, 77, 89, 112, 115, 116, 128
Marshall, A., 101, 174
Masculinity, 134, 140, 157
Martin, H.-J., 10
Mazer, N., 20, 104, 162
Mediation, 127
Meigs, C., 164
Mellor, F., 154
Mercer, C., 183
Miller-Lachmann, L., 185
Millett, K., 142
Millman, V., 16
Mills and Boon, 12
Mitchell, W., 181
Models of action, 135
Modleski, T., 149, 176, 184
Moi, T., 5, 117
Monaco, J., 147
Moral Majority, 123
Morley, D., 99
Motherhood, 2

Index

Mothers, 35, 38, 66, 89, 120, 124
Motion Picture Magazine, 46
Mr. & Mrs. Bo Jo Jones, 22, 33–34. 40. 70, 88, 127, 161, 177–179
Mrs. Mike, 75, 159, 179, 181
Mussell, K., 81
My darling, my hamburger, 20, 22, 33–34, 37, 40–41, 50, 88–89, 92, 124–125, 127, 161, 177–179
My first love and other disasters, 19, 26–27, 34, 37, 39–41, 50, 64, 105, 109, 163, 174, 177, 182
Mystery books, 100–101

Narrative, 80, 96, 148; elements, 96; and femininity, 180–181; form, 80, 133–35; and gender, class and race, 91; as ideological, 96; in teen romance novels, 80–81, 95–96, 134
National Consumers League, 184
The National Book Award, 161
Nesbitt, E., 164
Neville, M., 145, 148, 158, 164
New Advocate, 139
Newbery Award, 161, 183
The New Right, 2–3, 6, 14, 122–123, 126–127, 142; and femininity, 26
Nilsen, A., 145, 158–162, 164
Non-directive questioning, 154
Notable Books, 153, 183

Oakley, A., 60, 78
Official knowledge, see knowledge, valid
Ogilvie, E., 47, 159
Olson, D., 98
Opposition, see resistance
Oppositional readings, 112, 130
Oppositional structure, see binary oppositions
Oppositional texts, 139, 185
Other girl, 4, 6, 20, 81, 84–86, 134
Otto, W., 99
Outside over there, 185

Paintbox summer, 18, 25, 27, 33, 47, 63, 73–74, 76, 90, 159, 177, 179, 181
Paradigmatic plane, 146
Pascal, F., 19, 104, 109, 163, 174
A passing game, 174

Paterson, K., 140
Patriarchy, 3, 43, 96, 122–123, 132, 134
Patterson, E., 144
Period 1 novels, discussion, 4, 16, 19, 20–21, 32–33, 36, 46–47, 49, 62–63, 65, 68–89, 71–72, 74–77, 81–82, 85–86, 90, 92, 96, 123–125, 177–178
Period 2 novels, discussion, 4, 16, 12, 21–22, 24, 32, 36, 40–41, 46–47, 49–50, 92–64, 66, 68–69, 72, 74–75, 77–78, 81–82, 85–90, 92, 95–96, 124–125, 177–178
Period 3 novels, discussion, 4, 16, 20, 33, 40, 46, 63–64, 66, 72, 74, 77, 82–83, 86, 90, 92, 96, 113, 125–127, 177–178
Perfect Summer, 174
Personal life, see private life
Peters, C., 99
Peters, R., 99
Pevsner, S., 26, 47, 104, 163, 174
Picturing and imaging, 136–137
Pleasure, 34–35, 38–41, 43, 50, 52, 105, 109, 112, 127, 142; and danger, 30–31, 41
Plotke, D., 2
Politics, 4, 141, 144; of reading, 141–142; of sexuality, 42; and women, 117–123
Pollack, P., 176
Pollowitz, M., 18, 163
Popular culture, 6–7, 9, 116, 130, 141–142, 183; and the economy, 116; politics of, 2
Popular fiction, 9, 80, 117, 150; and gender, class, sex and age, 117, 130; and historical context, 126–127, 129; and society, 16, 127, 129
Popular literature, see popular fiction
The popularity plan, 163, 179
Possessive individualism, 128–129, 132
Poulantzas, N., 56
Powell, W., 2, 10–11, 175
Power, 5, 22, 29, 31, 54, 88, 118, 130; and beauty, 44; and control, 9–10, 16; formal, 25; and identity, 30; informal, 17, 26; and knowledge, 39; and

Index

romance, 16, 25–27, 29; relations, 3, 99; in schools, 99, 112; and sexuality, 30, 35, 38, 40
Practically seventeen, 26–27, 32, 36, 40, 47, 52, 63, 85, 158, 177–178, 181
Pregnancy, 20, 33, 35, 41, 88–89, 178
Princess Amy, 18, 22, 40, 51,66, 73–75, 77, 113, 125, 163, 177–178
Private life, 16, 28
Production, 57
Promises, 183
Property, girls as, 19, 26, 84
P. S. I love you, 1, 34, 40, 49, 64, 66, 72, 77, 125, 163, 174, 177–178
Publishing, 2, 4–5, 10; business of, 10; children's, 127; economic factors of, 10–15; mass market, 10–15; mergers in, 10–11; ownership, 10–11, 131, 176; of romance novels, 2, 12–15
Puzo, M., 11

Quercus, 99
Quin-Harkin, J., 163, 174

Race, 4–6, 8, 63–64, 67, 124, 127, 133, 135, 139, 141–143, 150; and class, 67, 75, 78; and education, 78, 181; and gender, 37, 46, 68, 71–76, 78
Radway, J., 3, 105, 112, 132, 134, 150, 153, 166, 176, 183
Readability, 182
READ teenage book club, 15, 176
Reader interests, of middle school and junior high girls, 14, 100–101, 104; of middle school and junior high teachers, 102–103
Reader communities, 136
Reader-text-context relations, 111
Reading courses, time structure and procedures of, 132
Reading instruction, 176; in middle and junior high school, 99–100; for reluctant readers, 99–100, 106, 157
Reading specialist, 151–152, 157
Reading Survey, 166–73
Reading the romance, 150

Reaganism, 2
Reagan, R., 2
Reagan administration, 122–123
Reagan Revolution, 122
Reis, D., 145, 164
Reluctance Variant, 92, 94–95
Reluctant readers, 99, 101, 106, 108, 112, 116, 156
Residual cultural forms, 130
Resistance, 9, 37–40, 51, 88, 112, 116, 123, 126, 133, 156
Response, see adult romance readers, teenage romance readers
Response journals, 136–137
Reproductive rights, 125
Reverby, S., 120
Rich, A., 43
Right to Life, 3
Right-wing organizations, 184
Roberts, H., 152
Robinson, E., 138
Robinson, L., 3, 181
Roe vs. Wade, 122
Roman, L., 175
Romance, 9, 15–16, 21, 24–25, 84–85, 90–91, 93–95, 133, 139, 148, 182; code of, 4–5, 8, 16–29, 79, 81, 87, 97, 149; controls sexuality, 22–23, 32–33, 40; and economic factors, 19; and femininity, 15, 17; as heterosexuality, 20–22; as a market relationship, 18–20, 22
Romance fiction, see adult and teen romance novels
Romance readers, adult women, 105, 112, 132, 134, 150; by age, 98, 101, 105–108; 110, 113; by class, 98, 101, 103–108, 110, 113; by race, 98, 101, 103–108, 110, 113; teenage girls, 3, 5–6, 100, 109, 115, 128, 134–136, 138, 140–141, 152, 156
Rose, J., 127, 150
Rosen, M., 118, 184
Rosenblatt, L., 133
Ruby, 21–22, 41, 53, 64, 67, 77, 87, 92–93, 124–125, 161, 179, 181
Runaway to freedom, 140

Sampling, 152–153; techniques, 144–145; theoretical sampling, 152

Index

Sarsby, J., 177
Sawicki, J., 178
Schecter, 158–163
Scherr, R., 43–44, 46
Schneider, K., 3
Schniedewind, N., 141
Schlafly, P. 3, 122
Scholastic, 2, 13–15, 142, 158, 176–177
School book clubs, 13, 99, 101, 103, 153; see also TAB and READ
Schooling, see schools
School libraries, 101, 145
School library journal, 139,160–164
Schools, 6, 8, 15, 100–102, 105, 112–113, 115–116, 131–132, 135, 141, 150, 152, 154, 176, 182–183
Scott, H., 61, 180
Screen stories, 46
Seamless text, 52, 97, 179
Seidler, V., 178
Selection tools, 145, 164
Selective tradition, 126
Selfless/mercenary coding, 85–89
Semiotics, 8, 146–149, 176
Sendak, M., 155
Senior high school library catalog, 158–162, 164
Service-domestic context, 75
Service-sector, 58–60, 100; work, 62, 72, 116, 135, 181
Seven days to a brand-new me, 26, 46, 82, 885, 91, 125, 163, 178–179, 181
Seventeen, 8
Seventeenth summer, 1, 18, 22, 25, 30, 34, 36, 63, 76, 81, 84, 90, 124, 144, 158, 178–179, 181–182
Sexism, 142, 179
Sexual exploitation, 51
Sexual intercourse, see sexuality, genitality
Sexual objectification, 6, 49–50, 54, 121
Sexual orientation, 4, 21–22, 41
Sexuality, 4–5, 8, 20, 88, 92, 113, 125–127, 133, 135, 141–143, 142–143, 148, 178; code of, 4, 16, 30–42, 79, 81, 87, 97, 133, 149; deployment of, 30–31; genitality, 17, 23, 32–41, 178; portrayal of heterosexuality, 5, 8, 22, 40–41, 112, 124–125; portrayal of homophobia, 21; portrayal of lesbianism, 21, 78, 124–125, 133
Sharpe, S., 177
Sheldon, S., 11
Sherwood Park Middle School, 100–102, 105, 108, 110, 113, 131–132, 138, 151, 157
Shrewsbury, C., 141
Sign, 146–147
Silhouette, 3, 12–14, 104, 185
Simon and Schuster, 13–14
Sister of the bride, 26, 41, 63, 66, 72, 77, 160, 178–179
Smart, B., 178
Smith, J., 59, 180
Smith, L., 164
Smith, W., 14
Smucker, B., 140
Snitow, A., 31, 115, 176
Sobol, R., 140
Social class, see class
Sohn, D., 145, 164
Sorority girl, 22–24, 36, 40–41, 73–74, 124, 159, 182
Specialness, 2, 23–25, 28, 40, 48, 106, 113, 134, 177
Spelman, E., 43
Sprint, 99
Square One Publishers, 142, 185
Stacy, J., 142
Standardized testing, 100, 102, 131
Stansell, C., 31
Starrs, C., 58–59
State testing, see standardized testing
Stignant, P., 127
Stolz, M., 48, 160
Story, see narrative
Strauss, A., 152, 155
Strong/Weak opposition, 4, 80, 89–91, 95, 149
Subject, see subjectivity
Subject positions, see subjectivity
Subjectivity, 4, 7, 9, 28, 109–113, 129, 142, 150
Subordination, 25, 28–29, 178
A summer's lease, 140

Index

Sundance, 99
Sweet Dreams, 13–14, 104, 142, 174
Sweet Valley High, 3, 143, 174
Swerdlow, A., 180
Swingewood, A., 127
Syntagmatic plane, 146–147

TAB teenage book club, 13–14, 176
Taxel, J., 126, 135, 139, 142
Teachers, 99, 101–104, 106, 108, 116, 131–132, 152–154, 157, 182; authority of, 104, 150
Teen romance fiction reading, see teen romance novels, see romance readers, teenage girls
Teen romance novels, 2–3, 13, 31, 76, 79, 89, 102–108, 111–112, 115–116, 128, 131, 133–135, 144–145, 150–151, 177; controversy over, 14–15, 102, 142, 176; development of, 2, 13–14, 144; and femininity, 123; and race, 183; in schools, 98–116, 135–151, 156; and society, 127–129; structural characteristics of, 107, 156; and teachers, 101–104, 107–108, 116, 131, 135–139
Textbooks, see texts
Texts, 15, 22, 96, 109, 132–133, 135–136, 146, 177; authority of, 98–100, 103, 131–132; closed, 132, 185; and gender, 109; legitimate, 132; and meaning, 126; open, 185; pleasure of, 105, 115, 132; and school, 98–100
Textual analysis, 4, 147; techniques of, 147–149
Thompson, S., 31, 177
Thorne, B., 178
Thurston, C., 3, 12, 153, 166, 176
Tip Sheets, 134, 185
Tracking, 100, 106
Trade paperbacks, 131, 135, 176
Transformation, 143; of gender relations, 145; of goods, 60; of the heroine, 17, 28, 46, 89–91 96
Trial Valley, 139
True womanhood, 3, 118, 183
Turkey trot, 174
The twenty-six minutes, 185

Two-paycheck family, 115, 120, 126
Tyler, T., 174

Unions, 11, 118–119
Up a road slowly, 1, 18, 22, 24, 33, 41, 63–64, 66, 72, 77, 88, 161, 181
Up in Seth's room, 20, 22, 32, 37, 39–41, 50, 72, 87–88, 124, 127, 162, 174, 177–179, 181, 182

Vacca, J., 137
Vacca, R., 137
Valuing and evaluating, 136, 138–139
The Vamp, 19, 177
Vance, C., 30–31, 126
Vaugh, J., 99
Vernon, R., 163, 179
Very far away from anywhere else, 22, 27, 38, 40, 77, 124, 162, 182
Viglucci, P., 139
Viguers, R., 164
Vogue, 46
Volosinov, V., 140

Wainwright, H., 58
Wait for Marcy, 18–20, 36, 47, 52–53, 71, 124, 159, 177–178, 181
Wages, by gender, class and race, 59–61, 118–23, 184
Walker, E., 165
Walker, J., 145, 158–161, 165
Walkerdine, V., 9, 150
Weinbaum, B., 60
Weiner, G., 150
Welter, B., 183
Wertheheimer, B., 117
West, T., 183
Wexler, P., 28
White, H., 80
Whiteside, T., 11, 176
Widdowson, P., 127
Wigutoff, S., 139
Wildfire, 2
Wilkinson, B., 26, 162
Willard, C., 145, 160, 165
Williams, R., 130
Willis, P., 8, 175–176
Winning consent, 2, 7, 28, 129
Winship, J., 9, 54

207

Index

Wodiwiss, K., 176
Wollacott, J., 183
Wolpe, A. M. 78
Woman chief, 140
Woman warrior, 140
Women's Bureau of the Department of Labor, 118–120, 184
Women's History Collective, 142
Women's Liberation movement, see feminist movement
Women's movement, see feminist movement
Women take issue, 8
World War I, 119
World War II, 118–119, 184
Work, 71–76, 115-ll6, 144; by class, 56, 59–60, 71–76, 100, 114–115, 117–124; domestic, 73–76, 180; and families, 56; by gender, 59–60; 63, 71–76, 100, 114–115, 119, 121–123, 128, 183–184; history of, 117–123 by race, 59–60, 71–76, 114–115, 117–123; unpaid, 57–59, 74–75.
Workforce stratification, 59–60
Wright, E., 56–57, 62, 180
Wylie, R. 151

Xerox, 14–15, 176

Yalom, M., 178
Young Adult Service Division (YASD) Notable Books, 145, 160–163
Young adult literature, 145
Young, C., 138
Young Love, 13–14
Your reading, 145
Yuval-Davis, N., 180

Zindel, P., 20, 161